The best tomatoes

The biggest squash

The tallest corn

The reddest radishes

The sweetest carrots

Every year Jerry Baker, America's Master Gardener, gets thousands of letters from impatient gardeners asking him how to lay out their vegetable gardens better, how to pick the right spot, what to do to improve the soil, when, what, where and how to plant in a particular season and locale. Now he's written this book answering those questions and more to help every vegetable gardener get started. He finds fresh solutions to such common problems as what to grow in a shady corner, what to do about aphids and leaf blight, how to water and still keep the foliage dry, and when to fertilize, and spells out practical, safe and easy tips for growing healthy, fabulous vegetables.

When the growing gets tough,
the tough get growing with Jerry Baker!

"Everything Jerry does seems
to mushroom . . . Everything grows!"
—*Detroit Sunday News Magazine*

Jerry Baker's FAST, EASY VEGETABLE GARDEN

JERRY BAKER, America's Master Gardener, is known to millions as the gardening spokesperson for K-Mart and for his daily show on Cable Health Network. The bestselling author of PLANTS ARE LIKE PEOPLE, TALK TO YOUR PLANTS, and THE IMPATIENT GARDENER, he has educated and entertained millions with his simple, down-to-earth, step-by-step appro

Jerry Baker's FAST, EASY VEGETABLE GARDEN

ILLUSTRATIONS BY ERV ZACHMANN

A PLUME BOOK

PLUME
Published by the Penguin Group
Penguin Putnam Inc., 375 Hudson Street, New York,
New York 10014, U.S.A.
Penguin Books Ltd, 27 Wrights Lane, London W8 5TZ,
England
Penguin Books Australia Ltd, Ringwood, Victoria, Australia
Penguin Books Canada Ltd, 10 Alcorn Avenue, Toronto,
Ontario, Canada M4V 3B2
Penguin Books (N.Z.) Ltd, 182–190 Wairau Road,
Auckland 10, New Zealand

Penguin Books Ltd, Registered Offices:
Harmondsworth, Middlesex, England

Published by Plume, a member of Penguin Putnam Inc.

First Printing, March, 1985
          20   21   22   23   24   25

 REGISTERED TRADEMARK—MARCA REGISTRADA

Library of Congress Cataloging-in-Publication Data
Baker, Jerry.
   Jerry Baker fast, easy vegetable garden.
   Includes index.
   ISBN 0-452-28104-0
   1. Vegetable gardening.   I. Title.   II. Title:
fast, easy vegetable garden.
   SB321.B23   1985   635   84-20667

PRINTED IN THE UNITED STATES OF AMERICA

Designed by Barbara Huntley

To my wife Ilene,
the sunshine of my life

Acknowledgments

Whenever I complete a manuscript for a new book, I turn my attention to the pleasant task of *thanking* those who have contributed their efforts, energy, and talents and others who have imparted their wisdom and knowledge over the years to help me learn about, enjoy, and protect the green scene that all of us cherish.

I particularly want to thank Carole Compton, my manuscript typist, who has spent hundreds of hours over the past few years deciphering my handwritten hieroglyphics preparing scripts, pamphlets, and books (with never a complaint). And the amazing Grace Smith, who always has the right answers, words of encouragement, and corrective advice for me, and always at the right time.

Thanks to John Schwartz, a best friend, who always teaches me something new and exciting about this growing world.

Thanks to the Park Seed Company, which always makes vegetable gardening the most delicious hobby, by creating new easy-to-grow varieties.

Thanks also to the United States Department of Agriculture, Cooperative Extension Service, and super agricultural colleges that are always curious and creative in finding new ways to improve our health, happiness, and way of life—for their unending sources of information.

Contents

Introduction

There seems to be an inherent need for most human beings at some time in their life to plant seeds and grow their own food. All children beg their parents to let them have a little spot in the yard for their own little garden—though as a rule the garden is soon forgotten as their interests change. Dad or Mom is often left with the responsibility of raising a stalk of corn or hill of beans along with the new puppy or kitten that the child just had to have or perish from sadness. "Honest, Mom and Dad, we'll take care of all their needs—you won't have to do a thing." If you fell for that line, you are in the majority with most parents.

As you grow older, mature, and move into your own house or apartment, that urge returns to grow something again. This time, however, you make your promises to yourself—not to your parents.

I will take care of my garden and fight the weeds, bugs, plagues, and blights every day. I'll water, feed, mulch, and hoe. I am going to have the best tomatoes, biggest squash, tallest corn, reddest radishes, and sweetest carrots in the whole apartment building, even if I am on the twenty-sixth floor.

Again, even though you are now a big kid, your interests change and your growing charges are soon left to fend for themselves. These same green-scene dreams and self-promises are also made by those of you with a little or a lot of land surrounding your home, so don't laugh at the apartment dweller.

The reason why most of you lose interest is that you become impatient and your original pride wanes because you don't have overnight results. By the end of the second week your persistence has slowed to a snail's pace; by the end of the third week your patience has run completely out. The heck with it! Anyone for tennis? But this does not have to be the story at your house with a small amount of pre-planning, obtainable goals, common sense steps, and not a heck of a lot of hard work (after you spade the first time). Remember Kipling's verse?

Oh, Adam was a gardener, and God who made him sees
That half a proper gardener's work is done upon his knees.

Even this need not be totally true—I mean about *half* on your knees.

You must always remember that the formula for a healthy, happy, and abundant vegetable garden is pride, patience, persistence, and prayer. I've always loved this one:

THE GARDENER'S PRAYER

Oh Lord, grant that my garden may have a little rain each day,
say from about three o'clock in the morning until five A.M. . . .
Make it gentle and warm so that it can soak in.
Grant that there may be plenty of dew and little wind,
enough worms, no plant lice or snails, no mildew . . .
And that once a week thin liquid manure and guano may
fall from Heaven!

Won't you please join me and your 35 million other home garden neighbors and put a little love back into the land that has been so good to you. Always remember this old play on words: *When the growing gets tough, the tough get growing.*

You will find a good number of amazingly easy solutions to many of your common problems in this book. Most of these solutions call for the use of a common household product that you have never before related to garden insects, disease control, or homemade plant food formulas.

Many of you who have never met me through my other books or TV and radio appearances may even wonder if I am gardening with a full deck.

As in the past, my objective in this book is to make home gardening fun, fast, safe, and economical. Garden chemicals, as we know most of them today, are safe and effective when used as recommended. I will make chemical recommendations, but I have learned through years of experience that soap, water, beer, wine, Epsom salts, and chewing tobacco can save time, money, and plants. So I use them liberally. Give it a chance and try a couple of my suggestions and you will be respectfully surprised.

I am but a humble servant of my maker and his garden lady, Mother Nature. I have learned a great deal over the years, but I don't have all the answers and am still learning. I find no fault with other people's recommendations and avoid making criticisms.

If you have an immediate need for a solution to a problem that I have not covered or have not explained to your satisfaction, please do your garden and yourself a favor and contact the greatest bunch of guys and gals ever assembled, the U.S. Cooperative Extension Service. There is an office near you. Just check the phone book and call or write to the office in your state. Ask for a copy of a general list of publications available or for helpful literature on home vegetable gardening. The addresses of the U.S. Cooperative Extension Service in each state are listed in Chapter 15 of this book.

JERRY BAKER

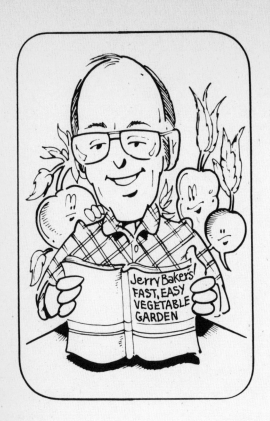

1

Basic Training

THE PLANNING STAGE

If you want to have a fun, fast, easy vegetable garden, you need to do some planning before you do your planting. So I'm going to give you a few things to think about to get you started.

In this chapter you'll learn the basics of planning a vegetable garden: how to lay out your garden, how to pick the right spot, what to do with the soil you have, and when, what, where, and how to plant. After you've read this chapter, you'll be ready for action.

Remember that a beautiful vegetable garden doesn't actually start in the ground. It begins as an urge or an idea. It begins in your mind!

Request a Few Catalogs While You're in the Mood

In most cases, we begin to think about, dream about, or in the case of old-timers at vegetable gardening (that's the second year) actually plan the future crop about the middle of January, when we first begin to see ads for free vegetable catalogs or the first one arrives in the mail. Usually after your first year, or your first request for a catalog, your name will make the rounds and you will receive more seed catalogs than you know what to do with. But then again, the more the merrier.

To get you off on the right foot, here is a list of the seed companies that send me catalogs.

CATALOGS ARE A GARDENER'S DREAMBOOK

Agway Inc.
Box 4933
Syracuse, NY 13221

Applewood Seed Company
Box 10761 Edgemont Station
Golden, CO 80401

Burgess Seed Company
905 Four Seasons Road
Bloomington, IL 61701

Burpee Seed Company
300 Park Avenue
Warminister, PA 18974

Dominion Seed House
Georgetown
Ontario, Canada L7GYA2

Farmer Seed Company
818 N.W. 4th Street
Fairbault, MN 55021

Field Seed Company
407 Sycamore Street
Shenandoah, IA 51602

Grace's Gardens
Autumn Lane
Hackettstown, NJ 07840

Gurney Seed
Yanktown, SD 47079

Joseph Harris Company
Moreton Farm
Rochester, NY 14624

Hart Seed Company
304 Main Street
Wethersfield, CT 06109

Herbst Brothers Seeds
1000 N. Main Street
Brewster, NY 10509

Jung Seed Company
Randolph, WI 53956

Olds Seed Company
Box 7790
Madison, WI 53707

Park Seed Company
Greenwood, SC 29647

Thompson & Morgan Inc.
Box 100
Farmingdale, NJ 07727

Versey's Seeds Ltd
York Prince Edwards Island
Canada C0 AIP0

Wyatt-Quaries Seed
  Company
Box 2131
Raleigh, NC 27602

These catalogs will supply lots of information and inspiration, even though you may find some dates and soil conditions that don't pertain to you and product recommendations that are not available to you in your garden outlets.

Your Ambition and the Land Available Will Determine the Size

The size and shape of your vegetable garden will depend on several things. First and foremost, how much space can you designate to a garden? Second, how much time are you willing to give the garden? Third, how much time will other members of the family devote, if any? Fourth, how much of your yard is in full sun? Sun is what it takes for an abundant vegetable garden. Fifth, what do you truly expect from your garden for fresh and preserved produce? All of these are things that you must ask yourself before you ever put a seed in the ground.

So, What's a Shape Got to Do with a Garden?

"A whole lot!" is the answer to this question if some of you are to have a vegetable garden at all. Because of existing trees, shrubs, walks, and buildings, the available sunny spots can be in some unusual locations, making it virtually impossible to have square, rectangular, or triangular areas to garden in. Or perhaps your taste in design does not run to straight sharp lines. That is super! Vegetable gardens, flower beds, and evergreen and shrub areas should live in harmony, and a curving winding vegetable garden well planned for looks as well as production is one of the most exciting sights a gardener can see. Since most of your annuals, perennials, roses, and other flowers will also require full sun, it stands to reason that sharing is the key word.

Let your imagination be your only restriction. Well, you had better consider the length of your arms and hoe handle too. Most of us comfortably reach up to 5 feet with a long-handled tool. So keep that in mind when you decide the size of the beds. You might also border your beds with the new plastic log edging from Custom Plastics and add a few foot paths to your layout.

X Marks the Spot Before You Begin to Dig

Your garden location must receive no less than 6 full hours of sunlight, and 8 hours would shove the odds in your favor. If this is not possible, you should consider container gardening, which we will discuss at great length later on. Don't give up here; turn to the pages on container gardening.

Moving right along, I hear others discourage folks from planting near shrubs and trees. Their objection is that the trees and shrubs will rob the vegetables of water and food.

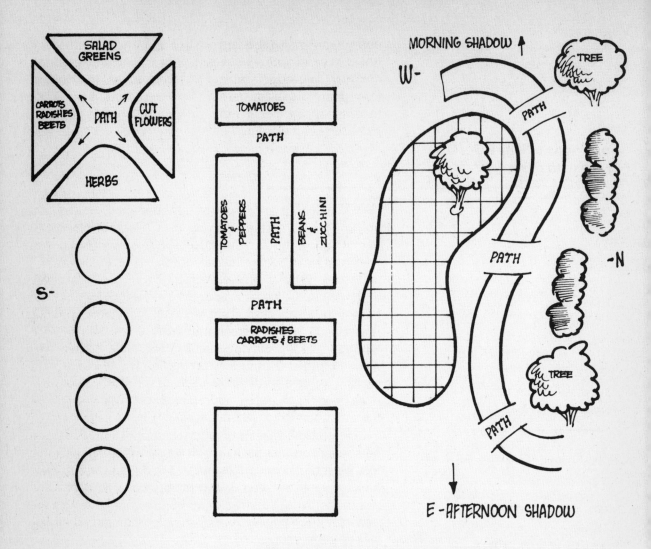

In most cases, it's the other way around. The only thing you must keep in mind when planting near trees and shrubs is their shadows. Remember, 6 to 8 hours of full sun! As for the food-and-water squabble, treat your trees, shrubs, and vegetables as separate groups.

It is handy as heck to end up with a spot for your vegetable garden as close to the house as possible, and if you can, do. Looks, availability, sunlight, traffic, and drainage all play a big part in site selection. Also remember that the farther from the house the more garden hose you will need.

The directions of the prevailing winds will also influence garden location. Avoid open southwest winds in summer and north-northwest winds in early spring. Also try to stay out of low-lying areas where cold frosty air is trapped.

By the same token, to avoid disease, make sure that the location has some air movement. A slight turtleshell shape to the land is best for proper drainage; if land is swaled, then it must be built up. Sloping land can be attractively tiered, and this also makes it easier to work on.

Put It on Paper

Now draw a picture of your garden plot to some sort of scale. Let's say you use ½ inch equals 10 feet. Or buy graph paper wherever school supplies are sold. While you are buying the graph paper, buy an 8½ × 11-inch spiral notebook. Use this for notes and to store your layouts.

This preplanned, well-thought-out drawing can save you lots of time, effort, heartache, and money if you will just make it a serious endeavor to get the most action out of the least amount of space. It's also helpful to keep you from becoming a slave to your garden instead of the master.

Any Dirt Will Do!

Since most of you call garden soil dirt, that's what we will refer to it as. The heading of this paragraph will raise a few eyebrows from my peers; so be it! I have seen bumper crops grown all over the world on what is considered totally untillable dirt, but with a little imagination, effort, work, and common sense, you and I will get your ground growing, even if we end up on your cement driveway.

No matter what the soil base is, we must have *good drainage*. This means that water can't sit more than an hour after a rain or watering. If we can't build the quality of the soil up to this expectation, then we will raise the garden up. If it's clay, we will build a 10-to-12-inch mound up all the way around and fill it with leaves, peat, soil, grass, compost, table scraps, and any other organic material we can find. Or let's use boards or blocks. Sandy soil will be enriched and firmed with the same organic materials year after year.

Your present soil condition will not prevent you from having a garden. Trust me!

You can start on soil preparation as soon as you can comfortably get a shovel into the ground. As for planting the seeds, that depends on the seeds themselves and when Jack Frost goes into hibernation for the summer.

READY, SET, GROW!

Refer to the following chart, which has the average first and last frost dates for your area.

HARD-FROST DATES
(from USDA Weather Records)

State	First Frost in Fall	Last Frost in Spring
Alabama—almost frost-free		
Alaska—irregular conditions		
Arizona—almost frost-free		
Arkansas, N	Oct. 23	Apr. 7
Arkansas, S	Nov. 3	Mar. 25
California		
Imperial Valley	Dec. 15	Jan. 25
Interior Valley	Nov. 15	Mar. 1
Southern Coast	Dec. 15	Jan. 15
Central Coast	Dec. 1	Feb. 25
Mountain Sections	Sept. 1	Apr. 25
Colorado, W	Sept. 18	May 25

State	First Frost in Fall	Last Frost in Spring
Colorado, NE	Sept. 27	May 11
Colorado, SE	Oct. 15	May 1
Connecticut	Oct. 20	Apr. 25
Delaware	Oct. 25	Apr. 15
District of Columbia	Oct. 23	Apr. 11
Florida, N	Dec. 5	Feb. 25
Florida, Cen.	Dec. 28	Feb. 11
Florida, south of Lake Okeechobee—almost frost-free		
Georgia, N	Nov. 1	Apr. 1
Georgia, S	Nov. 15	Mar. 15
Hawaii—almost frost-free		
Idaho	Sept. 22	May 21
Illinois, N	Oct. 8	May 1
Illinois, S	Oct. 20	Apr. 15
Indiana, N	Oct. 8	May 1
Indiana, S	Oct. 20	Apr. 15
Iowa, N	Oct. 2	May 1
Iowa, S	Oct. 9	Apr. 15
Kansas	Oct. 15	Apr. 20
Kentucky	Oct. 20	Apr. 15
Louisiana, N	Nov. 10	Mar. 13
Louisiana, S	Nov. 20	Feb. 20
Maine	Sept. 25	May 25
Maryland	Oct. 20	Apr. 19
Massachusetts	Oct. 25	Apr. 25
Michigan, Upper Pen.	Sept. 15	May 25
Michigan, N	Sept. 25	May 17
Michigan, S	Oct. 8	May 10
Minnesota, N	Sept. 15	May 25
Minnesota, S	Oct. 30	Mar. 25
Mississippi, N	Oct. 30	Mar. 25
Mississippi, S	Nov. 15	Mar. 15
Missouri	Oct. 20	Apr. 20
Montana	Sept. 22	May 21

HARD-FROST DATES (continued)
(from USDA Weather Records)

State	First Frost in Fall	Last Frost in Spring
Nebraska, W	Oct. 4	May 11
Nebraska, E	Oct. 15	Apr. 15
Nevada, W	Sept. 30	May 19
Nevada, E	Sept. 14	June 1
New Hampshire	Sept. 25	May 23
New Jersey	Oct. 25	Apr. 20
New Mexico, N	Oct. 17	Apr. 23
New Mexico, S	Nov. 1	Apr. 1
New York, W	Oct. 8	May 10
New York, E	Oct. 15	May 1
New York, N	Oct. 1	May 15
N. Carolina, W	Oct. 25	Apr. 15
N. Carolina, E	Nov. 1	Apr. 8
N. Dakota, W	Sept. 13	May 21
N. Dakota, E	Sept. 20	May 16
Ohio, N	Oct. 15	May 6
Ohio, S	Oct. 20	Apr. 20
Oklahoma	Nov. 2	Apr. 2
Oregon, W	Oct. 25	Apr. 17
Oregon, E	Sept. 22	June 4
Pennsylvania, W	Oct. 10	Apr. 20
Pennsylvania, Cen.	Oct. 15	May 1
Pennsylvania, E	Oct. 15	Apr. 17
Rhode Island	Oct. 25	Apr. 25
S. Carolina, NW	Nov. 8	Apr. 1
S. Carolina, SE	Nov. 15	Mar. 15
S. Dakota	Sept. 25	May 15
Tennessee	Oct. 25	Apr. 10
Texas, NW	Nov. 1	Apr. 15
Texas, NE	Nov. 10	Mar. 21
Texas, S	Dec. 15	Feb. 10
Utah	Oct. 19	Apr. 26

State	First Frost in Fall	Last Frost in Spring
Vermont	Sept. 25	May 23
Virginia, N	Oct. 25	Apr. 15
Virginia, S	Oct. 30	Apr. 10
Washington, W	Nov. 15	Apr. 10
Washington, E	Oct. 1	May 15
W. Virginia, W	Oct. 15	May 1
W. Virginia, E	Oct. 1	May 15
Wisconsin, N	Sept. 25	May 17
Wisconsin, S	Oct. 10	May 1
Wyoming, W	Aug. 20	June 20
Wyoming, E	Sept. 20	May 21

I am going to suggest that you refer to this next listing of *cool-season vegetable crops* for early and late planting in the cooler areas.

Artichokes	Collards	Parsnips
Asparagus	Cress	Peas
Beets	Endives	Potatoes
Broccoli	Garlic	Radishes
Brussels sprouts	Kale	Rhubarb
Cabbage	Kohlrabi	Rutabaga
Carrots	Leeks	Shallots
Cauliflower	Lettuce	Spinach
Celery	Mustard greens	Swiss chard
	Onions	Turnips

SOME LIKE IT HOT...

In the *frost-free areas* of the country, like southern Florida, the Gulf Coast parts of Alabama, Mississippi, Louisiana, and Texas, the lower elevations of Arizona and the lower elevations of southern California, you can plant in fall and harvest the following all winter:

Beets	Lettuce	Spinach
Broccoli	Greens	Radishes
Cabbage	(American	Turnips
Cauliflower	and Oriental)	
Celery	Peas	

Don't forget to stop and shop at your local garden shop or call your County Extension Area Agent for specific recommendations for your area.

What You Plant Just Depends on Your Taste and Needs

I can't help you here a great deal, because of lot of factors come into play: ethnic background, style of cooking, likes and dislikes, and end use. Later, I will tell you more about the uses of some of the vegetables to make your selection a little easier. But here are a few ideas to consider right now.

Fast-Growing	Eat Both Ends	A Lot for Your Money	For Storage
Herbs	Beets	Beans	Horseradish
Lettuce	Kohlrabi	Brussels	Artichokes
Mustard and	Onions	sprouts	Parsnips
turnip greens	Rutabaga	Cucumbers	Rutabaga
Oriental greens	Turnips	Herbs	Turnips
Radishes		Greens	Potatoes
Scallions		Peas	
Spinach		Radishes	
		Spinach	
		Squash	
		Tomatoes	
		Zucchini	

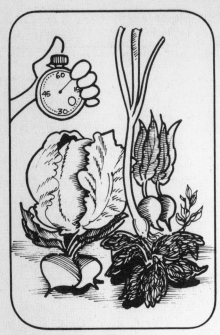

FIRST TO THE TABLE

I ATE THE WHOLE THING?

Where Do You Plant What, or Is It What Do You Plant Where?

That is the question. To begin, plant in dirt, but not necessarily in the ground. How's that for a riddle? The question is really "What location in the garden should you plant the whats?" Remember what I said about the hot southwest wind in the beginning. You had better remember, because it's a killer. Plant corn and sunflowers to the west/southwest as a screen. Next to that plant peppers, eggplants, then greens. Next plant beans, radishes, beets, parsnips, and rutabaga. Now, we go to lettuce, followed to the east by zucchini, tomatoes, peas, and finally on the far east side vine crops, cucumbers and squash.

The reason for this garden pecking system is to protect plants from each other. Vining crops grow to the east and tend to crawl all over the plants.

Oh, the riddle! When you plant in hanging baskets and containers. I know! Go west, young man, 'cause that's where the "corn" is.

How to Plant Is for Beginners

That's what you think! I am really referring to whether you begin from seed or pregrown bedding plants. I encourage all home gardeners to propagate seeds indoors, in cold frames, and in their own greenhouse; this is especially true in the warmer climates of the country. Sowing directly into the open soil is also a great idea, but time and space will play a great part in your selection. In the northern areas where the season is shorter, pregrown bedding plants and vegetables are the answer. These are healthy, happy, well-rooted plants, grown by professional growers in greenhouses and then hardened off so they are ready to be off and growing when you and your garden are. It's true they are more expensive than seeds, but then when you consider the advantage of earlier harvest so that you can roll over the space to a second and third planting, they end up to be a far better investment.

Basic Training Is Over and You Have Survived!

YOU'VE EARNED IT

In any competitive sport they always say that you must learn the basics and then constantly practice them. What you have just read is just that; the basics of vegetable gardening. It's time now to refine your techniques and add a little fancy footwork if you are to win the garden game.

2

Go Right to the Source

GARDEN SEEDS AND GREENHOUSE-GROWN PLANTS

If you don't have the space, time, confidence, or interest in starting seeds indoors, it's no big thing; as a matter of fact, you are in the majority. Vegetable gardeners sow seeds directly into the open ground or transplant seedlings that they purchase from their local garden department. In the last few years, so much progress has been made in commerical growing procedures that the cost and quality of pregrown vegetables makes bedding plants, as they are referred to, a better bet than garden seeds for most of you impatient vegetable gardeners.

When you buy pregrown plants they have been hardened off (prepared for the open garden) by the professional grower, and unless Jack Frost pays an unexpected visit or you completely ignore their need for water after planting, they will take hold quickly and produce much, much earlier than seed.

Seeds Are the Cheapest Way

Garden seeds, both vegetable and flower, are generally available in any garden department either in small seed packets or in seed tapes and seed pellets. In some cases, bulk quantities of seeds like mustard, turnip, collard, spinach, and lettuce are available. You need only worry about one thing when you purchase seeds: Make sure they bear a

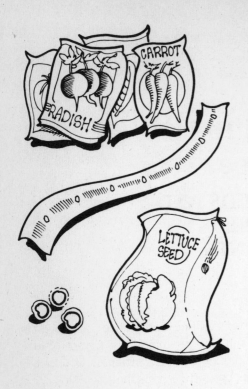

current-year packing-date stamp. This also applies to tapes and bulk purchases.

Seed packets can be purchased from seed racks, are found in many types of retail outlets, and are constantly restocked during the season by company representatives. You can be pretty sure that any reputable retailer will sell only the top quality, so look for bargains. The difference between buying from a seed rack and from a catalog house is that more varieties are available from catalogs than racks. You will also find the newer varieties much earlier in mail-order catalogs.

Seed tapes have been around for only a few years, but prove to be a quick, handy way to plant. Seeds are pre-spaced in a water-soluble material that dissolves from the moisture in the soil. I like them and have had excellent luck with them.

Seed pellets were developed for the commercial vegetable grower. Small seeds like carrots and lettuce can now be planted by a seed drill. The pellet is a light clay coating over the seed, which dissolves in the moist soil. Seed pellets are not widely available to the general garden public as yet.

Bulk seed is practical only if you are going to grow large quantities of leafy plants and as a rule are available only at a few garden centers or seed stores.

The Deeper the Better Is Deadly!

Most losses of vegetable seeds are the result of planting them too deep. i have listed the average plant depths of the most popular vegetables and herb seeds. If you try to conform, the results will be positive and pleasing.

VEGETABLE AND HERB SEED AVERAGE PLANTING DEPTH

Artichoke	½″	Kale	¼″
Asparagus	½″	Kohlrabi	½″
Beans, broad	2″	Leeks	½″
Beans, cow	1 ½″	Lettuce	¼″
Beans, lima	2″	Mustard	½″

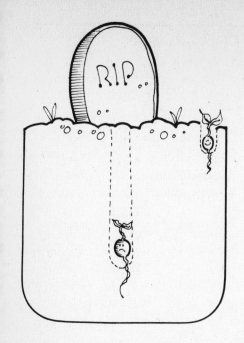

Beans, scarlet	1 ½″	Okra	½″
Beans, shelling	1 ½″	Onion	¼″
Beans, snap	1″	Parsley	⅛″
Beets	¼″	Parsnips	¼″
Broccoli	¼″	Peas	1 ½″
Brussels sprouts	¼″	Peanuts	1 ½″
Cabbage	¼″	Peppers	¼″
Cantaloupe	½″	Potatoes	¼″
Carrots	⅛″	Pumpkins	1″
Cauliflower	¼″	Radishes	½″
Celeriac	⅛″	Rutabaga	½″
Celery	⅛″	Salsify	½″
Chard, Swiss	½″	Spinach	½″
Collards	¼″	Squash	1″
Corn	1″	Tomatoes	¼″
Cucumber	1″	Turnips	½″
Eggplant	¼″	Watermelon	1″
Endive	¼″		

SPRING DATES TO PLANT IF LAST FREEZE IS—

Crop	Jan. 30	Feb. 8	Feb. 18	Feb. 28	Mar. 10	Mar. 20	Mar. 30
Asparagus[1]	——	——	——	——	1/1–3/1	2/1–3/10	2/15–3/20
Beans, lima	2/1–4/15	2/10–5/1	3/1–5/1	3/15–6/1	3/20–6/1	4/1–6/15	4/15–6/20
Beans, snap	2/1–4/1	2/1–5/1	3/1–5/1	3/10–5/15	3/15–5/15	3/15–5/25	4/1–6/1
Beets	1/1–3/15	1/10–3/15	1/20–4/1	2/1–4/15	2/15–6/1	2/15–5/15	3/1–6/1
Broccoli, sprouting[1]	1/1–1/30	1/1–1/30	1/15–2/15	2/1–3/1	2/15–3/15	2/15–3/15	3/1–3/20
Brussels sprouts[1]	1/1–1/30	1/1–1/30	1/15–2/15	2/1–3/1	2/15–3/15	2/15–3/15	3/1–3/20
Cabbage[1]	1/1–1/15	1/1–2/10	1/1–2/25	1/15–2/25	1/25–3/1	2/1–3/1	2/15–3/10
Cabbage, Chinese	——	——	——	——	——	——	——
Carrots	1/1–3/1	1/1–3/1	1/15–3/1	2/1–3/1	2/10–3/15	2/15–3/20	3/1–4/10
Cauliflower[1]	1/1–2/1	1/1–2/1	1/10–2/10	1/20–2/20	2/1–3/1	2/10–3/10	2/20–3/20
Celery and celeriac	1/1–2/1	1/10–2/10	1/20–2/20	2/1–3/1	2/20–3/20	3/1–4/1	3/15–4/15
Chard	1/1–4/1	1/10–4/1	1/20–4/15	2/1–5/1	2/15–5/15	2/20–5/15	3/1–5/25
Chervil and chives	1/1–2/1	1/1–2/1	1/1–2/1	1/15–2/15	2/1–3/1	2/10–3/10	2/15–3/15
Chicory, witloof	——	——	——	——	6/1–7/1	6/1–7/1	6/1–7/1
Collards[1]	1/1–2/15	1/1–2/15	1/1–3/15	1/15–3/15	2/1–4/1	2/15–5/1	3/1–6/1
Cornsalad	1/1–2/15	1/1–2/15	1/1–3/15	1/1–3/1	1/1–3/15	1/1–3/15	1/15–3/15

[1] Plants

Crop	Jan. 30	Feb. 8	Feb. 18	Feb. 28	Mar. 10	Mar. 20	Mar. 30
Corn, sweet	2/1–3/15	2/10–4/1	2/20–4/15	3/1–4/15	3/10–4/15	3/15–5/1	3/25–5/15
Cress, upland	1/1–2/1	1/1–2/15	1/15–2/15	2/1–3/1	2/10–3/15	2/20–3/15	3/1–4/1
Cucumbers	2/15–3/15	2/15–4/1	2/15–4/15	3/1–4/15	3/15–4/15	4/1–5/1	4/10–5/15
Eggplant[1]	2/1–3/1	2/10–3/15	2/20–4/1	3/10–4/15	3/15–4/15	4/1–5/1	4/15–5/15
Endive	1/1–3/1	1/1–3/1	1/15–3/1	2/1–3/1	2/15–3/15	3/1–4/1	3/10–4/10
Fennel, Florence	1/1–3/1	1/1–3/1	1/15–3/1	2/1–3/1	2/15–3/15	3/1–4/1	3/10–4/10
Garlic	——	——	——	——	——	2/1–3/1	2/10–3/10
Horseradish[1]	——	——	——	——	——	——	3/1–4/1
Kale	1/1–2/1	1/10–2/1	1/20–2/10	2/1–2/20	2/10–3/1	2/20–3/10	3/1–3/20
Kohlrabi	1/1–2/1	1/10–2/1	1/20–2/10	2/1–2/20	2/10–3/1	2/20–3/10	3/1–4/1
Leek	1/1–2/1	1/1–2/1	1/1–2/15	1/15–2/15	1/25–3/1	2/1–3/1	2/15–3/15
Lettuce, head[1]	1/1–2/1	1/1–2/1	1/1–2/1	1/15–2/15	2/1–2/20	2/15–3/10	3/1–3/20
Lettuce, leaf	1/1–2/1	1/1–2/1	1/1–3/15	1/1–3/15	1/15–4/1	2/1–4/1	2/15–4/15
Muskmelon	2/15–3/15	2/15–4/1	2/15–4/15	3/1–4/15	3/15–4/15	4/1–5/1	4/10–5/15
Mustard	1/1–3/1	1/1–3/1	2/15–4/15	2/1–3/1	2/10–3/15	2/20–4/1	3/1–4/15
Okra	2/15–4/1	2/15–4/15	3/1–6/1	3/10–6/1	3/20–6/1	4/1–6/15	4/10–6/15
Onion[1]	1/1–1/15	1/1–1/15	1/1–1/15	1/1–2/1	1/15–2/15	2/10–3/10	2/15–3/15
Onion, seed	1/1–1/15	1/1–1/15	1/1–1/15	1/1–2/15	2/1–3/1	2/10–3/10	2/20–3/15
Onion, sets	1/1–1/15	1/1–1/15	1/1–1/15	1/1–3/1	1/15–3/10	2/1–3/20	2/15–3/20
Parsley	1/1–1/30	1/1–1/30	1/1–1/30	1/15–3/1	2/1–3/10	2/15–3/15	3/1–4/1
Parsnip	——	——	1/1–2/1	1/15–2/15	1/15–3/1	2/15–3/15	3/1–4/1
Peas, garden	1/1–2/15	1/1–2/15	1/1–3/1	1/15–3/1	1/15–3/15	2/1–3/15	2/1–3/20
Peas, black-eyed	2/15–5/1	2/15–5/15	3/1–6/15	3/10–6/20	3/15–7/1	4/1–7/1	4/15–7/1
Pepper[1]	2/1–4/1	2/15–4/15	3/1–5/1	3/15–5/1	4/1–6/1	4/10–6/1	4/15–6/1
Potatoes	1/1–2/15	1/1–2/15	1/15–3/1	1/15–3/1	2/1–3/1	2/10–3/15	2/20–3/20
Radishes	1/1–4/1	1/1–4/1	1/1–4/1	1/1–4/1	1/1–4/15	1/20–5/1	2/15–5/1
Rhubarb[1]	——	——	——	——	——	——	——
Rutabaga	——	——	——	1/1–2/1	1/15–2/15	1/15–3/1	2/1–3/1
Salsify	1/1–2/1	1/10–2/10	1/15–2/20	1/15–3/1	2/1–3/1	2/15–3/1	3/1–3/15
Shallot	1/1–2/1	1/1–2/10	1/1–2/20	1/1–3/1	1/15–3/1	2/1–3/10	2/15–3/15
Sorrel	1/1–3/1	1/1–3/1	1/15–3/1	2/1–3/10	2/10–3/15	2/10–3/20	2/20–4/1
Soybeans	3/1–6/30	3/1–6/30	3/10–6/30	3/20–6/30	4/10–6/30	4/10–6/30	4/20–6/30
Spinach	1/1–2/15	1/1–2/15	1/1–3/1	1/1–3/1	1/15–3/10	1/15–3/15	2/1–3/20
Spinach, New Zealand	2/1–4/15	2/15–4/15	3/1–4/15	3/15–5/15	3/20–5/15	4/1–5/15	4/10–6/1

[1] Plants

Crop	Jan. 30	Feb. 8	Feb. 18	Feb. 28	Mar. 10	Mar. 20	Mar. 30
Squash, summer	2/1–4/15	2/15–4/15	3/1–4/15	3/15–5/15	3/15–5/1	4/1–5/15	4/10–6/1
Sweet potatoes	2/15–5/15	3/1–5/15	3/20–6/1	3/20–6/1	4/1–6/1	4/10–6/1	4/20–6/1
Tomatoes	2/1–4/1	2/20–4/10	3/1–4/20	3/10–5/1	3/20–5/10	4/1–5/20	4/10–6/1
Turnips	1/1–3/1	1/1–3/1	1/10–3/1	1/20–3/1	2/1–3/1	2/10–3/10	2/20–3/20
Watermelon	2/15–3/15	2/15–4/1	2/15–4/15	3/1–4/15	3/15–4/15	4/1–5/1	4/10–5/15

SPRING DATES TO PLANT IF LAST FREEZE IS—

Crop	Apr. 10	Apr. 20	Apr. 30	May 10	May 20	May 30	June 10
Asparagus[1]	3/10–4/10	3/15–4/15	3/20–4/15	3/10–4/30	4/20–5/15	5/1–6/1	5/15–6/1
Beans, lima	4/1–6/30	5/1–6/20	5/15–6/15	5/25–6/15	——	——	——
Beans, snap	4/10–6/30	4/25–6/30	5/10–6/30	5/10–6/30	5/15–6/30	5/25–6/15	——
Beets	3/10–6/1	3/20–6/1	4/1–6/15	4/15–6/15	4/25–6/15	5/1–6/15	5/15–6/15
Broccoli, sprouting[1]	3/15–4/15	3/25–4/20	4/1–5/1	4/15–6/1	5/1–6/15	5/10–6/10	5/20–6/10
Brussels sprouts[1]	3/15–4/15	3/25–4/20	4/1–5/1	4/15–6/1	5/1–6/15	5/10–6/10	5/20–6/10
Cabbage[1]	3/1–4/1	3/10–4/1	3/15–4/10	4/1–5/15	5/1–6/15	5/10–6/15	5/20–6/1
Cabbage, Chinese	——	——	——	4/1–5/15	5/1–6/15	5/10–6/15	5/20–6/1
Carrots	3/10–4/20	4/1–5/15	4/10–6/1	4/20–6/15	5/1–6/1	5/10–6/1	5/20–6/1
Cauliflower[1]	3/1–3/20	3/15–4/20	4/10–5/10	4/15–5/15	5/10–6/15	5/20–6/1	6/1–6/15
Celery and celeriac	4/1–4/20	4/10–5/1	4/15–5/1	4/20–6/15	5/10–6/15	5/20–6/1	6/1–6/15
Chard	3/15–6/15	4/1–6/15	4/15–6/15	4/20–6/15	5/10–6/15	5/20–6/1	6/1–6/15
Chervil and chives	3/1–4/1	3/10–4/10	3/20–4/20	4/1–5/1	4/15–5/15	5/1–6/1	5/15–6/1
Chicory, witloof	6/1–7/1	6/15–7/1	6/15–7/1	6/1–6/20	6/1–6/15	6/1–6/15	6/1–6/15
Collards[1]	3/1–6/1	3/10–6/1	4/1–6/1	4/15–6/1	5/1–6/1	5/10–6/1	5/20–6/1
Cornsalad	2/1–4/1	2/15–4/15	3/1–5/1	4/1–6/1	4/15–6/1	5/1–6/15	5/15–6/15
Corn, sweet	4/10–6/1	4/25–6/15	5/10–6/15	5/10–6/1	5/15–6/1	5/20–6/1	——
Cress, upland	3/10–4/15	3/20–5/1	4/10–5/1	4/20–5/20	5/1–6/1	5/15–6/1	5/15–6/15
Cucumbers	4/20–6/1	5/1–6/15	5/15–6/15	5/20–6/15	6/1–6/15	——	——
Eggplant[1]	5/1–6/1	5/10–6/1	5/15–6/1	5/20–6/15	6/1–6/15	——	——
Endive	3/15–4/15	3/25–4/15	4/1–5/1	4/15–5/15	5/1–5/30	5/1–5/30	5/15–6/30
Fennel, Florence	3/15–4/15	3/25–4/15	4/1–5/1	4/15–5/15	5/1–5/30	5/1–5/30	5/15–6/1
Garlic	2/20–3/20	3/10–4/1	3/15–4/15	4/1–5/1	4/15–5/15	5/1–5/30	5/15–6/1
Horseradish[1]	3/10–4/10	3/20–4/20	4/1–4/30	4/15–5/15	4/20–5/20	5/1–5/30	5/15–6/1
Kale	3/10–4/1	3/20–4/10	4/1–4/20	4/10–5/1	4/20–5/10	5/1–5/30	5/15–6/1

[1] Plants

SPRING DATES TO PLANT IF LAST FREEZE IS—(continued)

Crop	Apr. 10	Apr. 20	Apr. 30	May 10	May 20	May 30	June 10
Kohlrabi	3/10–4/10	3/20–5/1	4/1–5/10	4/10–5/15	4/20–5/20	5/1–5/30	5/15–6/1
Leek	3/1–4/1	3/15–4/15	4/1–5/1	4/15–5/15	5/1–5/20	5/1–5/15	5/1–5/15
Lettuce, head[1]	3/10–4/1	3/20–4/15	4/1–5/1	4/15–5/15	5/1–6/30	5/10–6/30	5/20–6/30
Lettuce, leaf	3/15–5/15	3/20–5/15	5/1–6/1	4/15–6/15	5/1–6/30	5/10–6/30	5/20–6/30
Muskmelon	5/20–6/1	5/1–6/15	5/15–6/15	6/1–6/15	——	——	——
Mustard	3/10–4/20	3/20–5/1	4/1–5/10	4/15–6/1	5/1–6/30	5/10–6/30	5/20–6/30
Okra	4/20–6/15	5/1–6/1	5/10–6/1	5/20–6/10	6/1–6/20	——	——
Onion[1]	3/1–4/1	3/15–4/10	4/1–5/1	4/10–5/1	4/20–5/15	5/1–5/30	5/10–6/10
Onion, seed	3/1–4/1	3/15–4/1	3/15–4/15	4/1–5/1	4/20–5/15	5/1–5/30	5/10–6/10
Onion, sets	3/1–4/1	3/10–4/1	3/10–4/10	4/1–5/1	4/20–5/15	5/1–5/30	5/10–6/10
Parsley	3/10–4/10	3/20–4/20	4/1–5/1	4/15–5/15	5/1–5/20	5/10–6/1	5/20–6/10
Parsnip	3/10–4/10	3/20–4/20	4/1–5/1	4/15–5/15	5/1–5/20	5/10–6/1	5/20–6/10
Peas, garden	2/20–3/20	3/10–4/10	3/20–5/1	4/1–5/15	4/15–6/1	5/1–6/15	5/10–6/15
Peas, black-eyed	5/1–7/1	5/10–6/15	5/15–6/1	——	——	——	——
Pepper[1]	5/1–6/1	5/10–6/1	5/15–6/1	5/20–6/10	5/25–6/15	6/1–6/15	——
Potatoes	3/10–4/1	3/15–4/10	3/20–5/10	4/1–6/1	4/15–6/15	5/1–6/15	5/15–6/1
Radishes	3/1–5/1	3/10–5/10	3/20–5/10	4/1–6/1	4/15–6/15	5/1–6/15	5/15–6/1
Rhubarb[1]	3/1–4/1	3/10–4/10	3/20–4/15	4/1–5/1	4/15–5/10	5/1–5/20	5/15–6/1
Rutabaga	——	——	5/1–6/1	5/1–6/1	5/1–5/20	5/10–5/20	5/20–6/1
Salsify	3/10–4/15	3/20–5/1	4/1–5/15	4/15–6/1	5/1–6/1	5/10–6/1	5/20–6/1
Shallot	3/1–4/1	3/15–4/15	4/1–5/1	4/10–5/1	4/20–5/10	5/1–6/1	5/10–6/1
Sorrel	3/1–4/15	3/15–5/1	4/1–5/15	4/15–6/1	5/1–6/1	5/10–6/10	5/20–6/10
Soybeans	5/1–6/30	5/10–6/20	5/15–6/15	5/25–6/10	——	——	——
Spinach	2/15–4/1	3/1–4/15	3/20–4/20	4/1–6/15	4/10–6/15	4/20–6/15	5/1–6/15
Spinach, New Zealand	4/20–6/1	5/1–6/15	5/1–6/15	5/10–6/15	5/20–6/15	6/1–6/15	——
Squash, summer	4/20–6/1	5/1–6/15	5/1–5/30	5/10–6/10	5/20–6/15	6/1–6/20	6/10–6/20
Sweet potatoes	5/1–6/1	5/10–6/10	5/20–6/10	——	——	——	——
Tomatoes	4/20–6/1	5/5–6/10	5/10–6/15	5/15–6/10	5/25–6/15	6/5–6/20	6/15–6/30
Turnips	3/1–4/1	3/10–4/1	3/20–5/1	4/1–6/1	4/15–6/1	5/1–6/15	5/15–6/15
Watermelon	4/20–6/1	5/1–6/15	5/15–6/15	6/1–6/15	6/15–7/1	——	——

[1] Plants

SUMMER DATES TO PLANT IF FIRST FREEZE IS—

Crop	Aug. 30	Sept. 10	Sept. 20	Sept. 30	Oct. 10	Oct. 20
Asparagus[1]	——	——	——	——	10/20–11/15	11/1–12/15
Beans, lima	——	——	——	6/1–6/15	6/1–6/15	6/15–6/30
Beans, snap	——	5/15–6/15	6/1–7/1	6/1–7/10	6/15–7/20	7/1–8/1
Beets	5/15–6/15	5/15–6/15	6/1–7/1	6/1–7/10	6/15–7/25	7/1–8/5
Broccoli, sprouting	5/1–6/1	5/1–6/1	5/1–6/15	6/1–6/30	6/15–7/15	7/1–8/1
Brussels sprouts	5/1–6/1	5/1–6/1	5/1–6/15	6/1–6/30	6/15–7/15	7/1–8/1
Cabbage[1]	5/1–6/1	5/1–6/1	5/1–6/15	6/1–7/10	6/1–7/15	7/1–7/20
Cabbage, Chinese	5/15–6/15	5/15–6/15	6/1–7/1	6/1–7/15	6/15–8/1	7/15–8/15
Carrots	5/15–6/15	5/15–6/15	6/1–7/1	6/1–7/10	6/1–7/20	6/15–8/1
Cauliflower[1]	5/1–6/1	5/1–7/1	5/1–7/1	5/10–7/15	6/1–7/25	7/1–8/5
Celery[1] and celeriac	5/1–6/1	5/15–6/15	5/15–7/1	6/1–7/5	6/1–7/15	6/1–8/1
Chard	5/15–6/15	5/15–7/1	6/1–7/1	6/1–7/5	6/1–7/20	6/1–8/1
Chervil and chives	5/10–6/10	5/1–6/15	5/15–6/15	——	——	——
Chicory, witloof	5/15–6/15	5/15–6/15	5/15–6/15	6/1–7/1	6/1–7/1	6/15–7/15
Collards[1]	5/15–6/15	5/15–6/15	5/15–6/15	6/15–7/15	6/1–8/1	6/15–8/15
Cornsalad	5/15–6/15	5/15–7/1	6/15–8/1	7/15–9/1	8/15–9/15	9/1–10/15
Corn, sweet	——	——	6/1–7/1	6/1–7/1	6/1–7/10	6/1–7/20
Cress, upland	5/15–6/15	5/15–7/1	6/15–8/1	7/15–9/1	8/15–9/15	9/1–10/15
Cucumbers	——	——	6/1–6/15	6/1–7/1	6/1–7/1	6/1–7/15
Eggplant[1]	——	——	——	5/20–6/10	5/15–6/15	6/1–7/1
Endive	6/1–7/1	6/1–7/1	6/15–7/15	6/15–8/1	7/1–8/15	7/15–9/1
Fennel, Florence	5/15–6/15	5/15–7/15	6/1–7/1	6/1–7/1	6/15–7/15	6/15–8/1
Garlic	——	——	——	——	——	——
Horseradish[1]	——	——	——	——	——	——
Kale	5/15–6/15	5/15–6/15	6/1–7/1	6/15–7/15	7/1–8/1	7/15–8/15
Kohlrabi	5/15–6/15	6/1–7/1	6/1–7/15	6/15–7/15	7/1–8/1	7/15–8/15
Leek	5/1–6/1	5/1–6/1	——	——	——	——
Lettuce, head[1]	5/15–7/1	5/15–7/1	6/1–7/15	6/15–8/1	7/15–8/15	8/1–8/30
Lettuce, leaf	5/15–7/15	5/15–7/15	6/1–8/1	6/1–8/1	7/15–9/1	7/15–9/1
Muskmelon	——	——	5/1–6/15	5/15–6/1	6/1–6/15	6/15–7/20
Mustard	5/15–7/15	5/15–7/15	6/1–8/1	6/15–8/1	7/15–8/15	8/1–9/1
Okra	——	——	6/1–6/20	6/1–7/1	6/1–7/15	6/1–8/1
Onion[1]	5/1–6/10	5/1–6/10	——	——	——	——
Onion, seed	5/1–6/1	5/1–6/10	——	——	——	——

[1] Plants

SUMMER DATES TO PLANT IF FIRST FREEZE IS—(continued)

Crop	Aug. 30	Sept. 10	Sept. 20	Sept. 30	Oct. 10	Oct. 20
Onion, sets	5/1–6/1	5/1–6/10	——	——	——	——
Parsley	5/15–6/15	5/1–6/15	6/1–7/1	6/1–7/15	6/15–8/1	7/15–8/15
Parsnip	5/15–6/1	5/1–6/15	5/15–6/15	6/1–7/1	6/1–7/10	——
Peas, garden	5/10–6/15	5/1–7/1	6/1–7/15	6/1–8/1	——	——
Peas, black-eyed	——	——	——	——	6/10–7/1	6/1–7/1
Pepper[1]	——	——	6/1–6/20	6/1–7/1	6/1–7/1	6/1–7/10
Potatoes	5/15–6/1	5/1–6/15	5/1–6/15	5/1–6/15	5/15–6/15	6/15–7/15
Radishes	5/1–7/15	5/1–8/1	6/1–8/15	7/1–9/1	7/15–9/15	8/1–10/1
Rhubarb[1]	9/1–10/1	9/15–10/15	9/15–11/1	10/1–11/1	10/15–11/15	10/15–12/1
Rutabaga	5/15–6/15	5/1–6/15	6/1–7/1	6/1–7/1	6/15–7/15	7/10–7/20
Salsify	5/15–6/1	5/10–6/10	5/20–6/20	6/1–6/20	6/1–7/1	6/1–7/1
Shallot	——	——	——	——	——	——
Sorrel	5/15–6/15	5/1–6/15	6/1–7/1	6/1–7/15	7/1–8/1	7/15–8/15
Soybeans	——	——	——	5/25–6/10	6/1–6/25	6/1–7/5
Spinach	5/15–7/1	6/1–7/15	6/1–8/1	7/1–8/15	8/1–9/1	8/20–9/10
Spinach, New Zealand	——	——	——	5/15–7/1	6/1–7/15	6/1–8/1
Squash, summer	6/10–6/20	6/1–6/20	5/15–7/1	6/1–7/1	6/1–7/15	6/1–7/20
Squash, winter	——	——	5/20–6/10	6/1–6/15	6/1–7/1	6/1–7/1
Sweet potatoes	——	——	——	——	5/20–6/10	6/1–6/15
Tomatoes	6/20–6/30	6/10–6/20	6/1–6/20	6/1–6/20	6/1–6/20	6/1–7/1
Turnips	5/15–6/15	6/1–7/1	6/1–7/15	6/1–8/1	7/1–8/1	7/15–8/15
Watermelon	——	——	5/1–6/15	5/15–6/1	6/1–6/15	6/15–7/20

DATES TO PLANT IF FIRST FREEZE IS—

Crop	Oct. 30	Nov. 10	Nov. 20	Nov. 30	Dec. 10	Dec. 20
Asparagus[1]	11/15–1/1	12/1–1/1	——	——	——	——
Beans, lima	7/1–8/1	7/1–8/15	7/15–9/1	8/1–9/15	9/1–9/30	9/1–10/1
Beans, snap	7/1–8/15	7/1–9/1	7/1–9/10	8/15–9/20	9/1–9/30	9/1–11/1
Beets	8/1–9/1	8/1–10/1	9/1–12/1	9/1–12/15	9/1–12/31	9/1–12/31
Broccoli, sprouting	7/1–8/15	8/1–9/1	8/1–9/15	8/1–10/1	8/1–11/1	9/1–12/31
Brussels sprouts	7/1–8/15	8/1–9/1	8/1–9/15	8/1–10/1	8/1–11/1	9/1–12/31
Cabbage[1]	8/1–9/1	9/1–9/15	9/1–12/1	9/1–12/31	9/1–12/31	9/1–12/31

[1] Plants

Crop	Oct. 30	Nov. 10	Nov. 20	Nov. 30	Dec. 10	Dec. 20
Cabbage, Chinese	8/1–9/15	8/15–10/1	9/1–10/15	9/1–11/1	9/1–11/15	9/1–12/1
Carrots	7/1–8/15	8/1–9/1	9/1–11/1	9/15–12/1	9/15–12/1	9/15–12/1
Cauliflower[1]	7/15–8/15	8/1–9/1	8/1–9/15	8/15–10/10	9/1–10/20	9/15–11/1
Celery[1] and celeriac	6/15–8/15	7/1–8/15	7/15–9/1	8/1–12/1	9/1–12/31	10/1–12/31
Chard	6/1–9/10	6/1–9/15	6/1–10/1	6/1–11/1	6/1–12/1	6/1–12/31
Chervil and chives	——	——	11/1–12/31	11/1–12/31	11/1–12/31	11/1–12/31
Chicory, witloof	7/1–8/10	7/10–8/20	7/20–9/1	8/15–9/30	8/15–10/15	8/15–10/15
Collards[1]	8/1–9/15	8/15–10/1	8/25–11/1	9/1–12/1	9/1–12/31	9/1–12/31
Cornsalad	9/15–11/1	10/1–12/1	10/1–12/1	10/1–12/31	10/1–12/31	10/1–12/31
Corn, sweet	6/1–8/1	6/1–8/15	6/1–9/1	——	——	——
Cress, upland	9/15–11/1	10/1–12/1	10/1–12/1	10/1–12/31	10/1–12/31	10/1–12/31
Cucumbers	6/1–8/1	6/1–8/15	6/1–8/15	7/15–9/15	8/15–10/1	8/15–10/1
Eggplant[1]	6/1–7/1	6/1–7/15	6/1–8/1	7/1–9/1	8/1–9/30	8/1–9/30
Endive	7/15–8/15	8/1–9/1	9/1–10/1	9/1–11/15	9/1–12/31	9/1–12/31
Fennel, Florence	7/1–8/1	7/15–8/15	8/15–9/15	9/1–11/15	9/1–12/1	9/1–12/1
Garlic	——	8/1–10/1	8/15–10/1	9/1–11/15	9/15–11/15	9/15–11/15
Horseradish[1]	——	——	——	——	——	——
Kale	7/15–9/1	8/1–9/15	8/15–10/15	9/1–12/1	9/1–12/31	9/1–12/31
Kohlrabi	8/1–9/1	8/15–9/15	9/1–10/15	9/1–12/1	9/15–12/31	9/1–12/31
Leek	——	——	9/1–11/1	9/1–11/1	9/1–11/1	9/15–11/1
Lettuce, head[1]	8/1–9/15	8/15–10/15	9/1–11/1	9/1–12/1	9/15–12/31	9/15–12/31
Lettuce, leaf	8/15–10/1	8/25–10/1	9/1–11/1	9/1–12/1	9/15–12/31	9/15–12/31
Muskmelon	7/1–7/15	7/15–7/30	——	——	——	——
Mustard	8/15–10/15	8/15–11/1	9/1–12/1	9/1–12/1	9/1–12/1	9/15–12/1
Okra	6/1–8/1	6/1–8/20	6/1–9/10	6/1–9/20	8/1–10/1	8/1–10/1
Onion[1]	——	9/1–10/15	10/1–12/31	10/1–12/31	10/1–12/31	10/1–12/31
Onion, seed	——	——	9/1–11/1	9/1–11/1	9/1–11/1	9/15–11/1
Onion, sets	——	10/1–12/1	11/1–12/31	11/1–12/31	11/1–12/31	11/1–12/31
Parsley	8/1–9/15	9/1–11/15	9/1–12/31	9/1–12/31	9/1–12/31	9/1–12/31
Parsnip	——	——	8/1–9/1	9/1–11/15	9/1–12/1	9/1–12/1
Peas, garden	8/1–9/15	9/1–11/1	10/1–12/1	10/1–12/31	10/1–12/31	10/1–12/31
Peas, black-eyed	6/1–8/1	6/15–8/15	7/1–9/1	7/1–9/10	7/1–9/20	7/1–9/20
Peppers[1]	6/1–7/20	6/1–8/1	6/1–8/15	6/15–9/1	8/15–10/1	8/15–10/1
Potatoes	7/20–8/10	7/25–8/20	8/10–9/15	8/1–9/15	8/1–9/15	8/1–9/15
Radishes	8/15–10/15	9/1–11/15	9/1–12/1	9/1–12/31	8/1–9/15	10/1–12/31
Rhubarb[1]	11/1–12/1	——	——	——	——	——

[1] Plants

DATES TO PLANT IF FIRST FREEZE IS—(continued)

Crop	Oct. 30	Nov. 10	Nov. 20	Nov. 30	Dec. 10	Dec. 20
Rutabaga	7/15–8/10	7/15–8/15	8/1–9/1	9/1–11/15	10/1–11/15	10/15–11/15
Salsify	6/1–7/10	6/15–7/20	7/15–8/15	8/15–9/30	8/15–10/15	9/1–10/31
Shallot	——	8/1–10/1	8/15–10/1	8/15–10/15	9/15–11/1	9/15–11/1
Sorrel	8/1–9/15	8/15–10/1	8/15–10/15	9/1–11/15	9/1–12/15	9/1–12/31
Soybeans	6/1–7/15	6/1–7/25	6/1–7/30	6/1–7/30	6/1–7/30	6/1–7/30
Spinach	9/1–10/1	9/15–11/1	10/1–12/1	10/1–12/31	10/1–12/31	10/1–12/31
Spinach, New Zealand	6/1–8/1	6/1–8/15	6/1–8/15	——	——	——
Squash, summer	6/1–8/1	6/1–8/10	6/1–8/20	6/1–9/1	6/1–9/15	6/1–10/1
Squash, winter	6/10–7/10	6/20–7/20	7/1–8/1	7/15–8/15	8/1–9/1	8/1–9/1
Sweet potatoes	6/1–6/15	6/1–7/1	6/1–7/1	6/1–7/1	6/1–7/1	6/1–7/1
Tomatoes	6/1–7/1	6/1–7/15	6/1–8/1	8/1–9/1	8/15–10/1	9/1–11/1
Turnips	8/1–9/15	9/1–10/15	9/1–11/15	9/1–11/15	10/1–12/1	10/1–12/31
Watermelon	7/1–7/15	7/15–7/30	——	——	——	——

[1] Plants

Plants, Like People, Like a Warm Bed

In order for seeds to germinate, whether indoors or out, they need heat and moisture. Soil temperature indoors can be adjusted and controlled by heating cable and thermostat. Soil temperature control is possible outdoors also by using

LOVE IS A WARM BED

soil-heating cables, but they are practical only in small areas or in cold frames and greenhouse benches. For more information on the uses and prices, write to my longtime good friends at Wrap-On Company, 341 West Superior, Chicago, Il 60610.

Our major source of heat in the soil will come from the sun. Most vegetable seeds need a soil temperature of 55° to 75° for a period of 10 days to 2 weeks.

Plants that prefer 50°–55° to germinate
Broad beans   Lettuce

Plants that prefer 55°–65°
Peas   Radish   Salsify   New Zealand Spinach

Plants that prefer 65°–70°
Celeriac   Celery

Plants that like real comfort, 70°–75°

Beans	Corn	Onion	Rutabaga
Beets	Endive	Parsley	Spinach
Broccoli	Kale	Parsnips	Squash
Brussels sprouts	Kohlrabi	Peanuts	Swiss chard
Cabbage	Leek	Peppers	Tomatoes
Cauliflower	Mustard	Potatoes	Turnips
Collards	Okra	Pumpkins	

Some even like it hot, 70° to 80°
Asparagus   Cantaloupe   Watermelon   Eggplant (demands 75° to 80°)

A SEED SAUNA

Warm Bath Does Wonders

Seed can be assisted on its journey to sprout by placing it in a lukewarm cup of tea for a few hours. Overnight will help. Then spread it out to dry enough to handle and plant. You can get from a 3-to-5-day jump on sprouting and a week or two on harvest.

NO TIGHT SPOTS

Each garden seed is an embryo, just like embryos of people, pets, fish, and fowl, and we all need room to grow. With this in mind, plan to plant each seed as an individual. No, I'm not kidding! Use seed tape, seed pellets, or a dibble. Believe me, the results will amaze you and will eliminate the need to thin out.

Plant 3 inches apart

Beets	Kohlrabi	Onion	Peas
Carrots	Leek	Parsnips	Turnips

Plant 6 inches apart

Parsley   Rutabaga   Spinach   Beans   Lettuce, leaf

Plant 12 inches apart

Asparagus	Celery	Cucumbers	Okra
Cabbage	Swiss chard	Endive	Potatoes
Cantaloupe	Collards	Lettuce, head	New salad
Celeriac	Corn	Mustard	squash

Plant 18 inches apart

Brussels sprouts   Eggplant   Kale   Peanuts   Peppers

Plant 24 inches apart

Tomatoes (even up to 36 inches)

Plant 36–48 inches apart

Squash

Plant 5–6 feet apart

Watermelon   Pumpkins

I want you to understand that these planting distances are ballpark distances not chiseled in stone. Grandma Putt, the lady that taught me to garden, always said that a plant with room to grow will do your garden proud. These figures will also keep you from biting off more garden than your family can chew.

Cover Your Seedbed with a Silk Sheet!

If you've ever had the pleasure of sleeping between silk sheets, you know true comfort. I have discovered that if I cover my newly planted seeds with a light cover of damp Pro Mix (soilless planter mix), my new seeds are so comfortable that they pop right up—no stress, no strain. This material will control moisture and lightly feed your new plants. Try it; your plants will love it and you.

A Little Baby Food Really Helps

As soon as my seeds are planted, I put an ounce of Super K-Gro Fish Emulsion in a hose-end sprayer, add a shot glass of liquid soap, and dampen my garden well. This keeps the soil from crusting and discourages most insects in the area while the fish food begins its action in the soil to be available for the new babies when they come out of their shells.

PLANT PABLUM

Take Your Time When Planting!

It is not necessary to plant all of your seeds and plants in one day. If you get tired, you may get careless; that can cost you and your seeds. Never walk on newly planted seeds, and be sure to keep on the paths that you designed into your layout.

Space Is No Excuse

Anyone who can turn on a light bulb or open a window can have a vegetable garden. If you have a small balcony, patio, or path along the driveway or sidewalk, you can plant in a planter, tub, wastebasket or old drum to have fresh vegetables.

Space Savers for Container Gardens

Today's trend toward city living and homes with smaller gardens has tremendously increased the interest in vegetables suitable for intensive gardening and container growing —those that are highly productive in a small place. The varieties I have suggested fill those requirements and more.

Beet, Green Top Bunching. 55 days. A dual-purpose beet useful for its finely flavored tops, which keep their green color, and for its tender roots—so good fresh, canned, or pickled.

Broccoli, Green Dwarf #36, Hybrid. A great space saver for the limited-area garden. Plants just 8 inches tall bear large, dome-shaped 5½-inch heads of exceptionally fine flavor. Surrounding leaves are short and grow as a dense rosette around the stem. And because the plants are so compact, you can plant more and harvest more for your table. Stem is thick and solid. Resistant to downy mildew. 90 days.

Cabbage, Darkri, Hybrid. 3 weeks earlier than any cabbage in our spring trials; firm 6-to-8-inch heads in just 47 days from setting out, 75 days from sowing. Exterior leaves are short and few, allow high yields in less space. Flavor is mild and sweet, heads are creamy white and densely curled at the center, high in quality even in summer.

Cantaloupe, Musketeer. Now you can enjoy juicy, sweet, delicious cantaloupes in even the smallest garden! Plants measure only 2 to 3 feet across, yet bear a bountiful crop of 5½-to-6-inch round fruits of mouth-watering quality. Each fruit is heavily netted to prevent splitting. And it's extra early—matures in just 90 days. The combination of great taste, earliness, and amazingly compact growth makes Musketeer the perfect answer for the limited-space gardener, and a superb melon for container growing, too.

Carrot, Lady Finger. A real gourmet's delight! Tiny, tender roots, 4 inches long and ½ to ⅝ inch across, golden orange, high in sugar, crisp and a joy to eat. A good choice for heavy soils, too. 65 days.

Sweet Corn, Golden Midget. Midget, 4-inch butter-yellow ears of highest sugar content, on miniature 30-inch plants, in less than 60 days!

Sweet Corn, Miniature Hybrid. 66 days. Dwarf plants take little space, but bear abundant 5-inch ears, well filled with golden kernels on a slim cob. Perfect for freezing.

Cucumber, Bush Whopper. Whopping big cucumbers, 6 to 8 inches long, on dwarf, mound-shaped plants. Vines are short, with no runners at all, excellent for small garden or for containers. Bush Whopper cukes are thick, deliciously crisp, and luscious in salads. The variety bears profusely in any climate. 55 days.

Eggplant, Morden Midget. Sturdy, small bushy plants bear smooth, medium-sized, deep purple fruits of the highest quality. 65 days from setting out. 6,000 seeds per ounce.

Honeydew, Oliver's Pearl Cluster. The first bush honeydew, ideal for the home garden where space is limited. Plants are just 2 feet across, bear fruits 4 to 5 inches in diameter, with sweet green flesh of exceptional flavor. 110 days.

Lettuce, Tom Thumb. A miniature butterhead type that's exceptionally crisp and sweet. These midget, tennis-ball-size heads are served whole with dressing as individual salads at the Waldorf and other famous hotels. Ideal for window box or garden. 65 days.

Parsley, Paramount. 70 days. Unusually dark green, triple-curled and handsome. Does not tip-burn. Excellent for flavoring and garnishing and as an attractive basket plant.

Pepper, Park's Pot, Hybrid. Handsome plants, just 10-12 inches tall, bear a heavy crop of delicious crisp medium fruits, just 45 days after setting out, 90 days from sowing. Remarkably productive in smaller gardens, pots, or hanging baskets.

Squash, Park's Creamy Hybrid. 55 days. High quality, performance, and dwarf habit make Creamy a true Park High Performer™. Space-saving dwarf plants, only 18 inches across, bear creamy-yellow 6-to-8-inch straight-neck fruits, firm and tender, wonderfully delicious. Prolific over a long season, it withstands extremes of temperature. A fine performer for the large and small garden.

Tomato, City Best VFN, Hybrid. This determinate or bush-type tomato bears an abundance of very tasty medium-size red fruit. Plants have lush foliage with self-supporting branches. A great container plant. Fruit begins to ripen in just 60 days.

Tomato, Minibel. High yield of bright red, 2-inch fruit glows on a background of cascading dark green foliage. Excellent table quality, with cool tomato flavor, thin palatable skin, and appealing color, deluxe for salad or appetizer. An attractive basket plant and a red companion to Goldie.

Watermelon, Bushbaby, Hybrid. The perfect watermelon for the small home garden. Dwarf determinate plants generously produce round-oval 8-pound fruit of the highest table quality—high in sugar, low in fiber, juicy and delectable. Light-green-striped skin, rich pink flesh. Plants are prolific and ripen their fruit in just 80 days.

Sow What?

There are hundreds and hundreds of vegetable garden varieties for the home gardener to pick from. Seed racks in your local community or seed catalogs make this great selection available to you.

The following varieties are a few in each vegetable catalog that I am familiar with and find adapt to most parts of the areas you folks live in; so, let this be a guide. In Chapter 15, which contains information on each state's vegetable garden habits, you will find a few special recommendations by the Agricultural Cooperative Extension Service that do best in your growing condition. All of the plant varieties in this section can be secured from George W. Park Seed Company, Inc., Cokesbury Road, Greenwood, SC 29647.

Park Seed continually keeps me coming back year after year with its new tasty, easy-to-grow varieties each year as well as a never-ending supply of the old stand-by varieties.

VARIETIES OF VEGETABLES
Artichoke

Green Globe. A perennial plant, grown for its flavorful flower heads with large scales, thick and heavy. May be boiled or steamed.

Jerusalem. A species of perennial sunflower *(Helianthus tuberosus)*, with crisp nutty flavor, for salads, relishes, and pickles. Among the easiest of all vegetables to grow, the plants yield small, white, edible tubers, much as do potatoes. Hardy in the South; requires mulching in cold areas.

Asparagus

Mary Washington. Delicious, tender green asparagus spears for eating, canning, or freezing. Thick, heavy shoots highly resistant to rust.

Brock's Imperial Hybrid. Extra-long tasty stalks in quick succession. Moderately rust-resistant.

Garden Beans

Bush Beans
Remus. 65 days.

Blue Lake 274. 55 days.
Blue Lake 141. 56 days.
Roma. 53 days.
Slenderette. 53 days.
Commodore. Bush Kentucky Wonder, 58 days.
Contender. 49 days.
Improved Tendergreen. 55 days.
Mountaineer White Half Runners. 57 days.
Royal Burgundy. 51 days.
Tenderette. 55 days.
Tendercrop. 53 days.
Topcrop. 50 days.

Wax Beans
Goldrop Bush Wax. 65 days.
Golden Wax Improved. 50 days.

Pole Beans
These bear later than bush varieties but with heavier yield. The 5-to-8-foot vines need support of pole, trellis, or fence.
Kentucky Wonder. 65 days.
Blue Lake FM-1. 60 days.
Romano. 66 days.
Selma Star. 60 days.
Selma Zebra. 55 days.

Bush Lima Beans
Plants need no support, therefore are easier to grow. Bear earlier than pole varieties. Excellent canned, frozen, and, of course, fresh. 1 pound plants to 100-foot row. Sow when soil is warm after last frost.
Early Thorogreen. 68 days.
Bridgeton. 65 days.
Fordhook 242. 75 days.
Henderson's Bush. 65 days.
Jackson Wonder. 65 days.
Dixie Butterpea. 75 days.
Dixie Butterpea Speckled. 75 days.

Pole Lima Beans
King of the Garden. 88 days.
Large Speckled Christmas. 88 days.

Bush Shell Beans
    Red Kidney. 95 days.
    Pinto. 88 days.
    Garbanzo. 88 days.

Beets

Readily grown, beets make one of the most attractive and delicious dishes of all vegetables and contain more iron than most. Sow thinly as early in spring as soil can be worked in rows 18 to 24 inches apart.
Detroit Dark Red, Short Top. 60 days.
Ruby Queen. 52 days.
Early Wonder. 52 days.
Cylindra. 60 days.
Green Top Bunching. 55 days.
Burpee's Golden Beet. 55 days.

Broccoli

Easily grown, broccoli has a rich, delicious flavor and is very rich in vitamins. Sow indoors 5 to 7 weeks before setting out. Set out 2 weeks before last spring frost, 2 feet apart in rows 2 feet apart. Approximately 9,000 seeds per ounce. Days to maturity are from setting out.
Green Dwarf. 90 days.
Premium Crop Hybrid. 58 days.
Green Duke Hybrid. 69 days.
De Cicco. 60 days.
Cleopatra Hybrid. 55 days.
Green Comet Hybrid. 55 days.
Green Sprouting. 55 days.

Brussels Sprouts

Sow indoors 4 to 6 weeks prior to planting date. Prefers cool soil. Set out as soon as soil can be worked, spacing 18 to 24 inches apart in rows 24 to 30 inches apart. Set out in June or July for fall crop. A touch of frost improves flavor. Days to maturity are from setting out.
Prince Marvel Hybrid, New. 90 days.
Jade Cross Hybrid. 85 days.
Long Island Improved. 90 days.

Cabbage

Sow indoors 5 to 7 weeks prior to planting. Requires cool soil. Set out plants as soon as soil can be worked, 15 to 18 inches apart in rows 24 to 30 inches apart. For fall crop, set out plants June to August. Days to maturity are from setting out.

Golden Cross Hybrid, New. 50 days.
Heavy Weighter Hybrid, New. 75 days.
Darkri Hybrid. 47 days.
All Seasons Wisconsin. 85 days.
Early Jersey. 64 days.
Golden Acre. 64 days.
Mammoth Red Rock. 100 days.
Harvester Queen Hybrid. 60 days.
Red Head Hybrid. 80 days.
Savoy Ace Hybrid. 85 days.
Savoy King Hybrid. 90 days.
Emerald Cross Hybrid. 67 days.
Stonehead Hybrid. 50 days.
Morden Dwarf. 55 days.

Chinese Cabbage

Michihli Jade Pagoda Hybrid. 60 days. The earliest, thickest, most succulent Chinese cabbage. Core is white and thick, creamy, deeply savoyed at center, mild and sweet. Big, clean, rot-free plants cylindrical in shape, very heat-resistant and able to tolerate all kinds of weather. Height 2 feet.
Chinese Michihli. 70 days.

Cantaloupe (Muskmelon)

Cantaloupes should ripen on the vine for best flavor. They're ripe when stem begins to part from the vine and separates with a slight pull. After danger of frost, sow seed in rich, well-drained sandy loam, in hills 4 feet apart with two to four seeds per hill. Thin to the two strongest plants per hill. Seed may be started indoors in "One-Steps" for an early start, particularly in short-season areas.
Musketeer. 90 days.

Luscious Hybrid. 90 days.
Scoop Hybrid. 61 days.
Short 'N' Sweet. 75 days.
Oval Chaca Hybrid. 78 days.
Saticoy Hybrid. 80 days.
Edisto. 90 days.
Samson Hybrid. 85 days.
Minnesota Midget. 60 days.
Bushwhopper Hybrid. 70 days.

Honey Dew
Pineapple Hybrid. 80 days.
Fruit Punch. 85 days.
Ogden. Flavor of pears. 80 days.
Honey Drip Hybrid. 85 days.
Oliver's Pearl Cluster. 110 days.
Tam Dew. 90 days.

Carrots

Rich in food value, carrots are delicious in all stages, and a treat when pulled young and eaten raw. They may be planted early as a spring crop, grown for fall harvest and stored over winter, or even forced in the cold frame as a wintertime delicacy. They do best in a rich, well-worked sandy soil, although the shorter kinds do well in heavy soils. Plant seeds ½ inch deep every 1 to 3 inches.
Lady Fingers. 65 days.
Nandor Hybrid. 66 days.
Amstel. 62 days.
Nantes Coreless. 68 days.
Kundulus, New. 68 days.
Royal Chantenay. 70 days.
Danvers Half Long. 75 days.
Royal Cross Hybrid. 70 days.
Golden Ball. 70 days.
Tendersweet. 75 days.

Cauliflower

Cauliflower is grown as broccoli is and is fine as a fall or spring crop. Sow seed in "One-Steps" or Jiffy Pots covering ¼ inch. Transplant to garden when roots emerge.

Early Hybrids
Snow King Hybrid. 50 days.
Snow Crown Hybrid. 53 days.

Self-Blanching
Early Super Snowball. 55 days.
Royal Purple. 95 days.
Snowball Self-Blanching. 70 days.
Alert, New. 48 days.

Celery

Sow indoors 10 to 12 weeks before planting out, about last frost date, 12 inches apart in trenches 12 inches wide and 18 inches deep.
Giant Pascal. 120 days.

Celeriac, Celery Knob or Root

Grown like celery, the root is eaten either raw or cooked, and its fine celery flavor and unique texture is a welcome addition to salads.
Celeriac Large Smooth Prague. 110 days.

Chard

Sow thinly in early spring in rows 15 to 18 inches apart. Stands hot weather, freezes well.
Rhubarb Chard. 60 days.
Lucullus Light Green. 60 days.
Swiss Chard of Geneva. 60 days.

Collards

Full of vitamins and very few calories, easily grown and winter-hardy except in extremely cold areas. Their flavor improves after frost. Grow like Brussels sprouts.

Hicrop Hybrid. 80 days.
Georgia. 80 days.
Vates Non-heading. 75 days.

Sweet Corn

Delicious vitamin-filled corn! Sow after danger of frost, 1 inch deep and 10 to 14 inches apart in rows 24 to 30 inches apart. Plant several rows together for proper pollination. Sow every 2 weeks until mid-July.

Super Sweet Corn Hybrids
Their special genetic makeup gives these varieties higher sugar content and keeps them sweet longer. To keep these properties, isolate from other varieties.
Butterfruit. 72 days.
Early Xtra Sweet. 70 days.
Illini Xtra Sweet. 83 days.
Golden Sweet EH. 78 days.
Florida Staysweet. 87 days.

White Sweet Corn Hybrids
Silver Queen Hybrid. 85 days.
White Lightning. 96 days.

Yellow Sweet Corn Hybrids
Seneca Chief Hybrid. 82 days.
Candystick Hybrid. 70 days.
Gold Rush Hybrid. 65 days.
Iochief Hybrid. 83 days.
Seneca Sentry. 89 days.
Early Sunglow. 62 days.
Merit. 75 days.
Golden Queen. 92 days.

Bicolor Sweet Corn Hybrids
Butter & Sugar. 73 days.
Seneca Pinto. 85 days.

Open Pollinated Corn
Trucker's Favorite White. 65 days.

Popcorn

Hybrid Popcorn South American. 105 days.
Hybrid Popcorn White Cloud. 83 days.

Cucumber

These varieties grow the long cylindrical fruit for slicing. Also useful for pickling when picked young. May be sown indoors 4 weeks prior to planting date. Set out in very fertile, light, well-drained, warm soil 4 feet apart each way, or 12 inches apart in rows 4 feet apart. Vines may be supported on trellis or fence. Keep soil moist. Germination: 7 to 10 days at 70° to 75° soil temperature.

Hybrid Salad Cucumbers

Park's Whopper Hybrid. 70 days.
Park's Comanche Hybrid. 50 days.
Patio Pik Hybrid. 51 days.
Saladin Hybrid. 55 days.
Early Surecrop Hybrid. 58 days.
Gemini Hybrid. 60 days.
Cherokee 7 Hybrid. 60 days.
Spartan Valor Hybrid. 60 days.
Damascus Hybrid. 60 days.

Burpless Hybrids

Park's Burpless Bush. 42 days.
Euro-American. 45 days.
Burpless Tasty Green No. 26 Hybrid. 62 days.
Sweet Slice Hybrid. 62 days.

Standard Salad Cucumbers

Marketmore 70. 55 days.
Poinsett 76. 63 days.
Bush Whopper. 55 days.

Pickling Cucumber

Mature fruits stay small on the vine, perfect for making sweet or sour pickles. Very productive.
Pickle-Dilly Hybrid. 50 days.

Liberty Hybrid. 50 days.
Spartan Dawn Hybrid. 51 days.
Pioneer Hybrid. 50 days.
Tiny Dill. 55 days.

Eggplant

Sow indoors 6 weeks before setting out. Set out after all danger of frost has passed in warm soil 30 inches apart in rows 36 inches apart. About 6,000 seeds per ounce. Days to maturity are from setting-out time.
Beauty Hybrid. 67 days.
Black Beauty. 80 days.
Ichiban Hybrid. 61 days.
Black Bell Hybrid. 68 days.
Dusky Hybrid. 63 days.
Morden Midget. 60 days.

Endive

Sow as soon as soil can be worked. Thin 10 to 12 inches apart. Sow in August for fall crop.
Green Curled Ruffec. 95 days.
Salad King. 98 days.

Garlic, Giant French Mild

Elephant Garlic. So named because of the very large cloves, weighing 4 to 5 ounces each. Of delicious aroma, milder than regular garlic and more intense than onion. One clove, when planted, produces five.

Kale

Plant out as soon as soil can be worked in the spring or September for fall crop. Thin to 12 inches apart in rows.
Dwarf Blue Curled Scotch Vates. 70 days.

Kohlrabi

Bulbous, above-ground stem bases are delicious raw and resemble water chestnuts in flavor and texture. Boiled, they combine the best qualities of turnip and cabbage. Sow indoors 4 to 6 weeks prior to setting out. Prefers cool soil; plant as soon as ground can be worked, 4 inches apart in rows. Days to maturity are from setting out.

Grand Duke Hybrid. 45 days.
Early White Vienna. 55 days.
Azur Star. 50 days.

Lettuce

Homegrown lettuce far surpasses in flavor, texture, and vitamin content lettuce you can get at the supermarket. Grow some for yourself for a true taste treat. Start in spring as soon as the soil reaches 52° F. Sow thinly, on top of the soil in rows 18 inches apart. Do not cover seeds; they need light for best germination. Prefers a rich, moist soil with good drainage. Sow again in August for a fall crop.

Loose-Leaf Lettuce
    Black Seeded Simpson. 45 days.
    Salad Bowl. 48 days.
    Red Salad Bowl. 50 days.
    Oak Leaf. 40 days.
    Pricehead. 45 days.
    Ruby. 47 days.
    Crispy Sweet. 40 days.

Butterhead Lettuce
    Augusta. 68 days.
    Bibb. 57 days.
    Buttercrunch. 65 days.
    Dark Green Boston W.S. 73 days.
    Butter King. 70 days.
    Tom Thumb. 65 days.

Romaine Lettuce
    Valmaine Cos. 70 days.
    Barcarolle. 70 days.

Crisp Heading Iceberg Types
    Mission, New. 74 days.
    Van Guard. 90 days.
    Slo-Bolt. 48 days.
    Great Lakes W.S. 75 days.
    Green Lake. 71 days.

Mustard for Greens

Sow seed outdoors in early spring. For fall crop sow 6 to 8 weeks before first fall frost. Sow 1 to 2 inches apart, in rows.
Southern Giant Curled (Mustard India). 50 days.
Tendergreens (Mustard Spinach). 28 days.

Okra

High in flavor and protein; delicious rolled in meal and fried, or used in soups and stews. Easy to grow; sow when soil and nights are warm. Starts bearing when just 1 foot tall, continues to frost. Relatively free of disease and insects.
Lee. 55 days.
Park's Candelabra Branching. 50–60 days.
Clemson Spineless. 56 days.
Spineless Green Velvet. 58 days.
Red Okra. 60 days.

Onions

Grow onions in your home garden. You'll get far better quality than any you can buy. To grow onions from seed, start indoors in flats about 8 weeks prior to date of last expected frost. Grow in sunny window or under lights. Set seedlings out 2 to 3 inches apart, thinning for green onions. Sets of plants should be set out 3 inches apart as soon as soil can be worked. Varieties marked SD are short-day types, best for winter culture in the South. Varieties marked LD are long-day types, best for spring planting.
Southport Red Globe. 110 days LD.
Grainex Hybrid. 80 days SD.
Crystal Wax. 95 days SD.
Spano Hybrid. 95 days SD.
Ringmaster. 110 days LD.
Ebenezer. 105 days LD.
Snow White Hybrid. 105 days LD.
Red Hamburger. 100 days LD.
Fiesta Hybrid. 110 days LD.
Patti King Hybrid. 100 days LD.

Onion Sets (Ebenezer). Plant 1 pound of the ¼-inch bulbs per 50-foot row in early spring and pull delicious green onion stalks within a few weeks or harvest bulbs from midsummer on.

Parsley

Beautiful, decorative garden plant, and a flavorful seasoning; easily grown.
Paramount. 70 days.
Italian Dark Green Plain Leaf. 72 days.
Curlina. 70 days.
Compact Curled. 70 days.
Evergreen. 70 days.

Peanuts

Nutritious and tasty, peanuts can be grown anywhere they get 4 months of growing season. Sow in a light, well-drained soil, 4 to 6 inches apart and 2 inches deep, then thin plants to 12 inches apart. To harvest, dig entire plant and let dry in the air.
Park's Whopper. 110 days.
Valencia Tennessee Red. 120 days.
Spanish. 110 days.

Garden Peas

Peas are a cool-weather crop. Plant as soon as the ground can be worked, in 3-foot-apart rows, ½ inch deep and 2 inches apart.
Patriot. 65 days.
Green Arrow. 70 days.
Laxton's Progress. 70 days.
Alaska. 55 days.
Midseason Freezer. 63 days.

Dwarf Vine Varieties
No staking. An entirely new plant type which supports itself when planted in a double row. Instead of leaves, the dwarf 20-inch vines have a profusion of strong tendrils which provide support with little weight, and permit good light penetration.

Novella. 70 days.
Knight. 61 days.
Little Marvel. 63 days.

Snap Peas (Edible-Podded)
Sugarbon. 60 days.
Sugarsnap. 70 days.
Sugar Rae. 72 days.

Snow Peas (Edible-Podded)
Giant Melting Sugar. 68 days.
Dwarf Gray Sugar. 65 days.

Cowpeas
Mississippi Silver. 70–80 days.
Mississippi Purple. 70–80 days.
Purple Hull. 70–80 days.
Big Boy. 70–80 days.
Magnolia Blackeye. 70–80 days.
California Blackeye. 70–80 days.

Peppers

Sweet Pepper
Hybrids yield a much larger crop on stronger plants than the standard varieties. For early peppers, start indoors, 6 weeks before planting out. Days to maturity are from setting out.
Park's Whopper Hybrid. 65 days.
Park's Early Thickset Hybrid. 48 days.
Bellboy Hybrid. 70 days.
Big Bertha Hybrid. 72 days.
Golden Gladiator Hybrid. 71 days.
Early Prolific Hybrid. 72 days.
California Wonder. 75 days.
Sweet Banana. 65 days.
Cherry Sweet. 78 days.
Dutch Treat. 70 days.
Yolo Wonder. 78 days.
Pimiento Select. 75 days.
Gypsy Hybrid. 62 days.
Cubanelle. 65 days.
Park's Sweet Banana Whopper Hybrid. 60 days.

Park's Pot. 90 days.

Hot Pepper
    Pepper Thai Hot. 72 days.
    Cayenne Long Red Slim. 72 days.
    Cayenne Large Red Thick. 75 days.
    Hungarian Yellow Wax. 65 days.
    Jalapeno M. 73 days.

Potato Explorer Seed

One of the most exciting horticultural achievements ever! Explorer is productive! It works! Sow early, 4 weeks before last anticipated frost. You'll harvest lots of 2-to-3-inch new boiling-size potatoes in 90 days and big 4-to-6-inch bakers a month later. Explorer escapes most tuber-borne diseases, is far cheaper per plant than spuds, and avoids the separate cold-weather tilling of starting spuds.

Seed Potatoes

Certified, heavy-yielding, blight-resistant, tasty varieties for baking, creaming, boiling, or frying. These are higher-yielding and more disease-resistant than potato sets. Plant in early spring, 2 weeks before last frost date in furrow 8 inches deep. Space 12 inches apart in rows.
Red McClure. 90 days.
Russet Burbank. 120 days.

Pumpkin

Plant two or three seeds in hills 5 to 7 feet apart each way when soil warms.
Big Moon. 110 days.
Big Max. 120 days.
Jack-O'-Lantern. 110 days.
Lady Godiva. 110 days.

Radishes

Sow as early as soil can be worked in early spring. Space rows 15 to 24 inches apart.

Red Prince. 22 days.
Champion. 28 days.
Cherry Belle. 22 days.
Icicle. 28 days.
Pax. 28 days.

Rutabaga

Sow thinly in rows 15 to 24 inches apart, 3 to 3½ months before first fall frost. Best used as a fall crop.
American Purple Top. 80 days.

Spinach

Sow very early in spring in rows 15 to 18 inches apart. Likes cool weather. For fall use sow in late summer.
Melody Hybrid. 42 days.
America Bloomsdale Extra Long. 50 days.
Early Smooth No. 424 Hybrid. 50 days.
New Zealand. 50 days.

Summer Bush Squash

When danger of frost has passed, plant two or three seeds in hills 4 feet apart in rich soil.
Kuta Hybrid. 42 days.
Peter Pan Hybrid. 49 days.
Seneca Butterbar Hybrid. 49 days.
Seneca Prolific Hybrid. 49 days.
Early Yellow Summer Crookneck. 53 days.
Dixie Hybrid. 50 days.
Sundance Hybrid. 53 days.
Patty Green Tint Hybrid. 50 days.
Scallopini Hybrid. 50 days.
Park's Creamy Hybrid. 55 days.

Winter Squash

Hard-shelled fruit for fall and winter use. Plant after danger of frost, two or three seeds in hills 24 to 48 inches apart.
Show King. Giant show-size "pumpkin." Some have weighed over 400 pounds. Skins vary in color.

Jersey Golden Acorn. 50 days.
Sweet Mama Hybrid. 85 days.
Blue Hubbard. 115 days.
Hubbard Improved Green. 100 days.
Early Butternut Hybrid. 85 days.
Waltham Butternut. 80 days.
Tahitian. 80 days.
Gold Nugget. 85 days.
Table Ace Hybrid. 80 days.
Table King. 85 days.

Zucchini Summer Squash

When danger of frost has passed, plant three or four seeds in hills 4 feet apart, in rich deep soil. For quicker starts, plant in pots indoors. Set in garden when 3 to 4 inches high after frost.
Black Magic. 44 days.
Aristocrat Hybrid. 53 days.
Ambassador Hybrid. 48 days.
Dark Green Zucchini (bush). 50 days.
Park's Green Whopper. 70 days.
Gold Rush Hybrid. 50 days.
Seneca Gourmet. 46 days.
Gourmet Globe, Hybrid. 50 days.
Vegetable Marrow. 60 days.

Sweet Potato Plants

These are among the easiest of all vegetables to grow. They're near the top in food value and can be prepared in countless tempting ways, adding color and a festive touch to the meal. They store well, and the taste improves each day in storage. These are sunshine-grown plants that live, grow, and produce high yields of tasty, sweet, and delicious potatoes. Set plants 2 feet apart in a sunny well-drained location.
Vineless Puerto Rio. 150 days.
Vardaman. 150 days.
Centennial. 150 days.
New Jewel. 150 days.

Vigorous and productive. Now you can grow bigger and better tomatoes than you ever thought possible. The new hybrids are resistant to soil-borne diseases such as verticillium and fusarium wilt, as well as to nematodes and tobacco mosaic; vines stay healthy and bear an abundance of delicious fruits. With resistance, tomatoes can be grown in the same area year after year. These symbols after the name indicate resistance to: V, verticillium wilt; F, fusarium wilt; FF, Race 1 and Race 2 fusarium wilt; N, nematodes; T, tobacco mosaic; A, *Alternaria alternata* (crown wilt disease). Days indicate time from setting out plants to first ripe fruits. Sow indoors 5 to 7 weeks before setting out. Set out when weather is warm in light, deeply worked soil, 2 to 2½ feet apart.

Park's Whopper VFNT. 70 days.
Park's Extra Early VFNT. 52 days.
Beefmaster VFN. 70 days.
Better Boy VFN. 70 days.
Spring Giant VF. 68 days.
Fantastic. 70 days.
Early Girl. 54 days.
Burpee Big Boy. 78 days.
Golden Boy. 80 days.
Floramerica VF. 70 days.
The Duke VF. 75 days.
Bonus VFN. 75 days.
Bragger. 75 days.
Big Pick VFFNTA. 70 days.
Quick Pick VFFNTA. 65 days.
Terrific VFN. 70 days.
Easy Peel. 65 days.

Basket Tomatoes for Containers

Goldie Hybrid. 50 days.
Minibel. 55 days.
Tiny Time. 55 days.
Small Fry VFN Hybrid. 65 days.
Toy Boy VF Hybrid. 55 days.
Burgess Early Salad. 45 days.

Cherry Tomatoes
Little King VFFNTA Hybrid. 65 days.
Sugar Lump. 65 days.

Cooking and Canning Varieties
Roma VF. 76 days.

Patio Tomatoes
For containers or stakeless gardens.
Patio Prize VFN Hybrid. 67 days.
Patio F Hybrid. 70 days.
City Best. 60 days.
Bitsy VF Hybrid. 52 days.

Standard Tomatoes
Rutgers California Supreme. 73 days.
Marglobe Supreme F. 73 days.
Beefsteak Scarlet. 80 days.

Turnips

Turnips are a cool-season crop and should be planted in very early spring or late summer. They may be harvested in the fall and roots stored. Tops are delicious as "greens." May be canned or frozen. Sow thinly in rows 15 to 18 inches apart.
Shiro Hybrid, New. 57 days.
Purple Top White Globe. 57 days.
Seven Top. 45 days.
Just Right Hybrid. 60 days.
Tokyo Cross Hybrid. 35 days.

Watermelon

Watermelon is frost-tender and requires a long growing season. In the North, early-maturing varieties should be used, such as You Sweet Thing, Garden Baby, and Park's Whopper. Seed can be started early indoors for the extra growing time needed.
Park's Whopper Hybrid. 70 days.
Bush Baby Hybrid. 80 days.
Super Sweet Seedless Hybrid. 85 days.
You Sweet Thing Hybrid. 70 days.

Black Diamond. 88 days.
Garden Baby Hybrid, New. 75 days.
Kengarden. 75 days.
Sweet Favorite Hybrid. 85 days.
Sugar Baby. 73 days.
Yellow Baby Hybrid. 70 days.

3

Let Me Introduce You to a Vegetable

MORE VARIETIES AND SPECIAL PRECAUTIONS

You have seen from Chapter 2, "Go Right to the Source," that your selections of vegetables to grow in your garden are almost unlimited. What I have done with this section of the book is give you a common profile of the most widely grown home vegetables according to the Department of Agriculture, along with a few important reminders and widely available varieties.

PERENNIAL VEGETABLES

The larger vegetable gardens need a number of perennials. Asparagus, horseradish, and rhubarb are the most important, but chives, bottom multiplier onions, and some of the flavoring and condiment plants, chiefly sage and mint, are also desirable. Unfortunately, asparagus, horseradish, and rhubarb are not adapted to conditions in the lower South.

Asparagus

Asparagus is among the earliest of spring vegetables. An area about 20 feet square, or a row 50 to 75 feet long, will supply plenty of fresh asparagus for a family of five or six persons, provided the soil is well enriched and the plants are given good attention. More must be planted if some are to be canned or frozen.

Asparagus does best where winters are cold enough to freeze the ground to a depth of a few inches at least. In many southern areas the plants make a weak growth, producing small shoots. Elevation has some effect, but, in general, the latitude of south-central Georgia is the southern limit of profitable culture.

The crop can be grown on almost any well-drained, fertile soil, and there is little possibility of having the soil too rich, especially through the use of manure. Loosen the soil far down, either by subsoil plowing or by deep spading before planting. Throw the topsoil aside and spade manure, leaf mold, rotted leaves, or peat into the subsoil to a depth of 14 to 16 inches; then mix from 5 to 10 pounds of a complete fertilizer into each 75-foot row or 20-foot bed.

When the soil is ready for planting, the bottom of the trench should be about 6 inches below the natural level of the soil. After the crowns are set and covered to a depth of an inch or two, gradually work the soil into the trench around the plants during the first season. When set in beds, asparagus plants should be at least 1½ feet apart each way; when set in rows, they should be about 1½ feet apart with the rows from 4 to 5 feet apart.

Asparagus plants, or crowns, are grown from seed. *The use of 1-year-old plants only is recommended.* These should have a root spread of at least 15 inches, and larger ones are better. The home gardener will usually find it best to buy his plants from a grower who has a good strain of a recognized variety. Mary Washington and Waltham Washington are good varieties that have the added merit of being rust-resistant. Waltham Washington is an improved strain of Mary Washington. It contains very little of the purple overcast predominant in the Mary Washington, is a high yielder, and has good green color clear into the ground line. In procuring asparagus crowns, it is always well to be sure that they have not been allowed to dry out.

Clean cultivation encourages vigorous growth; it behooves the gardener to keep his asparagus clean from the start. In a large farm garden, with long rows, most of the work can be done with a horse-drawn cultivator or a garden tractor. In a small garden, however, where the rows are short or the asparagus is planted in beds, hand work is necessary.

For a 75-foot row, an application of manure and 6 to 8 pounds of a high-grade complete fertilizer, once each year, is recommended. Manure and fertilizer may be applied either before or after the cutting season.

Remove no shoots the year the plants are set in the permanent bed, and keep the cutting period short the year after setting. Remove all shoots during the cutting season in subsequent years; stop cutting about July 1 to 10 and let the tops grow. In the autumn, remove and burn the dead tops.

Asparagus rust and asparagus beetles are the chief enemies of the crop.

Horseradish

Horseradish is adapted to the north-temperate regions of the United States, but not to the South, except possibly in the high altitudes.

Any good soil, except possibly the lightest sands and heaviest clays, will grow horseradish, but it does best on a deep, rich, moist loam that is well supplied with organic matter. Avoid shallow soil; it produces rough, prongy roots. Mix organic matter with the soil a few months before the plants or cuttings are set. Some fertilizer may be used at the time of planting and more during the subsequent seasons. A topdressing of organic matter each spring is advisable.

Horseradish is propagated either by crowns or by root cuttings. In propagating by crowns a portion of an old plant consisting of a piece of root and crown buds is merely lifted and planted in a new place. Root cuttings are pieces of older roots 6 to 8 inches long and the thickness of a lead pencil. They may be saved when preparing the larger roots for grating, or they may be purchased from seedsmen. A trench 4 or 5 inches deep is opened with a hoe and the root cuttings are placed at an angle with their tops near the surface of the ground. Plants from these cuttings usually make good roots the first year. As a rule, the plants in the home garden are allowed to grow from year to year, and portions of the roots are removed as needed. Pieces of roots and crowns remaining in the soil are usually sufficient to reestablish the plants.

There is very little choice in the matter of varieties of horseradish. Be sure, however, to obtain good healthy planting stock of a strain that is giving good results in the area where it is being grown. New Bohemian is perhaps the best-known sort sold by American seedsmen.

Rhubarb

Rhubarb thrives best in regions having cool moist summers and winters cold enough to freeze the ground to a depth of several inches. It is not adapted to most parts of the South, but in certain areas of higher elevation it does fairly well. A few hills along the garden fence will supply all that a family can use.

Any deep, well-drained, fertile soil is suitable for rhubarb. Spade the soil or plow it to a depth of 12 to 16 inches and mix in rotted manure, leaf mold, decayed hardwood leaves, sods, or other form of organic matter. The methods of soil preparation suggested for asparagus are suitable for rhubarb. As rhubarb is planted in hills 3 to 4 feet apart, however, it is usually sufficient to prepare each hill separately.

Rhubarb plants may be started from seed and transplanted, but seedlings vary from the parent plant. The usual method of starting the plants is to obtain pieces of crowns from established hills and set them in prepared hills. Topdress the planting with a heavy application of organic matter in either early spring or late fall. Organic matter applied over the hills during early spring greatly hastens growth, or forces the plant.

A pound of complete commercial fertilizer high in nitrogen applied around each hill every year ensures an abundant supply of plant food. The plants can be mulched with green grass or weeds.

Remove seed stalks as soon as they form. No leaf stems should be harvested before the second year and but few until the third. Moreover, the harvest season must be largely confined to early spring. The hills should be divided and reset every 7 or 8 years. Otherwise, they become too thick and produce only slender stems.

Crimson, Red Valentine, MacDonald, Canada Red, and Victoria are standard varieties.

GREENS

Greens are usually the leaves and leaf stems of immature plants, which in their green state are boiled for food. Young, tender branches of certain plants—New Zealand spinach, for example—are also used this way. All the plants treated here as greens except New Zealand spinach are hardy vegetables, most of them adapted to fall sowing and winter culture over the entire South and in the more temperate parts of the North. Their culture may be extended more widely in the North by growing them with some protection, such as mulching or frames.

Chard

Chard, or Swiss chard, is a type of beet that has been developed for its tops instead of its roots. Crop after crop of the outer leaves may be harvested without injuring the plant. Only one planting is necessary, and a row 30 to 40 feet long will supply a family for the entire summer. Each seed cluster contains several seeds, and fairly wide spacing of the seeds facilitates thinning. The culture of chard is practically the same as that of beets, but the plants grow larger and need to be thinned to at least 6 inches apart in the row. Chard needs a rich, mellow soil, and it is sensitive to soil acidity.

Collards

Collards are grown and used about like cabbage. They withstand heat better than other members of the cabbage group, and are well liked in the South for both summer and winter use. Collards do not form a true head, but a large rosette of leaves, which may be blanched by tying together.

Kale

Kale, or cole, is hardy and lives over winter in latitudes as far north as northern Maryland and southern Pennsylvania and in other areas where similar winter conditions prevail. It is also resistant to heat and may be grown in summer. Its real merit, however, is as a cool-weather green.

Kale is a member of the cabbage family. The best garden varieties are low-growing, spreading plants, with thick, more or less crinkled leaves. Vates Blue Curled, Dwarf Blue Scotch, and Siberian are well-known garden varieties.

No other plant is so well adapted to fall sowing throughout a wide area of both North and South or in areas characterized by winters of moderate severity. Kale may well follow some such early-season vegetable as green beans, potatoes, or peas.

In the autumn the seed may be broadcast very thinly and then lightly raked into the soil. Except for spring sowings, made when weeds are troublesome, sow kale in rows 18 to 24 inches apart and later thin the plants to about a foot apart.

Kale may be harvested either by cutting the entire plant or by taking the larger leaves while young. Old kale is tough and stringy.

Mustard

Mustard grows well on almost any good soil. As the plants require but a short time to reach the proper stage for use,

frequent sowings are recommended. Sow the seeds thickly in drills as early as possible in the spring or, for late use, in September or October. The forms of Indian mustard, the leaves of which are often curled and frilled, are generally used. Southern Curled and Green Wave are common sorts.

Spinach

Spinach is a hardy cool-weather plant that withstands winter conditions in the South. In most of the North, spinach is primarily an early-spring and late-fall crop, but in some areas, where summer temperatures are mild, it may be grown continuously from early spring until late fall. It should be emphasized that summer and winter culture of spinach is possible only where moderate temperatures prevail.

Spinach will grow on almost any well-drained, fertile soil where sufficient moisture is available. It is very sensitive to acid soil. If a soil test shows the need, apply lime to the part of the garden used for spinach, regardless of the treatment given the rest of the area.

The application of 100 pounds of rotted manure and 3 to 4 pounds of commercial fertilizer to each 100 square feet of land is suitable for spinach in the home garden. Broadcast both manure and fertilizer and work them in before sowing the seed.

Long-standing Bloomsdale is perhaps the most popular variety seeded in spring. It is attractive, grows quickly, is very productive, and will stand for a moderate length of time before going to seed. Virginia Savoy and Hybrid No. 7 are valuable varieties for fall planting, as they are resistant to yellows, or blight. Hybrid No. 7 is also resistant to downy mildew (blue mold). These two varieties are very cold-hardy but are not suitable for the spring crop, as they produce seed stalks too early.

New Zealand Spinach

New Zealand spinach is not related to common spinach. It is a large plant, with thick, succulent leaves and stems, and grows with a branching, spreading habit to a height of 2 or more feet. It thrives in hot weather and is grown as a substitute in seasons when ordinary spinach cannot withstand the heat. New Zealand spinach thrives on soils suitable for common spinach. Because of their larger size, these plants must have more room. The rows should be at least 3 feet apart, with the plants about 1½ feet apart in the rows. As prompt germination may be difficult, the seeds should be soaked for 1 or 2 hours in water at 120° F. before being planted. They may be sown, 1 to 1½ inches deep, as soon as danger of frost is past. Successive harvests of the tips may be made from a single planting, as new leaves and branches are readily produced. Care must be taken not to remove too large a portion of the plant at one time.

Turnip Greens

Varieties of turnips usually grown for the roots are also planted for the greens. Shogoin is a good variety for greens. It is resistant to aphid damage and produces fine-quality white roots if allowed to grow. Seven Top is a leafy sort that produces no edible root. As a rule, sow turnips to be used for greens thickly and then thin them, leaving all but the greens to develop as a root crop. Turnip greens are especially adapted to winter and early-spring culture in the South. The cultural methods employed are the same as those for turnip and rutabaga.

SALAD VEGETABLES

The group known as salad crops includes vegetables that are usually eaten raw with salt, pepper, vinegar, and salad oil, or with mayonnaise or other dressings. This classification is entirely one of convenience; some vegetables not included in this group are used in the same way. Some members of this class may be cooked and used as greens.

Celery

Celery can be grown in home gardens in most parts of the country at some time during the year. It is a cool-weather crop and adapted to winter culture in the lower South. In the upper South and in the North it may be grown either as an early-spring or as a late-fall crop. Farther north in certain favored locations it can be grown throughout the summer.

Rich, moist but well-drained, deeply prepared, mellow soil is essential for celery. Soil varying from sand to clay loam and to peat may be used as long as these requirements are met. Unless the ground is very fertile, plenty of organic material, supplemented by liberal applications of commercial fertilizer, is necessary. For a 100-foot row of celery, 5 pounds of a high-grade complete fertilizer thoroughly mixed with the soil is none too much. Prepare the celery row a week or two before setting the plants.

The most common mistake with celery is failure to allow enough time for growing the plants. About 10 weeks are needed to grow good celery plants. Celery seed is small and germinates slowly. A good method is to place the seeds in a muslin bag and soak them overnight, then mix them with dry sand, distribute them in shallow trenches in the seed flats or seedbed, and cover them with leaf mold or similar material to a depth of not more than ½ inch. Keep the bed covered with moist burlap sacks. Celery plants are very delicate and must be kept free from weeds. They are made more stocky by being transplanted once before they are set in the garden, but this practice retards their growth. When they are to be transplanted before being set in the ground, the rows in the seed box or seedbed may be only a few inches apart. When they are to remain in the box until transplanted to the garden, however, the plants should be

about 2 inches apart each way. In beds, the rows should be 10 to 12 inches apart, with seedlings 1 to 1½ inches apart in the row.

For hand culture, celery plants are set in rows 18 to 24 inches apart. The plants are spaced about 6 inches in the row. Double rows are about 1 foot apart. Set celery on a cool or cloudy day, if possible; and if the soil is at all dry, water the plants thoroughly. If the plants are large, it is best to pinch off the outer leaves 3 or 4 inches from the base before setting. In bright weather it is well also to shade the plants for a day or two after they are set. Small branches bearing green leaves, stuck in the ground, protect the plants from intense sun without excluding air. As soon as the plants attain some size, gradually work the soil around them to keep them upright. Be careful to get no soil into the hearts of the plants. Early celery is blanched by excluding the light with boards, paper, drain tiles, or other devices. Late celery may be blanched also by banking with earth or by storing in the dark. Banking celery with soil in warm weather causes it to decay.

Late celery may be kept for early-winter use by banking with earth and covering the tops with leaves or straw to keep them from freezing, or it may be dug and stored in a cellar or a cold frame, with the roots well embedded in moist soil. While in storage it must be kept as cool as possible without freezing.

For the home garden, Golden Detroit, Summer Pascal (Waltham Improved), and Golden Plume are adapted for the early crop to be used during late summer, fall, and early winter. For storage and for use after the holiday season, it is desirable to plant some such variety as Green Light or Utah 52–70.

Endive

Endive closely resembles lettuce in its requirements, except that it is less sensitive to heat. It may be substituted for lettuce when the culture of lettuce is impracticable. In the South, it is mainly a winter crop. In the North, it is grown in spring, summer, and autumn and is also forced in winter. Full Heart Batavian and Salad King are good varieties. Broad-leaved endive is known in the markets as escarole.

Cultural details are the same as those for head lettuce. When the plants are large and well formed, draw the leaves together and tie them so that the heart will blanch. For winter use, lift the plants with a ball of earth, place them in a cellar or cold frame where they will not freeze, and tie and blanch them as needed.

Lettuce

Lettuce can be grown in any home garden. It is a cool-weather crop, being as sensitive to heat as any vegetable grown. In the South, lettuce culture is confined to late fall, winter, and spring. In colder parts of the South, lettuce may not live through the winter. In the North, lettuce culture is practically limited to spring and autumn. In some favored locations, such as areas of high altitude or in far-northern latitudes, lettuce grows to perfection in summer. Planting at a wrong season is responsible for most of the failures with this crop.

Any rich soil is adapted to lettuce, although the plant is sensitive to acid soil. A commercial fertilizer with a heavy proportion of phosphorus is recommended.

Start spring lettuce indoors or in a hotbed and transplant it to the garden when the plants have four or five leaves. Gardeners need not wait for the end of light frosts, as lettuce is not usually harmed by a temperature as low as 28° F., if the plants have been properly hardened. Allow about 6 weeks for growing the plants. For the fall crop the seed may be sown directly in the row and thinned; there is no gain in transplanting.

For hand culture, set lettuce plants about 14 to 16 inches apart. Where gardeners grow leaf lettuce or desire merely the leaves and not well-developed heads, the spacing in the rows may be much closer. In any case it is usually best to cut the entire plant instead of removing the leaves.

There are many excellent varieties of lettuce, all of which do well in the garden when conditions are right. Of the loose-leaf kinds, Black-Seeded Simpson, Grand Rapids, Slobolt, and Saladbowl are among the best. Saladbowl and Slobolt are heat-resistant and very desirable for warm-weather culture. Of the heading sorts, Buttercrunch, White Boston, Fulton, and Great Lakes are among the best. The

White Boston requires less time than the three others. Where warm weather comes early, it is seldom worthwhile to sow head lettuce seed in the open ground in the spring with the expectation of obtaining firm heads.

Parsley

Parsley is hardy to cold but sensitive to heat. It thrives under much the same temperature conditions as kale, lettuce, and spinach. If given a little protection it may be carried over winter through most of the North.

Parsley thrives on any good soil. As the plant is delicate during its early stages of growth, however, the land should be mellow.

Parsley seeds are small and germinate slowly. Soaking in water overnight hastens the germination. In the North, it is a good plan to sow the seeds indoors and transplant the plants to the garden, thereby getting a crop before hot weather. In the South, it is usually possible to sow the seed directly. For the fall crop in the North, row seeding is also practiced. After seeding, it is well to lay a board over the row for a few days until the first seedlings appear. After its removal, day-to-day watering will ensure germination of as many seeds as possible. Parsley rows should be 14 to 16 inches apart, with the plants 4 to 6 inches apart in the rows. A few feet will supply the family, and a few plants transplanted to the cold frame in the autumn will give a supply during early spring.

ROOT VEGETABLES

Potatoes in the North and sweet potatoes in the South are grown in almost every garden. Beets, carrots, and turnips are also widely grown in gardens. The vegetables in this group may be used throughout the growing season and may also be kept for winter.

Beet

The beet is well adapted to all parts of the country. It is fairly tolerant of heat; it is also resistant to cold. However, it will not withstand severe freezing. In the northern states, where winters are too severe, the beet is grown in spring, summer, and autumn.

Beets are sensitive to strongly acid soils, and it is wise to apply lime if a test shows the need for it. Good beet quality depends on quick growth; for this the land must be fertile, well drained, and in good physical condition.

Midsummer heat and drought may interfere with seed germination. Much of this trouble can be avoided by covering the seeds with sandy soil, leaf mold, or other material that will not bake and by keeping the soil damp until the plants are up. Make successive sowings at intervals of about 3 weeks in order to have a continuous supply of young, tender beets throughout the season.

Where cultivating is by hand, the rows may be about 16 inches apart; where it is by tractor, they must be wider. Beet seed as purchased consists of small balls, each containing several seeds. On most soils the seed should be covered to a depth of about 1 inch. After the plants are well established, thin them to stand 2 to 3 inches apart in the rows.

Early Wonder, Crosby Egyptian, and Detroit Dark Red are standard varieties suitable for early home garden planting, while Long Season remains tender and edible over a long season.

Carrot

Carrots are usually grown in the fall, winter, and spring in the South, providing an almost continuous supply. In the North, carrots can be grown and used through the summer and the surplus stored for winter. Carrots will grow on almost any type of soil as long as it is moist, fertile, loose, and free from clods and stones, but sandy loams and peats are best. Use commercial fertilizer.

Because of their hardiness, carrots may be seeded as early in the spring as the ground can be worked. Succession plantings at intervals of 3 weeks will ensure a continuous supply of tender carrots. Cover carrot seed about ½ inch on most soils; less, usually about ¼ inch, on heavy soils. With care in seeding, little thinning is necessary; carrots can stand some crowding, especially on loose soils. However, they should be no thicker than 10 to 15 plants per foot of row.

Chantenay, Nantes, and Imperator are standard sorts. Carrots should be stored before hard frosts occur, as the roots may be injured by cold.

Celeriac

Celeriac, or turnip-rooted celery, has been developed for the root instead of the top. Its culture is the same as that of celery, and the enlarged roots can be used at any time after they are big enough. The late-summer crop of celeriac may be stored for winter use. In areas having mild winters the roots may be left in the ground and covered with a mulch of several inches of straw or leaves, or they may be lifted, packed in moist sand, and stored in a cool cellar.

Parsnip

The parsnip is adapted to culture over a wide portion of the United States. It must have warm soil and weather at planting time, but does not thrive in midsummer in the South.

In many parts of the South, parsnips are grown and used during early summer. They should not reach maturity during midsummer, however. Furthermore, it is difficult to obtain good germination in the summer, which limits their culture during the autumn.

Any deep, fertile soil will grow parsnips, but light, friable soil, with no tendency to bake, is best. Stony or lumpy soils are objectionable; they may cause rough, prongy roots.

Parsnip seed must be fresh—not more than a year old— and it is well to sow rather thickly and thin to about 3 inches apart. Parsnips germinate slowly, but it is possible to hasten germination by covering the seed with leaf mold, sand, a mixture of sifted coal ashes and soil, peat, or some similar material that will not bake. Rolling a light soil over the row or trampling it firmly after seeding usually hastens and improves germination. Hollow Crown and All American are suitable varieties.

Parsnips may be dug and stored in a cellar or pit or left in the ground until used. Roots placed in cold storage gain in quality faster than those left in the ground, and freezing in the ground in winter improves the quality.

There is no basis for the belief that parsnips that remain in the ground over winter and start growth in the spring are poisonous. All reported cases of poisoning from eating so-called wild parsnips have been traced to water hemlock *(Cicuta),* which belongs to the same family and resembles the parsnip somewhat.

Be very careful in gathering wild plants that look like the parsnip.

Potato

Potatoes, when grown under favorable conditions, are one of the most productive of all vegetables in terms of food per unit area of land.

Potatoes are a cool-season crop; they do not thrive in midsummer in the southern half of the country. Any mellow, fertile, well-drained soil is suitable for potato production. Stiff, heavy clay soils often produce misshapen tubers. Potatoes respond to a generous use of commercial fertilizer, but if the soil is too heavily limed, the tubers may be scabby.

Commercial 5-8-5 or 5-8-7 mixtures applied at 1,000 to 2,000 pounds to the acre (approximately 7½ to 15 pounds to each 100-foot row) usually provide enough plant food for a heavy crop. The lower rate of application is sufficient for very fertile soils, the higher rate for less fertile ones. Commercial fertilizer can be applied at the time of planting, but it should be mixed with the soil in such a way that the seed pieces will not come in direct contact with it.

In the North, plant two types of potatoes—one to provide early potatoes for summer use, the other for storage and winter use. Early varieties include Irish Cobbler, Early Gem, Norland, Norgold Russet, and Superior. Best late varieties are Katahdin, Kennebec, Chippewa, Russet Burbank, Sebago, and the golden nematode-resistant Wanseon. Irish Cobbler is the most widely adapted of the early varieties and Katahdin of the late. In the Great Plains states, Pontiac and Red La Soda are preferred for summer use, the Katahdin and Russet Burbank for winter. In the Pacific Northwest, the Russet Burbank, White Rose, Kennebec, and Early Gem are used. In the Southern states, the Irish Cobbler,

Red La Soda, Red Pontiac, and Pungo are widely grown. The use of certified seed is always advisable.

In preparing seed potatoes for planting, cut them into blocky rather than wedge-shaped pieces. Each piece should be about 1½ ounces in weight and have at least one eye. Medium-sized tubers weighing 5 to 7 ounces are cut to best advantage.

Plant early potatoes as soon as weather and soil conditions permit. Fall preparation of the soil often makes it impossible to plant the early crop without delay in late winter or early spring. Potatoes require 2 to 3 weeks to come up, depending on depth of planting and the temperature of the soil. In some sections the ground may freeze slightly, but this is seldom harmful unless the sprouts have emerged. Prolonged cold and wet weather after planting is likely to cause the seed pieces to rot. Hence, avoid too early planting. Young potato plants are often damaged by frost, but they usually renew their growth quickly from uninjured portions of the stems.

Do not dig potatoes intended for storage until the tops are mature. Careful handling to avoid skinning is desirable, and protection from long exposure to light is necessary to prevent their becoming green and unfit for table use. Store in a well-ventilated place where the temperature is low, 45° to 50° if possible, but where there is no danger of freezing.

Radish

Radishes are hardy to cold, but they cannot withstand heat In the South, they do well in autumn, winter, and spring. In the North, they may be grown in spring and autumn, and in sections having mild winters they may be grown in cold frames at that season. In high altitudes and in northern locations with cool summers, radishes thrive from early spring to late autumn.

Radishes are not sensitive to the type of soil so long as it is rich, moist, and friable. Apply additional fertilizer when the seeds are sown; conditions must be favorable for quick growth. Radishes that grow slowly have a pungent flavor and are undesirable.

Radishes mature the quickest of our garden crops. They remain in prime condition only a few days, which makes small plantings at week or 10-day intervals advisable. A few yards of row will supply all the radishes a family will consume during the time the radishes are at their best.

There are two types of radishes—the mild, small, quick-maturing sorts such as Scarlet, Globe, French Breakfast, and Cherry Belle, all of which reach edible size in from 20 to 40 days; and the more pungent, large, winter radishes such as Long Black Spanish and China Rose, which require 75 days or more for growth. Plant winter radishes so that they will reach a desirable size in the autumn. Gather and store them like other root crops.

Salsify

Salsify, or vegetable oyster, may be grown in practically all parts of the country. It is similar to parsnips in its requirements but needs a slightly longer growing season. For this reason it cannot be grown as far north as parsnips. Salsify, however, is somewhat more hardy and can be sown earlier in the spring.

Thoroughly prepare soil for salsify to a depth of at least a foot. Lighten heavy garden soil by adding sand or comparable material. Salsify must have plenty of plant food.

Sandwich Island is the best-known variety. Always use fresh seed; salsify seed retains its vitality only 1 year.

Salsify may be left in the ground over winter or lifted and stored like parsnips or other root crops.

Sweet Potato

Sweet potatoes succeed best in the South, but they are grown in home gardens as far north as southern New York and southern Michigan. They can be grown even farther north, in sections having especially mild climates, such as the Pacific Northwest. In general, sweet potatoes may be grown wherever there is a frost-free period of about 150 days with relatively high temperatures. Jersey Orange, Nugget, and Nemagold are the commonest dry-fleshed varieties; Centennial, Puerto Rico, and Goldrush are three of the best of the moist type.

A well-drained, moderately deep sandy loam of medium fertility is best for sweet potatoes. Heavy clays and very deep loose-textured soils encourage the formation of long stringy roots. For best results the soil should be moderately fertilized throughout. If applied under the rows, the fertilizer should be well mixed with the soil.

In most of the area over which sweet potatoes are grown it is necessary to start the plants in a hotbed, because the season is too short to produce a good crop after the weather warms enough to start plants outdoors. Bed roots used for seed close together in a hotbed and cover them with about 2 inches of sand or fine soil, such as leaf mold. It is not safe to set the plants in the open ground until the soil is warm and the weather settled. Toward the last, ventilate the hotbed freely to harden the plants.

The plants are usually set on top of ridges, 3½ to 4 feet apart in the row. When the vines have covered the ground, no further cultivation is necessary, but some additional hand weeding may be required.

Dig sweet potatoes a short time before frost, on a bright, drying day when the soil is not too wet to work easily. On a small scale they may be dug with a spading fork, great care being taken not to bruise or injure the roots. Let the roots lie exposed for 2 or 3 hours to dry thoroughly; then put them in containers and place them in a warm room to cure. The proper curing temperature is 85° F. Curing for about 10 days is followed by storage at 50° to 55°.

Turnip and Rutabaga

Turnips and rutabagas, similar cool-season vegetables, are among the most commonly grown and widely adapted root crops in the United States. They are grown in the South chiefly in the fall, winter, and spring, and in the North largely in the spring and autumn. Rutabagas do best in the more northerly areas; turnips are better for gardens south of the latitude of Indianapolis, Indiana, or northern Virginia.

Turnips reach a good size in from 60 to 80 days, but rutabagas need about a month longer. Being susceptible to heat and hardy to cold, these crops should be planted as late as possible for fall use, allowing time for maturity before hard frost. In the South, turnips are very popular in the winter and spring. In the North, however, July to August seeding, following early potatoes, peas, or spinach, is the common practice.

Land that has been in a heavily fertilized crop, such as early potatoes, usually gives a good crop without additional fertilizing. The soil need not be prepared deeply, but the surface should be fine and smooth. For spring culture, row planting similar to that described for beets is the best practice. The importance of planting turnips as early as possible for the spring crop is emphasized. When seeding in rows, cover the seeds lightly; when broadcasting, rake the seeds in lightly with a garden rake. A half ounce of seed will sow a 300-foot row or broadcast 300 square feet. Turnips may be thinned as they grow, and the tops used for greens.

Although there are both white-fleshed and yellow-fleshed varieties of turnips and rutabagas, most turnips are white-fleshed and most rutabagas are yellow-fleshed. Purple Top White Globe and Just Right are the most popular white-fleshed varieties; Golden Ball (Orange Jelly) is the most popular yellow-fleshed variety. American Purple Top is the commonly grown yellow-fleshed rutabaga; Sweet German (White Swede, Sweet Russian) is the most widely used white-fleshed variety. For turnip greens, the Seven Top variety is most suitable. This winter-hardy variety overwinters in a majority of locations in the United States.

VINE VEGETABLES

The vine crops, including cucumbers, muskmelons, pumpkins, squashes, watermelons, and citrons, are similar in their cultural requirements. In importance to the home gardener they do not compare with some other groups, especially the root crops and the greens, but there is a place in most gardens for at least bush squashes and a few hills of cucumbers. They all make rank growth and require much space. In large gardens, muskmelons and watermelons are often desirable.

Cucumber

Cucumbers are a warm-weather crop. They may be grown during the warmer months over a wide portion of the country, but are not adapted to winter growing in any but a few

of the most southerly locations. Moreover, the extreme heat of midsummer in some places is too severe, and there cucumber culture is limited to spring and autumn.

The cucumber demands an exceedingly fertile, mellow soil high in decomposed organic matter from the compost pile. Also, an additional application of organic matter and commercial fertilizer is advisable under the rows or hills. Be sure the organic matter contains no remains of any vine crops; they might carry injurious diseases. Three or four wheelbarrow loads of well-rotted organic matter and 5 pounds of commercial fertilizer to a 50-foot drill or each ten hills are enough. Mix the organic matter and fertilizer well with the top 8 to 10 inches of soil.

For an early crop, the seed may be started in berry boxes or pots, or on sods in a hotbed, and moved to the garden after danger of late frost is past. During the early growth and in cool periods, cucumbers may be covered with plant protectors made of panes of glass with a top of cheesecloth, parchment paper, or muslin. A few hills will supply the needs of a family.

When the seed is planted in drills, the rows should be 6 or 7 feet apart, with the plants thinned to 2 to 3 feet apart in the rows. In the hill method of planting, the hills should be at least 6 feet apart each way, with the plants thinned to two in each hill. It is always wise to plant 8 or 10 seeds in each hill, thinned to the desired stand. Cover the seeds to a depth of about ½ inch. If the soil is inclined to bake, cover them with loose earth, such as a mixture of soil and coarse sand, or other material that will not harden and keep the plants from coming through.

When cucumbers are grown primarily for pickling, plant one of the special small-sized pickling varieties, such as Chicago Pickling or National Pickling; if they are grown for slicing, plant such varieties as White Spine or Straight Eight. It is usually desirable to plant a few hills of each type; both types can be used for either purpose.

Cucumbers require almost constant vigilance to prevent destructive attacks by cucumber beetles. These insects not only eat the foliage but also spread cucumber wilt and other serious diseases.

Success in growing cucumbers depends largely on the control of diseases and insect pests that attack the crop.

Removal of the fruits before any hard seeds form materially lengthens the life of the plants and increases the size of the crop.

Muskmelon

The climatic, soil, and cultural requirements of muskmelons are about the same as for cucumbers, except that they are less tolerant of high humidity and rainy weather. They develop most perfectly on light-textured soils. The plants are vigorous growers, and need a somewhat wider spacing than cucumbers.

Hearts of Gold, Hale's Best, and Rocky Ford, the last-named a type not a variety, are usually grown in the home garden. Where powdery mildew is prevalent, resistant varieties such as Gulf Stream, Dulce, and Perlita are better adapted. Osage and Pride of Wisconsin (Queen of Colorado) are desirable home-garden sorts, particularly in the northern states. Sweet Air (Knight) is a popular sort in the Maryland-Virginia area.

The casaba and honeydew are well adapted only to the West, where they are grown under irrigation.

Pumpkin

Pumpkins are sensitive to both cold and heat. In the North they cannot be planted until settled weather; in the South they do not thrive during midsummer.

The gardener is seldom justified in devoting any part of a limited garden area to pumpkins, because many other vegetables give greater returns from the same space. However, in gardens where there is plenty of room and where they can follow an early crop like potatoes, pumpkins can often be grown to advantage.

The pumpkin is one of the few vegetables that thrives under partial shade. Therefore it may be grown among sweet corn or other tall plants. Small Sugar and Connecticut Field are well-known orange-yellow-skinned varieties. The Kentucky Field has a grayish-orange rind with salmon flesh. All are good-quality, productive varieties.

Hills of pumpkins, containing one to two plants, should be at least 10 feet apart each way. Pumpkin plants among corn, potato, or other plants usually should be spaced 8 to 10 feet apart in every third or fourth row.

Gather and store pumpkins before they are injured by hard frosts. They keep best in a well-ventilated place where the temperature is a little above 50° F.

Squash

Squashes are among the most commonly grown garden plants. They do well in practically all parts of the United States where the soil is fertile and the moisture sufficient. Although sensitive to frost, squashes are more hardy than melons and cucumbers. In the warmest parts of the South they may be grown in winter. The use of well-rotted composted material thoroughly mixed with the soil is recommended.

There are two classes of squash varieties, summer and winter. The summer class includes the Bush Scallop, known in some places as the Cymling, the Summer Crookneck, Straightneck, and zucchini. It also includes the vegetable marrows, of which the best-known sort is Italian Vegetable Marrow (Cocozelle). All the summer squashes and the marrows must be used while young and tender, when the rind can be easily penetrated by the thumbnail. The winter squashes include varieties such as Hubbard, Delicious, Table Queen (Acorn), and Boston Marrow. They have hard rinds and are well adapted for storage.

Summer varieties, like yellow Straightneck, should be gathered before the seeds ripen or the rinds harden, but the winter sorts will not keep unless well matured. They should be taken in before hard frosts and stored in a dry, moderately warm place, such as on shelves in a basement with a furnace. Under favorable conditions such varieties as Hubbard may be kept until midwinter.

Watermelon

Only gardeners with a great deal of space can afford to grow watermelons. Moreover, they are rather particular in their soil requirements, a sand or sandy loam being best. Watermelon hills should be at least 8 feet apart. The plan of mixing a half wheelbarrow load of composted material with the soil in each hill is good, provided the compost is free from the remains of cucurbit plants that might carry diseases; ½ pound of commercial fertilizer should also be thoroughly mixed with the soil in the hill. It is a good plan to place several seeds in a ring about 1 foot in diameter in each hill. Later the plants should be thinned to two to each hill.

New Hampshire Midget, Rhode Island Red, and Charleston Gray are suitable varieties for the home garden. New Hampshire Midget and Sugar Baby are small, extra-early, widely grown, very productive varieties. The oval fruits are about 5 inches in diameter; they have crisp, red flesh and dark seeds. Rhode Island Red is an early variety. The fruits are medium in size, striped, and oval; they have a firm rind and bright pink-red flesh of choice quality. Charleston Gray is a large, long, high-quality, gray-green watermelon with excellent keeping and shipping qualities. It is resistant to anthracnose and fusarium wilt and requires a long growing season.

LEGUMES

Beans and peas are among our oldest and most important garden plants. The popularity of both is enhanced by their wide climatic and soil adaptation.

Beans

Green beans, both snap and lima, are more important than dry beans to the home gardener. Snap beans cannot be planted until the ground is thoroughly warm, but successive 7 or 8 weeks before frost. In the lower South and Southwest, green beans may be grown during the fall, winter, and spring, but they are not well adapted to midsummer. In the extreme South, beans are grown throughout the winter.

Green beans are adapted to a wide range of soils as long as the soils are well drained, reasonably fertile, and of such physical nature that they do not interfere with germination and emergence of the plants. Soil that has received a general application of manure and fertilizer should need no additional fertilization. When beans follow early crops that

have been fertilized, the residue of this fertilizer is often sufficient for the beans.

On very heavy lands it is well to cover the planted row with sand, a mixture of sifted coal ashes and sand, peat, leaf mold, or other material that will not bake. Bean seed should be covered not more than 1 inch in heavy soils and 1½ inches in sandy soils. When beans are planted in hills, they may be covered with plant protectors. These covers make it possible to plant somewhat earlier.

Tendercrop, Topcrop, Tenderette, Contender, Harvester, and Kinghorn Wax are good bush varieties of snap beans. Dwarf Horticultural is an outstanding green-shell bean. Brown-seeded or white-seeded Kentucky Wonders are the best pole varieties for snap pods. White navy or pea beans, white or red kidney, and the horticultural types are excellent for dry-shell purposes.

Two types of lima beans, called butter beans in the South, are grown in home gardens. Most of the more northerly parts of the United States, including the northerly New England States and the northern parts of other states along the Canadian border, are not adapted to the culture of lima beans. Lima beans need a growing season of about 4 months with relatively high temperatures; they cannot be planted safely until somewhat later than snap beans. The small butter beans mature in a shorter period than the large-seeded lima beans. The use of plant protectors over the seeds is an aid in obtaining earliness.

Lima beans may be grown on almost any fertile, well-drained, mellow soil, but it is especially desirable that the soil be light-textured and not subject to baking, as the seedlings cannot force their way through a hard crust. Covering with some material that will not bake, as suggested for other beans, is a wise precaution when using heavy soils. Lima beans need a soil somewhat richer than is necessary for kidney beans, but the excessive use of fertilizer containing a high percentage of nitrogen should be avoided.

Both the small- and large-seeded lima beans are available in pole and bush varieties. In the South, the most commonly grown lima bean varieties are Jackson Wonder, Nemagreen, Henderson Bush, and Sieva pole; in the North, Thorogreen, Dixie Butterpea, and Thaxter are popular small-seeded bush varieties. Fordhook 242 is the most popular midseason large, thick-seeded bush lima bean. King of the Garden and Challenger are the most popular large-seeded pole lima bean varieties.

Pole beans of the kidney and lima types require some form of support, as they normally make vines several feet long. A 5-foot fence makes the best support for pole beans. A more complicated support can be prepared from 8-foot metal fence posts, spaced about 4 feet apart and connected horizontally and diagonally with coarse stout twine to make a trellis. Bean plants usually require some assistance to get started on these supports. Never cultivate or handle bean plants when they are wet; doing so is likely to spread disease.

English Peas

English peas are a cool-weather crop and should be planted early. In the lower South they are grown in all seasons except summer; farther north, in spring and autumn. In the northern states and at high altitudes, they may be grown from spring until autumn, although in many places summer heat is too severe and the season is practically limited to spring. A few succession plantings may be made at 10-day intervals. The later plantings rarely yield as well as the earlier ones. Planting may be resumed as the cool weather of autumn approaches, but the yield is seldom as satisfactory as that from the spring planting.

Alaska and other smooth-seeded varieties are frequently used for planting in the early spring because of the supposition that they can germinate well in cold, wet soil. Thomas Laxton, Greater Progress, Little Marvel, Freezonia, and Giant Stride are recommended as suitable early varieties with wrinkled seeds. Wando has considerable heat resistance. Alderman and Lincoln are approximately 2 weeks later than Greater Progress, but under favorable conditions yield heavily. Alderman is a desirable variety for growing on brush or a trellis. Peas grown on supports are less vulnerable to destruction by birds.

Sugar Peas

Sugar peas (edible-podded peas) possess the tenderness and fleshy-podded qualities of snap beans and the flavor and sweetness of fresh English peas. When young, the pods are cooked like snap beans; the peas are not shelled. At this stage, pods are stringless, brittle, succulent, and free of fiber or parchment. However, if the pods develop too fast, they are not good to use like snap beans, but the seeds may be eaten as shelled peas and are of the best flavor before they have reached full size. Dwarf Gray Sugar is the earliest and smallest sugar pea. It is ideal for home gardens, especially where space is limited and seasons are short. A larger and later variety, Mammoth Melting Sugar, is resistant to fusarium wilt and requires support to climb upon.

Black-eyed Peas

Black-eyed or blackeye peas, also known as cowpeas and southern table peas, are highly nutritious, tasty, and easily grown. Do not plant until danger of frost has passed, because they are very susceptible to cold. Leading varieties are Dixilee, Brown Crowder, Lady, Conch, White Acre, Louisiana Purchase, Texas Purple Hull 49, Knuckle Purple Hull, and Monarch Blackeye. Dixilee is a later variety of southern pea. Quality is excellent and it yields considerably more than such old standbys as blackeyes and crowders. It is also quite resistant, or at least tolerant, to nematodes. This fact alone makes it a desirable variety wherever this pest is present. Monarch Blackeye is a fairly new variety of the blackeye type and much better adapted to southern conditions.

Heavy applications of nitrogen fertilizer should not be used for southern peas. Fertilize moderately with a low-nitrogen analysis such as 4-12-12.

For the effort necessary to grow them, few if any other vegetables will pay higher dividends than southern table peas.

CABBAGE GROUP

The cabbage, or cole, group of vegetables is noteworthy because of its adaptation to culture in most parts of the country having fertile soil and sufficient moisture and because of its hardiness to cold.

Broccoli

Heading broccoli is difficult to grow, and therefore only sprouting broccoli is discussed here. Sprouting broccoli forms a loose flower head (on a tall, green, fleshy, branching stalk) instead of the compact head or curd found on cauliflower or heading broccoli. It is one of the newer vegetables in American gardens, but has been grown by Europeans for hundreds of years.

Sprouting broccoli is adapted to winter culture in areas suitable for winter cabbage. It is also tolerant of heat. Spring-set plants in the latitude of Washington, D.C., have yielded good crops of sprouts until midsummer and later under conditions that caused cauliflower to fail. In the latitude of Norfolk, Virginia, the plant has yielded good crops of sprouts from December until spring.

Sprouting broccoli is grown in the same way as cabbage. Plants grown indoors in the early spring and set in the open about April 1 begin to yield sprouts in about 10 weeks. The fall crop may be handled in the same way as late cabbage, except that the seed is sown later. The sprouts carrying flower buds are cut about 6 inches long, and other sprouts arise in the axils of the leaves, so that a continuous harvest may be obtained. Green Comet, Calabrese, and Waltham 29 are among the best-known varieties.

Brussels Sprouts

Brussels sprouts are somewhat more hardy than cabbage and will live outdoors over winter in all the milder sections of the country. They may be grown as a winter crop in the South and as early and late as cabbage in the North. The sprouts, or small heads, are formed in the axils (the angle between the leaf stem and the main stalk) of the leaves. As the heads begin to crowd, break the lower leaves from the stem of the plant to give them more room. Always leave the top leaves; the plant needs them to supply nourishment. For winter use in cold areas, take up the plants that are well laden with heads and set them close together in a pit, a cold frame, or a cellar, with some soil tamped around the roots. Keep the stored plants as cool as possible without freezing.

Jade Cross, a true F_1 hybrid, has a wide range of adaptability.

Cabbage

Cabbage ranks as one of the most important home-garden crops. In the lower South, it can be grown in all seasons except summer, and in latitudes as far north as Washington, D.C., it is frequently set in the autumn, as its extreme hardiness enables it to live over winter in relatively low temperatures and thus become one of the first spring garden crops. Farther north, it can be grown as an early-summer crop and as a late-fall crop for storage. Cabbage can be grown throughout practically the entire United States.

Cabbage is adapted to widely different soils as long as they are fertile, of good texture, and moist. It is a heavy feeder; no vegetable responds better to favorable growing conditions. Quality in cabbage is closely associated with quick growth. Both compost and commercial fertilizer should be liberally used. In addition to the applications made at planting time, a side dressing or two of nitrate of soda, sulfate of ammonia, or other quickly available nitrogenous fertilizer is advisable. These may be applied sparingly to the soil around the plants at intervals of 3 weeks, not more than 1 pound being used to each 200 square feet of space, or, in terms of single plants, ⅓ ounce to each plant. For late cabbage the supplemental feeding with nitrates may be omitted. Good seed is especially important. Only a few seeds are needed for starting enough plants for the home garden, as 2 or 3 dozen heads of early cabbage are as many as the average family can use. Early Jersey Wakefield and Golden Acre are standard early sorts. Copenhagen Market and Globe are excellent midseason kinds. Flat Dutch and Danish Ballhead are largely used for late planting.

Where cabbage yellows is a serious disease, resistant varieties should be used. The following are a few of the wilt-resistant varieties adapted to different seasons: Wisconsin Hollander, for late storage; Wisconsin All Seasons, a kraut cabbage, somewhat earlier; Marion Market and Globe, round-head cabbages, for midseason; and Stonehead for an early, small, round-head variety.

Cabbage plants for spring setting in the North may be grown in hotbeds or greenhouses from seeding made 1 month to 6 weeks before planting time, or may be purchased from southern growers who produce them outdoors in winter. The winter-grown, hardened plants, sometimes referred to as frostproof, are hardier than hotbed plants and may be set outdoors in most parts of the North as soon as the ground can be worked in the spring. Northern gardeners can have cabbage from their gardens much earlier by using healthy plants grown in the South or well-hardened, well-grown hotbed or greenhouse plants. Late cabbage, prized by northern gardeners for fall use and for storage, is grown from plants produced in open seedbeds from sowings made about a month ahead of planting. Late cabbage may well follow early potatoes, peas, beets, spinach, or other early crops. Many gardeners set cabbage plants between potato rows before the potatoes are ready to dig, thereby gaining time. In protected places, or when plant protectors are used, it is always possible to advance dates somewhat, especially if the plants are well hardened.

Chinese Cabbage

Chinese cabbage is more closely related to mustard than to cabbage. It is variously called Crispy Choy, Chihili, Michili, and Wong Bok. Also, it is popularly known as celery cabbage, although it is unrelated to celery. The nonheading types deserve greater attention.

Chinese cabbage seems to do best as an autumn crop in the northern tier of states. When full-grown, it is an attractive vegetable. It is not especially successful as a spring crop, and gardeners are advised not to try to grow it at any season other than fall in the North or in winter in the South.

The plant demands a very rich, well-drained but moist soil. The seeds may be sown and the plants transplanted to the garden, or the seed may be drilled in the garden rows and the plants thinned to the desired stand.

Cauliflower

Cauliflower is a hardy vegetable, but it will not withstand as much frost as cabbage. Too much warm weather keeps cauliflower from heading. In the South, its culture is limited to fall, winter, and spring; in the North, to spring and fall. However, in some areas of high altitude and when conditions are otherwise favorable, cauliflower culture is continuous throughout the summer.

Cauliflower is grown on all types of land from sands to clay and peats. Although the physical character is unimportant, the land must be fertile and well drained. Manure and commercial fertilizer are essential.

The time required for growing cauliflower plants is the same as for cabbage. In the North, the main cause of failure with cauliflower in the spring is delay in sowing the seed and setting the plants. The fall crop must be planted at such time that it will come to the heading stage in cool weather. Snowball and Purple Head are standard varieties of cauliflower. Snow King is an extremely early variety with fair-sized, compact heads of good quality; it has very short stems. Always take care to obtain a good strain of seed; poor cauliflower seed is most objectionable. The Purple Head variety, well adapted for the home garden, turns green when cooked.

A necessary precaution in cauliflower culture with all varieties, except Purple Head, is to tie the leaves together when the heads, or buttons, begin to form. This keeps the heads white. Cauliflower does not keep long after the heads form; 1 or 2 dozen heads are enough for the average garden in one season.

Kohlrabi

Kohlrabi is grown for its swollen stem. In the North, the early crop may be started like cabbage and transplanted to the garden, but usually it is sown in place. In the South, kohlrabi may be grown almost anytime except midsummer. The seeds may be started indoors and the plants transplanted in the garden, or the seeds may be drilled in the garden rows and the plants thinned to the desired stand. Kohlrabi has about the same soil and cultural requirements as cabbage, principally a fertile soil and enough moisture. It should be harvested while young and tender. Standard varieties are Purple Vienna and White Vienna.

ONION GROUP

Practically all members of the onion group are adapted to a wide variety of soils. Some of them can be grown at one time of the year or another in any part of the country that has fertile soil and ample moisture. They require but little garden space to produce enough for a family's needs.

Chives

Chives are small onionlike plants that will grow in any place where onions do well. They are frequently planted as a border, but are equally well adapted to culture in rows. Being a perennial, chives should be planted where they can be left for more than one season.

Chives may be started from either seed or clumps of bulbs. Once established, some of the bulbs can be lifted and moved to a new spot. When left in the same place for several years the plants become too thick; occasionally dividing and resetting is desirable.

Garlic

Garlic is more exacting in its cultural requirements than are onions, but it may be grown with a fair degree of success in almost any home garden where good results are obtained with onions.

Garlic is propagated by planting the small cloves, or bulbs, which make up the large bulbs. Each large bulb contains about ten small ones. Carefully separate the small bulbs and plant them singly.

The culture of garlic is practically the same as that of onions. When mature the bulbs are pulled, dried, and braided into strings or tied in bunches, which are hung in a cool, well-ventilated place.

In the South, where the crop matures early, care must be taken to keep the garlic in a cool, dry place; otherwise it spoils. In the North, where the crop matures later in the season, storage is not so difficult, but care must be taken to prevent freezing.

Leek

The leek resembles the onion in its adaptability and cultural requirements. Instead of forming a bulb it produces a thick, fleshy cylinder like a large green onion. Leeks are started from seeds, like onions. Usually the seeds are sown in a shallow trench, so that the plants can be more easily hilled up as growth proceeds. Leeks are ready for use anytime after they reach the right size. Under favorable conditions they grow to 1½ inches or more in diameter, with white parts 6 to 8 inches long. They may be lifted in the autumn and stored like celery in a cold frame or a cellar.

Onion

Onions thrive under a wide variety of climatic and soil conditions, but do best with an abundance of moisture and a temperate climate, without extremes of heat or cold through the growing season. In the South, the onion thrives in the fall, winter, and spring. Farther north, winter temperatures may be too severe for certain types. In the North, onions are primarily a spring, summer, and fall crop.

Any type of soil will grow onions, but it must be fertile, moist, and in the highest state of tilth. Both compost and commercial fertilizer, especially one high in phosphorus and potash, should be applied to the onion plot. A pound of compost to each square foot of ground and 4 or 5 pounds of fertilizer to each 100 square feet are about right. The soil should be very fine and free from clods and foreign matter.

Onions may be started in the home garden by the use of sets, seedlings, or seed. Sets, or small dry onions grown the previous year—preferably not more than ¾ inch in diameter—are usually employed by home gardeners. Small green plants grown in an outdoor seedbed in the South or in a hotbed or a greenhouse are also in general use. The home garden culture of onions from seed is satisfactory in the North where the summers are comparatively cool.

Sets and seedlings cost about the same; seeds cost much less. In certainty of results the seedlings are best; practically none form seed stalks. Seed-sown onions are uncertain unless conditions are extremely favorable.

Several distinct types of onions may be grown. The potato (multiplier) and top (tree) onions are planted in the fall or early spring for use green. Yellow Bermuda, Granex, and White Granex are large, very mild, flat onions for spring harvest in the South; they have short storage life. Sweet Spanish and the hybrids Golden Beauty, Fiesta, Bronze, Perfection, and El Capitan are large, mild, globular onions suited for growing in the middle latitudes of the country; they store moderately well. Southport White Globe, Southport Yellow Globe, Ebenezer, Early Yellow Globe, Yellow Globe Danvers, and the hybrid Abundance are all firm-fleshed, long-storage onions for growing as a "main crop" in the Northeast and Midwest. Early Harvest is an early F_1 hybrid adapted to all northern regions of the United States. Varieties that produce bulbs may also be used green.

Shallot

The shallot is a small onion of the multiplier type. Its bulbs have a more delicate flavor than most onions. Its growth requirements are about the same as those of most other onions. Shallots seldom form seed and are propagated by means of the small cloves or divisions, into which the plant splits during growth. The plant is hardy and may be left in the ground from year to year, but best results are had by lifting the clusters of bulbs at the end of the growing season and replanting the smaller ones at the desired time.

FLESHY-FRUITED VEGETABLES

The fleshy-fruited, warm-season vegetables, of which the tomato is the most important, are closely related and have about the same cultural requirements. All must have warm weather and fertile, well-drained soil for good results.

Eggplant

Eggplant is extremely sensitive to the conditions under which it is grown. A warm-weather plant, it demands a growing season of from 100 to 140 days with high average day and night temperatures. The soil, also, must be well warmed up before eggplant can safely be set outdoors.

In the South, eggplants are grown in spring and autumn; in the North, only in summer. The more northerly areas, where a short growing season and low summer temperatures prevail, are generally unsuitable for eggplants. In very fertile garden soil, which is best for eggplant, a few plants will yield a large number of fruits.

Sow eggplant seeds in a hotbed or greenhouse or, in warm areas, outdoors about 8 weeks before the plants are to be transplanted. It is important that the plants be kept growing without check from low or drying temperatures or other causes. They may be transplanted like tomatoes. Good plants have stems that are not hard or woody; one with a woody stem rarely develops satisfactorily. Black Beauty, Early Beauty Hybrid, and Jersey King Hybrid are good varieties.

Pepper

Peppers are more exacting than tomatoes in their requirements, but may be grown over a wide range in the United States. Being hot-weather plants, peppers cannot be planted in the North until the soil has warmed up and all danger of frost is over. In the South, planting dates vary with the location, fall planting being practiced in some locations. Start pepper plants 6 to 8 weeks before needed. The seeds and plants require a somewhat higher temperature than those of the tomato. Otherwise they are handled in exactly the same way.

Hot peppers are represented by such varieties as Red Chili and Long Red Cayenne, and the mild-flavored ones by Penn Wonder, Ruby King, World-beater, California Wonder, and Yale Wonder, which mature in the order given.

Tomato

Tomatoes grow under a wide variety of conditions and require only a relatively small space for a large production. Of tropical American origin, the tomato does not thrive in very cool weather. It will, however, grow in winter in home gardens in the extreme South. Over most of the upper South and the North, it is suited to spring, summer, and autumn

culture. In the more northern areas, the growing season is likely to be too short for heavy yields, and it is often desirable to increase earliness and the length of the growing season by starting the plants indoors. By adopting a few precautions, the home gardener can grow tomatoes practically everywhere, given fertile soil with sufficient moisture.

A liberal application of compost and commercial fertilizer in preparing the soil should be sufficient for tomatoes under most conditions. Heavy applications of fertilizer should be broadcast, not applied in the row; but small quantities may be mixed with the soil in the row in preparing for planting.

Start early tomato plants from 5 to 7 weeks before they are to be transplanted to the garden. Enough plants for the home garden may be started in a window box and transplanted to small pots, paper drinking cups with the bottoms removed, plant bands (round or square), or other soil containers. In boxes, the seedlings are spaced 2 to 3 inches apart. Tomato seeds germinate best at about 70° F., or ordinary house temperature. Growing tomato seedlings, after the first transplanting, at moderate temperatures, with plenty of ventilation, as in a cold frame, gives stocky, hardy growth. If desired, the plants may be transplanted again to larger containers, such as 4-inch clay pots or quart cans with holes in the bottom.

Tomato plants for all but the early spring crop are usually grown in outdoor seedbeds. Thin seeding and careful weed control will give strong, stocky plants for transplanting. In the Southwest, Pearson, Early Pack No. 7, VF 36, California 145, VF 13L, and Ace are grown. A list of tomato varieties for home garden use in areas other than the Southwest is given at the end of Chapter 2.

Tomatoes are sensitive to cold. Never plant them until danger of frost is past. By using plant protectors during cool periods the home gardener can set tomato plants somewhat earlier than would otherwise be possible. Hot, dry weather, like midsummer weather in the South, is also unfavorable for planting tomatoes. Planting distances depend on the variety and on whether the plants are to be pruned and staked or not. If pruned to one stem, trained, and tied to stakes or a trellis, they may be set 18 inches apart in 3-foot-apart rows; if not, they may be planted 3 feet apart in rows 4 to 5 feet apart. Pruning and staking have many advantages for the home gardener. Cultivation is easier, and the fruits are always clean and easy to find. Staked and pruned tomatoes are, however, more subject to losses from blossom-end rot than those allowed to grow naturally.

MISCELLANEOUS VEGETABLES
Okra

Okra, or gumbo, has about the same degree of hardiness as cucumbers and tomatoes and may be grown under the same conditions. It thrives in any fertile, well-drained soil. An abundance of quickly available plant food will stimulate growth and ensure a good yield of tender, high-quality pods.

As okra is a warm-weather vegetable, the seeds should not be sown until the soil is warm. The rows should be from 3 to 3½ feet apart, depending on whether the variety is dwarf or large-growing. Sow the seeds every few inches and thin the plants to stand 18 inches to 2 feet apart in the rows. Clemson Spineless, Emerald, and Dwarf Green are good varieties. The pods should be picked young and tender, and none allowed to ripen. Old pods are unfit for use and soon exhaust the plant.

Sweet Corn

Sweet corn requires plenty of space and is suitable only to larger gardens. Although a warm-weather plant, it may be grown in practically all parts of the United States. It needs a fertile, well-drained, moist soil. With these requirements met, the type of the soil does not seem to be especially important, but a clay loam is almost ideal for sweet corn.

In the South, sweet corn is planted from early spring until autumn, but the corn earworm, drought, and heat make it difficult to obtain worthwhile results in midsummer. The ears pass the edible stage very quickly, and succession plantings are necessary to ensure a constant supply. In the North, sweet corn cannot be safely planted until the ground has thoroughly warmed up. Here, too, succession plantings need to be made to ensure a steady supply. Sweet corn is frequently planted to good advantage after early potatoes,

peas, beets, lettuce, or other early, short-season crops. Sometimes, to gain time, it may be planted before the early crop is removed.

Sweet corn may be grown in either hills or drills, in rows at least 3 feet apart. It is well to plant the seed rather thickly and thin to single stalks 14 to 16 inches apart or three plants to each 3-foot hill. Experiments have shown that in the eastern part of the country there is no advantage in removing suckers from sweet corn. Cultivation sufficient to control weeds is all that is needed.

Hybrid sweet corn varieties, both white and yellow, are usually more productive than the open-pollinated sorts. As a rule, they need a more fertile soil and heavier feeding. They should be fertilized with 5-10-5 fertilizer about every 3 weeks until they start to silk. Many are resistant to disease, particularly bacterial wilt. Never save seed from a hybrid crop for planting. Such seed does not come true to the form of the plants from which it was harvested.

Good yellow-grained hybrids, in the order of the time required to reach edible maturity, are Span-cross, Marcross, Golden Beauty, Golden Cross Bantam, and Ioana. White-grained hybrids are Evergreen and Country Gentleman.

Well-known open-pollinated yellow sorts are Golden Bantam and Golden Midget. Open-pollinated white sorts, in the order of maturity, are Early Evergreen, Country Gentleman, and Stowell Evergreen.

The Vegetable Garden Midwife

STARTING SEEDS INDOORS

No, Virginia, There Is No Plant Stork!

If you want healthy baby plants to grow up in your garden this summer, you have to be prepared to help with the delivery, and do a little pacing up and down in front of your newly sown seeds—sweating it out until they rear their little heads and stretch those first two leaves. You can then pat yourself on the back. As with all new babies, there is the adjustment period to their new surroundings, temperature and food formula. So, let's keep alert.

Taking a Chance with Seeds Indoors

Timing is the main consideration you must concern yourself with when you finally get up nerve to sprout your own seeds indoors—to save money and time and to experience the thrill that comes to all of us when we know that we played a part in this little miracle, when we harvest the end result of planting. It is important that new plants from seed not stay in our dry homes any longer than necessary. You can have healthy happy little baby plants one minute, take a coffee break, and come back to find them lying flat on their little leaves. This is called *damping-off disease.* Its cause is a fungus that lives in unsterilized dirt, or uncleaned pots. Because our homes are not designed as greenhouses, poor light, high temperatures, overwatering, and improper ventilation encourage this bad guy to come around. Don't get discouraged; we can handle him. I am just pointing out how important it is not to pen our growing babies up too long. The sooner we can turn them over to Mama Nature to baby-sit the better for all concerned.

How Do You Check Growing Time?

One of the easiest ways is to look at the back of most any seed packet, and it will tell you how many days to harvest provided that Jack Frost doesn't nip the little tender plants in the bud. So, you must check the weather reports and frost-free dates on the chart that I have provided for you. What this tells you is just about when you will start your seeds indoors so that they can be transplanted into the garden bed as early and safely as possible. In areas where you have fewer growing days, the earlier you get your cool crops in the sooner you can make your second planting with midseason crops.

Early Quick, Cool-Weather Crops

| Peas | Lettuce | Swiss chard | Cauliflower |
| Radishes | Spinach | Cabbage | Brussels sprouts |

Short-Season Plants (60 days)

Peas	Spinach	Swiss chard	Scallions
Beans	Mustard greens	Lettuce	Kohlrabi
Radishes			

Midseason Plants (70-80 days)

| Squash | Cabbage | Cucumbers | Beets | Some beans |

Need-a-Whole-Season Plants (90 days or more)

Corn	Leeks	Onions	Garlic
Carrots	Peppers	Celery	Leeks
Potatoes	Parsnips		

Soak the Seeds and Bake the Dirt

THIS RECEIPE WILL GROW ON YOU

In order to give the new seeds an even chance to survive, we have to make them comfortable, and since I believe in giving all of my seeds room to grow, I plant them one at a time.

First lay two layers of paper towel in the bottom of a pie tin or shallow tray. Soak the towels in a warm solution of weak tea (honest-to-goodness tea), 2 drops of liquid soap, and 2 drops of non-sweet mouthwash; 1 quart of mixture should do. Spread the seeds out with room in between on the wet paper towel. Next, spray the seeds with the wake-up tonic. Cover the seeds now with another two sheets of paper towel and soak it. Place in a dark, warm location overnight.

To ensure the safety of our new seeds, let's head damping-off disease off at the pass. If you are going to use your own garden soil for starting seeds indoors (which I don't recommend), fill up a cake tin or two with soil, wrap a potato in foil paper and place it on top of the soil, and bake the potato and soil at 325° for one hour or until the potato is done. Now you can take a break for dinner and eat the baked potato while the soil cools.

When the soil has cooled, spray it with the wake-up tonic (the solution of tea, soap, and mouthwash) and mix well until soil is damp, not wet.

If you are going to use your garden soil, you will mix 1 part soil, 2 parts sharp sand, and 3 parts peat moss and blend well. As a matter of fact, add 1 part perlite. Lastly, spray with a solution of Truban (Science Product) to prevent damping off.

I've said I don't recommend a beginner or for that matter a casual vegetable gardener to blend his or her own starter mix. The professionals have all discovered that the soilless potting mixes are safer, quicker, cheaper, and more responsive. Professional Mix from Hyponex Premier brands is available at most garden departments in both the United

YOU SURE FRED ASPARAGUS STARTED THIS WAY?

IT WAS JUST A NIGHT CRAWLER

States and Canada. I use Pro Mix myself. It contains seasoned Canadian sphagnum, peat moss, perlite, vermiculite, and other ingredients that are scientifically blended and enriched. It is an improved university formula, ready to use right from the bag. Just dampen it with the wake-up tonic. This Pro Mix is really better and safer than your own soil. It is also lighter than soil and retains moisture better and longer; no chance of fungi, weeds, or bugs. There are also others such as Jiffy Mix or Redi Earth.

Baby Needs a New Pair of Shoes

Since plants' roots are their feet, the pots they grow in are considered their shoes. Since we want to be very cautious about disease, we want everything spic and span for our new baby seeds. No dirty shoes or damping off will show up.

Use peat pots filled with Pro Mix, or compressed peat pellets which swell up when set in water. If you use peat pots or Pro Mix, make sure they are well moistened before you wake up the seeds and place them into the mix. I use peat pots for smaller seeds and peat pellets for the bigger seeds such as cucumbers, squash, and melons. Sow one seed per pot. Small seeds should be planted ¼ inch deep; big seeds should be dropped into the middle of the peat pellet and then pinched shut.

Tuck the New Seeds In!

What this means is that you should set the peat pots and/or peat pellets in a shallow tray and slip it into a clear plastic bag and secure the end. Place the seeds in a dark warm area for 24 hours at 70°. After 24 hours, open the bag each day to let fresh air in, and move to an area with a medium light.

As quick as the seeds sprout, remove the plastic bag and move into the sunlight. Keep them warm and damp—not hot and wet.

PLUG IN FOR PLEASURE

The Electric Blanket for Seeds Is Great

Soil-heating cables are specially designed wire with insulated cable that will not be injured by the enzyme action of the soil or by water. Soil-heating cables can be purchased in almost any lawn and garden department. The heating cables come with a built-in thermostat which automatically keeps the soil temperature in the 70s. Soil-heating cables are for cold frames and small soil areas.

Let's Put a Little Light on the Subject

Until the little guys and gals sprout, the sun and room temperature or heat cable keep them warm and comfortable. As soon as they stretch their little green arms, however, light as well as heat becomes a matter of life or death. It's light that activates photosynthesis for them to grow by.

With low-cost, easy-to-use grow lights available, you should invest. Place the plants 12 inches below the lights for 14 to 16 hours a day. If you raise the light, the plants will get tall and skinny. General Electric has a full line of economical, effective, and attractive lighting fixtures available for home gardens called Gro & Sho. I find them in all plant and garden departments.

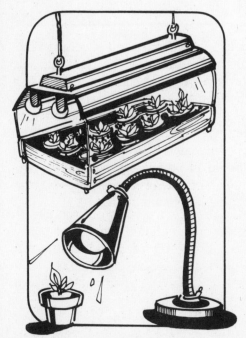

LET'S LOOK AT THE BRIGHT SIDE

Wet Their Whistle Regularly

Peat containers will dry out quickly indoors, so watch them closely. An hour of dry soil will wilt or kill a young seedling. Do not pour water onto the soil. Either spray or fill the container and let them take the water up. Remember— *damp*, not *drowned!*

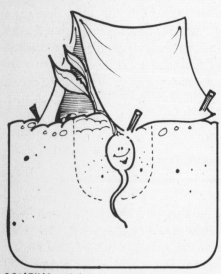

YOUR GREENHOUSE WORK FOR TONIGHT IS

CAMPING OUT

We Won't Put Them on Solid Food Indoors

There is sufficient nourishment in the Pro Mix or any of the other mixes to satisfy the little plants adequately until they go into the garden patch. Please don't be tempted to add any plant food to the water. I mean it! If you do, all your TLC will have been in vain.

It's Time to Go to Grow-and-Play School

You must not scare or shock the new seedlings. Don't just plunk them in the soil and walk away. As soon as the temperature gets up to a comfortable 70°, set the plants in their tray outdoors for an hour or two and extend the time each day until you can leave them out overnight. Now, wait two more days and then transplant.

Don't Bury Them, Just Plant Them!

Dig a hole only about ½ inch deeper and wider than the container. Fill the hole with water. Set the plant into the holes and add soil and firm, but don't squash.

It's a good idea to cover new transplants for at least a week to protect from both heat and cold. Cover with paper bags, cardboard boxes, plastic milk cartons with bottom cut out, plastic tent—any of these will help.

Now, aren't you proud of your accomplishment? You ought to be. Few home gardeners ever really try to grow from seed, at least indoors. I'm proud of you.

SO, WHO CARES?

5

The Groundwork for Success
PREPARING THE SOIL

I would not be doing the job you hired me to do if I did not make an issue of making bad dirt good, good dirt better, and all dirt more appetizing for the vegetables you are about to start growing. You have not read wrong. I referred to your garden soil as dirt because about 80 percent of you 35 million impatient vegetable gardeners call soil dirt. There's nothing the matter with the word.

Yes, I said you hired me to do a job for you. When you bought this book, you hired me to help you have a garden that provides you and your family with as much wholesome, tasty, attractive produce as is possible with the amount of land, effort, and money you are able to invest. And that, my garden friend, is exactly what I am going to try to do.

Choose the Best Garden Tools—Don't Go Cheap!

You will need very few tools for a small garden. It is better to buy a few simple, high-grade tools that will serve well for many years rather than tools that are poorly designed or made of cheap materials that won't last. In most cases, the only tools needed are a *spade* or *spading fork,* a *steel bow* rake, a *7-inch common hoe,* a *wheelbarrow,* and a *garden hose* long enough to water all parts of the garden. A *trowel* can be useful in transplanting, but is not necessary. If the soil is well prepared, plants can be planted more easily with the hands than with a trowel.

For gardens that are from 2,000 to 4,000 square feet, a *wheel hoe* is useful because it can be used for most work usually done with a common hoe and takes a lot less effort. The single-wheel type is probably the easiest to handle and best for use as an all-purpose wheel hoe. Other styles are available.

The cultivating tools, or attachments, for the wheel hoe should include one or more of the so-called *hoe blades.* They are best for weeding and are used more than the cultivator teeth or small plow usually supplied with a wheel hoe.

For gardens over 4,000 square feet, a *rotary garden tiller* is useful in preparing the soil for planting and controlling weeds. One brand is the Rototiller, and "rototilling" has become a generic word for the process.

Gardeners who do little farming have the choice of hiring equipment for garden-land preparation or buying their own. Equipment for hire is often unavailable when needed; so, a favorable season for planting may be missed.

The rotary tiller is capable of preparing light to medium soils for planting in one operation, and has been widely adopted by gardeners who have such soils. In the hands of a careful operator and on land that is not too hard and heavy and is reasonably free from stones, roots, and other obstructions, this machine has many desirable features. It can be adjusted to cultivate very shallowly or to plow the soil and fit it for planting. Tools such as *sweeps* may be attached, thereby adapting the machine to straddle-row cultivating.

Use of well-adapted implements in preparing garden land cuts down the work required in cultivating. Clean, sharp, high-grade tools greatly lessen garden labor.

BEST BUYS AREN'T ALWAYS BEST

Bum Dirt Is a Blessing!

HOE, BO

A whole bunch of you home gardeners are perfectly satisfied to settle for garden dirt that is really not ideal for growing vegetables. That's a shame, both for the vegetables that you are asking to try to live and produce there and for your own personal satisfaction in proving that you really do have a green thumb.

Any soil can be improved, from the thickest, heaviest clay to the driest sand to the hard, parched soil of the desert areas. All you have to remember is what it took to make fertile soil to begin with. Fallen leaves, decayed trees that fell from storms, withered grasses, weeds and flowers in the fall, and aging carcasses and wild animal waste are among the natural materials that go into enriching any of these types of soil. They are referred to as organic materials.

If you are just beginning a garden, mark out your plot and remove any common lawn grass and use it in other areas of your yard. Waste not!

If your garden area is going to be less than 200 square feet (that's 10×20 feet) and you and your back are in good shape, over a few days' time with an hour here and there you can hand-spade the soil to a depth of 12 inches. Anything larger I would have *plowed.* I stress "plowed" because I want it turned over. Look in your local paper for ads that offer this service in your neighborhood. Rototilling comes later.

There are two best times to incorporate organic material into gardens: spring (before spading) and fall (after harvest).

All Organic Material Does Some Good—Some More Than Others

Plants need N-P-K to survive and produce, and all plants don't need the same amounts of each. The N is nitrogen; the P is short for P_2O_5, phosphate; and the K is short for K_2O, potash. As we begin a new vegetable garden or continually fortify a long-producing plot, we will add organic materials that are high in humus and break down quickly so that the plants can get N-P-K.

NET WORTH OF ORGANIC MATERIALS

H = High L = Low M = Medium F = Fast S = Slow O = None

Material	Humus Range	Speed of Breakdown
Cattle manure	H	M
Horse manure (1 year old)	H	M
Pig manure	M	M
Sheep and goat manure (1 year old)	M	M
Duck manure	M	M
Chicken manure	M	M
Turkey manure	M	M
Rabbit manure (1 year old)	M	M
Bean straw	M	M
Oat straw	M	M
Rye straw	M	M
Wheat straw	M	M
Sawdust	M	M
Leaves	M	M
Peat moss (Add peat each year along with any other)	H	M
Table scraps	M	H
Coffee grounds	M	M
Tea leaves	M	M
Shredded cornstalks	M	M
Corn cobs	M	S
Peanut shells	M	M
Seaweed	L	M
Tobacco stems	M	M
Ashes	O	F
Dried blood	O	F
Bone meal (steamed)	O	S
Eggshells	O	S
Fish emulsion	M	F
Fish meal	L	M

Material	Humus Range	Speed of Breakdown
Fish scraps	L	M
Dried grass clippings	M	S
Green grass clippings	M	S

All of the aforementioned materials contribute more to the quality of soil than just humus, and we will cover this as needed.

Turn Over an Old Leaf

Throwing any of the soil-building materials I recommend on top of the garden plot won't do anything but make your neighbors mad, because it will blow into their yards. You must put it under. Here is how to do it by hand. Dig a trench the width of the shovel, across the narrow end of the garden, and throw the soil at least halfway back onto the garden. Fill the trench a quarter to a third full of any organic materials; now, throw the soil from the next row over the organic material. Repeat the organic material in the bottom of the next and continue until you have spaded the whole garden.

If you are plowing, spread on top and wet down only enough to keep it from blowing around and then plow under.

Liquid Compost Shake

You folks throw away dollars every week in the form of organic plant food—your table scraps! You will notice that garbage as a humus is only of medium value but is quick to break down. What your table scraps contribute is a good, mild, safe, clean source of food for your garden, and in most cases as it breaks down it provides 2.5 percent nitrogen, 1.5 percent phosphorus, and 1.5 percent potassium. After supper add all vegetable waste both cooked and raw that has not been fried or cooked in oil or salt, raw fish, seeds, peels, tops, and roots and put them in a blender and emulsify with water. Pour this into a plastic container and

I COULD HAVE HAD A V-8

add 1 capful of household ammonia per quart and ½ teaspoon of Epsom salts. Add each quart of compost shake to a gallon of warm water and pour onto an unmulched garden or pour through plant openings.

Carpet Your Walkways

Since you will be mulching your garden with grass clippings or plastic or woven mulch, moisture will be contained. On the area around the outside and path through the middle, the soil will dry and crack in the dry hot weather and be muddy, slippery, and dangerous when wet. So I suggest that you cover the paths with shredded bark, which can be added to the soil as humus in the fall. It looks great and makes walking more comfortable.

Add the Frosting

The frostings are fertilizers, lime, and gypsum when a new garden is started. I broadcast 1 quart of 5-10-5 or 4-12-4 per 100 square feet of garden, and 2 quarts of lime and 8 quarts of garden gypsum. On established gardens I take a soil test each fall and again in the spring to determine the pH factor, which means: Is the soil sweet or sour?

In order to test the soil for pH you can purchase a simple soil-testing kit or a pH meter, or send the soil to the Cooperative Extension Service. Most vegetables like a pH range between 6.3 and 7. If your soil test shows a range above 6.3, you don't need lime. In the high-rainfall areas of the country you will probably need lime every year. In hot, dry areas you probably won't need lime. To lower the soil pH, you would use sulfur, aluminum sulfate, or iron sulfate.

Crank Up the Tiller

Now it's time to fine-tune your garden dirt. That's done by blending all of the materials we have added on top and underneath. This is best done with a tiller. Tillers can be rented in most neighborhoods and are well worth the in-

vestment. If you have a big garden you may want to purchase one. Till north and south, east and west, crisscross and crisscross until you have darn near blended it smooth. Now, go rest and relax for a while.

Patience Is Not a Virtue, It's a Must!

If you will just keep adding leaves, grass, sawdust, manure, and any or all on the list to the soil, within three years at the most, you will have the best garden soil this side of Eden. Well, at least close.

Keep Your Garden in Shape

Keeping a garden in shape means maintaining the physical or constructive shape in which you build your garden. I

NO ONE LOVES A FAT PATCH

told you in the introduction and basic training chapter that your vegetable garden had to be in a sunny, well-drained location. The design makes no difference. I also said to put paths to walk on. Don't be stomping all over the dirt and in between your plants; you'll just cause problems.

Most professional vegetable gardens and knowledgeably designed home vegetable gardens are slightly raised above the normal level of the surrounding ground. They also have a slightly turtleback appearance. What this does is allow good drainage even on the heaviest soil. Never plant a garden in a location that water lies in; that's called swaled. Build it up by bringing in additional soil. As you add new organic material, leaves, and grass clippings each spring and fall, you will see your garden soil rise automatically.

Some Gardens Can Rise Above It

In areas where you have heavy rainfall, little soil area to work with, or other reasons why you cannot dig into the dirt, I think you should simply consider raised vegetable gardens.

Raised vegetable gardens are big kids' sandboxes. Build simple square or rectangular boxes out of redwood or Wolmanized (treated) wood. Build them 10 to 12 inches high and whatever length or width you desire. You can tier them along a patio to make a wall effect or lay them out in various designs.

Fill your raised bed with the same good rich organic growing dirt we have been talking about and you will have more to chew on than you ever dreamed of.

Cinder blocks, railroad ties, piled rock, and broken concrete blocks will also do to contain the soil and provide you with an attractive as well as a productive garden area.

GARDEN GOLD: COMPOST
Waste with a Purpose

In twenty-some years of writing and broadcasting gardening information, I have written and spoken thousands of words

on the wonderful contributions that a compost pile can contribute to your vegetable, flower, rose, and evergreen beds —as a matter of fact, to all of the soil in your "yarden" (yard and garden). As I travel around the country, however, I find very few of you keeping my advice on this subject, as well as that of my colleagues, who also highly recommend garden gold (compost). "It smells!" some say. "Draws flies!" comes from another. "Rats and mice will breed in it!" from yet another. It's the truth, and yet it's nonsense. If you simply build a scuzzy pile of trash, it will certainly have all the problems above and more. If you systematically add grass clippings, lettuce leaves, vegetable tops, dry leaves, sawdust, coffee grounds, eggshells, peels, green leaves, and flower heads you will have a fresh-smelling, rich, attractive pile of highly valuable earth food, or substrate as it is referred to in Europe.

If you are going to make a serious run at successful vegetable gardening, as your coach I insist that you try a *small* compost pile this year.

It's time to begin the pile. Add 6 to 8 inches of the organic material we talked about and sprinkle a light layer of garden soil on top. Mix 1 cup of household ammonia, ½ cup of liquid soap, and a shot glass of clear corn syrup in a 2-gallon sprinkling can of very warm water and sprinkle it over the layer of compost; this will speed up the decomposition action. You may also use stale beer or flat whiskey (when the alcohol has evaporated). From time to time stir or turn the pile with a spade fork. When your compost is dark brown to black, work it into the soil.

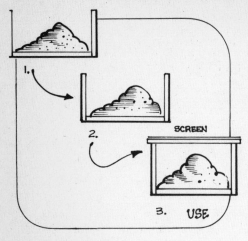

For the sake of this experiment, let's make a $3 \times 3 \times 3$-foot cube of cedar, redwood, or treated wood. Use 2×12 stock, and hardware cloth (also known as rat wire) in the middle of the sides and back wall to allow for air circulation.

The front gate will consist of three boards (12 inches high and 3 feet long) that will sit one on top of the other to be slid up and down to turn the pile or remove material. To hold them in place, drive a metal pipe or heavy stake into the ground at all six corners.

After you have tried it once, build two more boxes and transfer the working compost from box 1 to box 2 and start a new pile in box 1; then build a wire-screen frame to lay over box 3 to sift the compost from box 2 when it's time to move it again. Use the fine-screened compost from box 3 as needed. Believe me, it's worth the work!

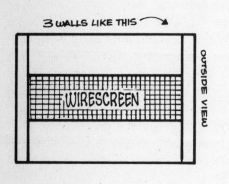

3 WALLS LIKE THIS

OUTSIDE VIEW

WIRESCREEN

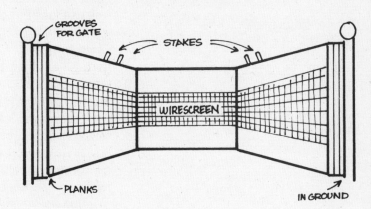

GROOVES FOR GATE

STAKES

WIRESCREEN

PLANKS

IN GROUND

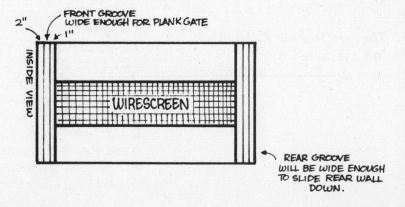

2"

1"

FRONT GROOVE
WIDE ENOUGH FOR PLANK GATE

INSIDE VIEW

WIRESCREEN

REAR GROOVE
WILL BE WIDE ENOUGH
TO SLIDE REAR WALL
DOWN.

YOU SURE YOU'RE NOT A TOMATO?

6

Tomatoes Are Fruit in Disguise
GROWING TOMATOES

Tomatoes are classified as fruit in every country in the world but the United States. Here the tomato was made a vegetable by an act of Congress to reduce its taxation base. Tomatoes were also thought to be a poison for generations until the godfather of home gardening in this country, Benjamin Franklin, discovered their tastiness and safety. The tomato has gone on to become the single most popular vegetable/fruit in the United States and Canada.

Tomatoes can be grown anywhere. These garden plants will grow both indoors and out. Tomatoes can be used in cooking in combination with almost any fish, fowl, and meat dishes. They are compatible with just about all other garden vegetables.

There Is Trouble Right Here in Vegetable City!

Many, many of you plant tomatoes, year in and year out, with less than spectacular results. They wilt, tilt, drop, blossom, and rot. The bugs beat them up and eat them up. It almost sounds as if they're not worth the work. Wrong!

Tomatoes are easy to grow, and disease and insects don't have to be a problem with a little preplanning. Select a

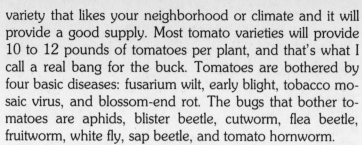

variety that likes your neighborhood or climate and it will provide a good supply. Most tomato varieties will provide 10 to 12 pounds of tomatoes per plant, and that's what I call a real bang for the buck. Tomatoes are bothered by four basic diseases: fusarium wilt, early blight, tobacco mosaic virus, and blossom-end rot. The bugs that bother tomatoes are aphids, blister beetle, cutworm, flea beetle, fruitworm, white fly, sap beetle, and tomato hornworm.

This list of bad guys sounds worse than it is. If you prepare the soil properly, the way I have suggested earlier in this book, if you select varieties of tomatoes that are resistant to viruses and wilts, and if you mulch properly, you won't have a worry in the gardening world. The insect problem can be licked with two products and a simple trick or two.

Varieties That Laugh at Trouble

There are nearly 500 different varieties of tomatoes in the world, with more to come. So you should have no problem finding one that fits your family needs and taste.

The following is a list of standbys that are pretty much disease-resistant. Be sure to check your seed racks, catalogs, and garden centers for new seeds and plants.

RUN BABY, RUN!

Variety	Climate Preferred	Disease-Resistant
Ace Hy	Humid	V, F, N
Beefmaster	Humid	V, F, N
Better Boy	Cool	V, F, N
Big Set	Cool	V, F, N
Bonus	Cool	V, F, N
Burpee VF	Humid	V, F
Burpee Super Steak	Cool	V, F, N
Fireball VF	Humid	V, F
Floramerica	Cool	V, F
Homestead 24	Humid	F
Hybrid Ace	Dry	V, F, N
Jet Star	Humid	V, F

Variety	Climate Preferred	Disease-Resistant
Manalucie	Humid	F, S, C
Monty Carlo	Cool	V, F, N
Moscow VR	Dry	V
Ramapo	Humid	V, F
Small Fry	Cool	V, F
Supersonic	Humid	V, F
Terrific	Cool	V, F, N
Toy Boy	Cool	V, F
Tropic	Humid	V, F, S
Walter	Humid	F_{1+2}, S
Wonder Boy	Humid	V, F, N

Code for Disease

V = Verticillium wilt

F = Fusarium wilt (1 and 2 means resistant to the common race and the recently discovered second race)

N = Root knot nematodes

S = Stemphylium (gray leaf spot)

C = Clodasparium (leaf mold)

Now don't forget, if you're having good luck with your own favorite variety, stick with it. If not, try one of these or another one recommended by your county agency or garden center.

The Other Ways to Fight Disease

A clean, neat garden will seldom suffer from disease. Make sure that the soil is rich with organic compost and plant healthy plants. Stake them up with metal poles, pipes, or cables, not wood. Tie them with pieces of nylon stockings, not wire, cloth, or plastic. Cover the soil with grass, straw, or plastic. Water at the roots, and don't wet foliage if possible. Feed with Super K-Gro Fish Emulsion and spray when necessary with Super K-Gro All Purpose Fruit Tree & Vegetable Spray; it contains Sevin, malathion, methoxy-

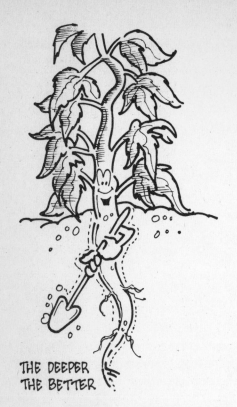

THE DEEPER
THE BETTER

ENOUGH IS ENOUGH

chlor, and captan. When you check the bug chart, you will note that one or more of each of these is suggested.

Plant Them Deep

In most parts of the country, especially the Midwest, East, and North, short-season areas are foolish to mess with tomato seeds sown into the ground. Your local greenhouse and garden center have rooted plants available at prices you can't grow your own for, so start with these.

Remove all but the top leaves and plant deep enough that these leaves are lying on the mulch or covering. Planting this way gives you stronger healthier plants.

You Have to Mulch Tomatoes

Blossom-end rot (gray moldy bottom) is the result of a real dry spell followed by a wet one; if soil is mulched, it will keep even moisture and no rot will appear.

Dropping Their Blossoms Is Not a Death Dance

Blossom drop means the temperature was too cold or too hot or the soil is too rich. There is nothing you can do but wait. Flowers will appear and set fruit, and your crop will be a little late. Rarely does the plant continue to drop its flowers indefinitely. Do not feed tomatoes until you can see the fruit form.

Don't Bug, D-Bug Your Tomatoes!

I give my tomatoes a bath on Tuesdays with liquid dish soap, chewing-tobacco juice, and a touch of mustard and tea. To 1 quart of weak tea add 3 teaspoons of liquid soap, 3 tablespoons of chewing-tobacco juice, and $\frac{1}{16}$ teaspoon of ordinary mustard. Shake well and spray. If this spray doesn't make your bugs sick, then use the Super K-Gro All Purpose Fruit Tree & Vegetable Spray. For tomato worms, spray with Dipel.

Best Tomato Sauce You Ever Froze

You will have so many tomatoes this season that I thought I would give you my favorite, fast, easy, tasty recipe for tomato sauce. You don't have to peel the tomatoes, just pour them into a blender after cooking and freeze.

TOMATO SAUCE FOR FREEZER

20 large tomatoes—washed, cored, cut in chunks

4 large onions—chopped (4 cups)

4 large carrots—pared, shredded

½ cup parsley, chopped

3 tablespoons sugar

2 tablespoons salt

¾ teaspoon pepper

Bring all ingredients to boil in a large pot and stir often. Simmer 30 minutes or until mixture thickens. Cool slightly. Pour into covered blender and blend on high speed for 1 minute.

Pour into freezer containers in serving size portions. Leave ½" headroom. Place in freezer. Keeps for a couple of years.

To serve: Place frozen block of sauce in medium-size heavy saucepan. Cover and bring to bubbling over very low heat or in a microwave with a piece of wax paper over top.

To season: Add 1 teaspoon of leaf basil, oregano, or thyme to each 2 cups of sauce.

IT'S PROBABLY JUST A FAD

7

Contain Your Vegetable Garden Enthusiasm
CONTAINER GARDENING

Many of you folks do not have an area to spade up and make a permanent vegetable garden, but you still have an interest in growing and enjoying fresh vegetables. Quit your worrying now, for cans, wooden boxes, wastebaskets, planters, bushel baskets, and hanging baskets will fill the bill for your growing grounds. As a matter of fact, plastic garbage bags filled with Hyponex Professional Mix are what the pros use.

You Have to Clean Up Your Act Here!

If you are going to get the best results in container growing, you should use a professional planter mix called a soilless mix. Pro Mix, Jiffy Mix, and Super Soil are a few of the best-known and are available in most areas. These are referred to as synthetic mixes. The reason I suggest this type of growing medium is that it is insect-free and disease-free and will last for several years. The ingredients you find in most of these mixes are peat moss, redwood sawdust, other wood by-products, perlite, vermiculite, and sand. The soilless mixes provide fast drainage and air in the soil and retain moisture. Most of the mixes on the market contain a mild source of starter food to get your plants off to a good start.

Size And Shape Don't Matter Much, But Depth Can Be a Killer!

The vegetable plants and I don't care about how wide, long, or big around the container you build or buy is, or even if it's heart- or kidney-shaped. We are both concerned as to how "deep" it is.

The size of your container will depend on the space you have or its portability. The depth of the container will determine how often you will need to water and feed. Shallow containers and hanging baskets will need closer watching for water, while the deep cans and boxes will retain more lower moisture.

Beets, lettuce, radishes, turnips, and herbs need a minimum depth of 6 inches.

Short carrots, Swiss chard, spinach, mustard, turnip greens, cabbage, bush beans, peppers, and eggplants need 8 to 10 inches of depth.

MIXED UP CAN
BE SMART

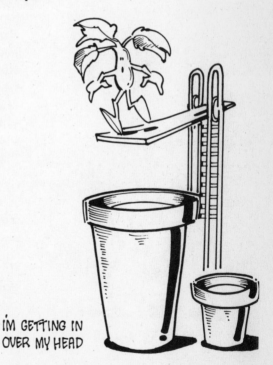

I'M GETTING IN
OVER MY HEAD

DON'T GET ROBBED OF SPACE

Carrots, parsnips, broccoli, cauliflower, Brussels sprouts, and tomatoes need 12 to 14 inches of depth.

Select Those Vegetables That Give the Biggest Bang for the Buck, on Space

Since your space is limited with container gardening, make your plant vegetables ones that return the most to eat for the space. Beets, carrots, chives, green onions, lettuce, spinach, collards, turnips, and mustard greens are a few that fit the bill.

Refer to "Space Savers for Container Gardens" in Chapter 2.

Looks Make a Difference!

Since you and your friends will be living among your garden containers, both plants and containers should be attractive. After all, most of them will be on the patio or balcony. Rubbermaid, the large manufacturer of housewares and planters, has all sizes and shapes of plastic garbage cans, planters, wastebaskets, and trays. The color choice is also unlimited, so put some thought into your display. If you are building your own boxes, paint or stain them to be attractive. Hanging baskets must fit the same criteria.

PUT WHEELS ON IT

Your Aching Back!

If you don't have one, you will with container gardening if you don't make the containers portable, retractable, and rotatable. Make plans to build or buy bases with casters to move the large boxes and containers. For hanging baskets you can purchase holders that hook onto your ceiling hooks

NO JER, FISH EMULSION IS GOOD BUT NOT THAT GOOD.

and let you pull the basket down for working on and watering and then send it back up. Large fishing swivels on ceiling hooks allow you to rotate baskets so that all sides get sun—especially on patios and porches.

Give a Shower, Don't Get One!

To make watering and feeding your containers easier, both on the ground and in the air, get a water wand with a flare-end rose head and a hose-on siphon. This will let you mix your plant food and chemicals in a bucket on the ground and then bring it up through your hose each time you water. A rose flare nozzle or bubble nozzle has a gentle water spray and does not disturb the soil or break the foliage. Always attach a cheap on-and-off connector at the nozzle.

Frequent Snacks Are Best for Containers

Since any of your container and hanging vegetable baskets will depend totally on you for survival, you have to stay alert. The reason their life is in your hands is that they are in a confined space, with a small amount of dirt to hold their dinner and drinks. Since they will be drinking at a rate of 1 quart to 2 gallons a day (tomatoes when mature) and eating every daylight hour (they sleep and grow in the dark), your job is cut out for you.

Feed and water at the same time. I add a small amount of Super K-Gro Fish Emulsion (1 capful to 10 gallons) and the same of liquid dish soap into a gallon bucket. Place the hose-on siphon into it and water through the bubble nozzle. Plants are like people. They will eat a little bit each time, digest it, enjoy it, not waste it and then grow their vegetables off for you.

THAT'S A BALANCED DIET?

SO WHAT IF I'M AN OLD BAG? BUSTER!

Who Should Hang Around?

As a rule, I always tell folks to let small vegetables and vining crops hang around in suspended baskets (cukes, beans, peas, cherry tomatoes). I recently saw a cute trick done by suspending one hanging basket from the other and planting small French forcing carrots in one, radishes in the other; did they ever look terrific! So let yourself and your growing friends grow. Hang out with anyone that looks good. Taste is taken for granted.

As a Last Resort, Bag It!

No, I don't mean throw it out. I mean simply fill heavy plastic trash liners with the professional mix, cut holes in the side for planting, then water, feed, and harvest. Nothing fancy, just functional. I have seen where an imaginative apartment gardener went to the carpet department and bought green Astroturf and covered the bags with a neat hole for the plant to grow through and made a super-looking "yardio"—yard and patio.

THE TASTE WILL TELL

8

What's the Difference Between a Chef and a Cook?
HERBS

When I visit a garden, whether it be that of a professional, active hobbiest, or early beginner, one of the first things I look for after maintenance practices is the presence of herbs. Any gardener who loves to garden will soon discover the enchanting world of herbs.

There are hundreds of herbs to choose from, as you can see from any of the seed catalogs, and you soon find yourself all wrapped up in your search for yet another seasoning or pleasant fragrance.

Herbs can be grown both indoors and out, in pots, pans, trays, and saucers or as borders around the vegetable garden or flower beds. Herbs can be grown alongside other plants to protect them from insects.

Fragrant herbs can be grown in hanging baskets outside windows or in tubs on patios or porches to send their pleasant scents riding on the gentle breezes into your rooms or even to apartment dwellers dozens of stories above the exhaust-filled streets of big cities. To really have a relaxing and pleasant experience, hang a wind chime alongside your herbs.

Never Turn Down a Dinner Invitation from an Herb Gardener!

Many, many folks tell me that I write like I talk or perform. Those of you who know me will know that I talk like I feel and when I am excited I talk fast and am animated as the dickens. Right this moment I am 34,000 feet above your gardens, in an airplane from Troy, Michigan, to Los Angeles, writing about herbs; the more I write the more excited I get, because tonight I am joining some friends for a home-cooked meal. It will be a gourmet meal no matter what we have, because they have over 185 different herbs growing at all times. They use them in all of their cooking; from scrambled eggs in the morning for an added touch of class to a can of soup at lunch to a gastronomic symphony for dinner. I can't wait, and neither should you to add herbs to your garden. Check my suggestions for a good start from your local garden center or Park Seed Company, Greenwood, SC 29647.

Herbs for the Home Gardener

The more the "now" generation travels about this old world, the more we become aware of the delights of well-seasoned cookery. The secrets lie chiefly in wise selection of kitchen herbs, too long overlooked and mostly forgotten by old-line American families.

Both seeds and plants are readily available, and only a few plants of any one kind, given reasonable care, will supply in abundance for year-long use. Best results for the drying of herbs are had by picking just before flowering, drying quickly in shaded but airy trays or screens, then covering tightly in screwtop jars. One cannot buy better seasonings at any price, anywhere.

And while we're about it: The true pronunciation sounds the H, as in Herbert; to the English, it's pure Cockney to call it "erb." But, when in Rome . . .

HERBS FOR THE HOME GARDEN

Herb	Height	Longevity	Soil	Fresh	Dried	Uses
Anise	1½–2'	Annual	Sandy loam	Leaves	Seeds	Leaves in salads and as garnish; seeds flavor candies, cakes, cookies, soups, stews, and cottage cheese
Caraway	2½'	Biennial	Sandy loam	——	Seeds	Warm, aromatic odor and flavor for cooking, pastries, cheese, sauces, and soups
Catnip	3–4'	Perennial	Sandy loam	Leaves	Leafy tips	For seasoning and tea; cats love this; also animal tonic
Chive	10"	Perennial	Sandy loam	Leaves	——	Adds delicious onion flavor to foods, soups; decorative flowers used as a border; plant in sun or light shade
Clary sage	9"	Biennial	Sandy loam	——	Leaves	Use in omelets and fritters, and for flavoring wines
Coriander	2'	Annual	Sandy loam	——	Seeds	Delicious perfumed taste and odor, for condiment and confections
Dill	3'	Annual	Rich loam	Leaves	Seeds	Flavoring for pickles (seeds) and leaves in soups, stews, sauces
Garlic	2'	Perennial	Sandy loam	——	Mature bulbs	Sections of bulbs, or "cloves," for flavoring in cookery
Horehound	14"	Perennial	Sandy loam	Leafy stems	Leaves	Fresh for juice in flavoring candies; dried for flavoring
Lavender	1½–3'	Perennial	Dry loam Sun, lime	——	Flower spikes	Fragrance for sachets, potpourris, perfumes; repels moths; border flower
Lovage	2–3'	Perennial	Rich, moist	Leaves	Leaves	Adds celery flavor to soups and salads
Marjoram, sweet	8–12"	Annual	Sandy loam	Leaves	Leafy stems	Flavoring for dressings, meats, soups, salads, stews, some vegetables; indispensable
Marjoram, wild	2'	Perennial	Light sandy	——	Leaves	Flavoring in cooking, tea
Nasturtium	Vine	Annual	Good loam	Leaves, flowers, pods	——	Fresh leaves, stems, and flowers have spicy peppery flavor for salads; green seed pods are pickled.
Parsley	12"	Biennial	Rich, moist	Leaves	Leaves	Fresh as garnish; grow in pots for winter use; dried to flavor cheese, eggs, fish.
Pennyroyal	4"	Perennial	Rich, moist	Leaves	——	Tea for coughs and colds; tender—protect in winter.

HERBS FOR THE HOME GARDEN

Herb	Height	Longevity	Soil	Fresh	Dried	Uses
Pineapple sage	4'	Perennial	Good loam	Leaves	Leaves	Fresh in iced tea; dried for pot-pourris; protect in winter.
Peppermint	2'	Perennial	Rich, moist	Leaves	Leaves	Tea and flavoring; oil in confections and medicines
Rosemary	3'	Perennial	Sandy loam, lime	———	Leaves	Flavoring for meats, dressings, sauces, soups; protect in winter.
Rue	3'	Perennial	Moist loam	Leaves	———	Aromatic, used in sandwiches; some may be allergic to this in summer.
Sage	2'	Perennial	Sandy loam	———	Leaves	Seasoning, for meats, dressings, stews, soups, fish chowder, and sauces; grow the best, at home.
Spearmint	1½–2'	Perennial	Rich, moist	Leaves	Leaves	Fresh leafy stems in cold drinks, in teas, mint sauce; oil in confectionery
Summer savory	18"	Annual	Rich loam	Leaves	Leafy tops	Condiment with meats and vegetables; flavoring in salads, stews
Sweet basil	18"	Annual	Rich, moist	Leaves	Leaves	Spicily scented for seasoning meats, fish, eggs, soups, sauces
Tarragon	2'	Perennial	Sandy, light shade	New leaves, stem tips	Leaves	In salads and other cookery; vinegar; flavor a little like anise
Thyme	6–10"	Perennial	Sandy loam	———	Leafy tips	Popular seasoning for foods of many kinds, soups; also in pot-pourris

Don't Just Look, Enjoy!

Even though most herbs are pleasant just to look at in a well-kept herb garden, the fun is learning how to use them in your cooking. Any bookstore has dozens of good cookbooks that specialize in the use of herbs and spices in cooking; check them out.

Since I travel thousands of miles each year all over the world, I am constantly alert for a new taste in food seasoning and often ask to talk to the chef for further information; most are very proud when you compliment them and ask.

This Spicy Group Is Never Taken Too Seriously

Do you know that wars were fought over spices? Ransoms and dowries have been exchanged as well as requests from royalty for spices in place of jewels.

Today less than one home garden family in fifty grows herbs in the garden—a shame as well as a waste. Many are missing a great deal of gardening enjoyment, with very little effort involved; the waste is the money that you spend over the years for a small package of herbs for cooking that you can grow yourself. Herbs contribute greatly to the quality of family living; they're pretty and their smell will fill your property with perfume. When you season your cooking with herbs, cooking becomes an art.

Here is a suggested list of both annual and perennial herbs for you to pick from to spice up your life and for cooking both indoors and out.

Perennial Herbs

Allium fistulosum (Welsh bunching onion). Sweet, mild bunching onions. Eat bulbs, stalks, and leaves raw in salads for a tangy treat.

Anthemis nobilis (Roman Chamomile). Used as a tea.

Balm (Melissa officianalis). 2 feet. Whitish blooms, lemon flavor. Often used in medicinal teas. Attractive to bees.

Basil (Holy, lemon, licorice, cinnamon). Four rare, fragrant herbs.

Burnet (Poterium sanguisorba). 1½ feet. Used to flavor salads and cold drinks.

Caper bush (Capparis spinosa). 3 feet. Flower buds are pickled and used in cooking and flavoring.

Carob tree (Ceratonia siliqua). Fruits and seeds source of a chocolate substitute. Tropical, grow like oranges.

Catmint (Nepeta mussinii superba). 1 foot. Showy border plants with fragrant lavender-blue flowers and aromatic silver foliage.

Catnip (Nepeta cataria). 3 feet. Tea from leaves said to aid digestion. Cats love it.

THEY TASTE AS GOOD AS THEY LOOK

Chicory, large-rooted Magdeburg *(coffee chicory).* Dried roots used as substitute for or to augment coffee.

Chives *(Allium schoenoprasum).* Delicate, onion-flavored foliage for flavoring and garnishing soups, potatoes, salads. The lavender flower heads are lovely in the garden, too.

Chrysanthemum cinerariifolium. Petals are primary source of pyrethrum, an important natural insecticide.

Comfrey, Russian *(Symphytum x uplandicum).* Leaves high in vitamins and minerals. Reputed remedy for sore throats, wounds, other internal and external problems.

Coriander *(Coriandrum sativum; cilantro).* Leaves and seeds used in Oriental and other cooking.

Curled cress (peppergrass). Bright green leaves add tang to salads. Can be grown indoors on sponge or blotter.

Curled mint *(Mentha aquatica crispa).* 3 feet. Used for flavoring.

Dandelion *(Taraxacum officinale).* Leaves make a popular spring salad. Also used for wine.

Fennel, sweet *(Foeniculum vulgare).* 4 feet. Leaves used in fish sauces and for garnishing.

Ginseng *(Panax quinquefolium).* 18 inches. Orientals consider ginseng to promote long life and virility and have used it as a cure-all. Here, roots are used mainly for their tranquilizing qualities. Prefers well-drained, moist location.

Hops *(Humulus lupulus).* Flower buds used to flavor beer.

Horehound *(Marribium vulgare).* 2 feet. Grayish leaves are used in candies and cough remedies.

Horseradish roots *(Armoracia rusticana).* Homemade, fresh-grated horseradish far surpasses in pungency and flavor the tired preparations you find at the grocery. Excellent with meats and in sauces.

Hyssop *(Hyssopus officinalis).* 1½ feet. Attractive plants with white, pink, or blue flowers. Makes good tea.

Jojoba *(Simmondisa chinesis).* Cosmetic and medicinal oil extracted from seed. Needs good drainage.

Lavender (Munstead strain). 1 foot. Deep lavender flowers, delightfully fragrant. Use in sachets.

Lavender vera *(Lavendula angustifolia)*. 2 feet. Lilac flowers, delightfully scented, dried to make sachets. Attractive gray-green foliage.

Lemon mint *(Monarda citriodora)*. Lemon-scented leaves and flowers that attract bees. Indians used oil to treat wounds.

Lovage *(Levisticum officinale)*. 6 feet. Aromatic seeds used in cakes.

Oregano *(Origanum vulgare)*. 2 feet. Thick green leaves, strongly aromatic, used in Italian dishes. Lavender-pink flowers.

Pennyroyal *(Mentha pulegium)*. Prostrate grower. Leaves steeped as tea to aid digestion.

Peppermint *(Mentha x piperita)*. 3 feet. Yields an essential oil used in flavoring candies.

Rosemary *(Rosmarinus officinalis)*. 3 feet. Evergreen sub-shrub with pale blue flowers. Used for seasoning, particularly pork and lamb.

Rue *(Ruta graveolens)*. 3 feet. Aromatic blue-green plants used to flavor cheese.

Safflower *(Carthamnus tinctorius)*. Orange flowers used for dye. Oil from seed used for cooking.

Sage *(Salvia officinalis)*. Broad leaves, 2½-foot plants with blue flowers. Widely used for seasoning poultry stuffing, meats, and sausages.

Saponario ocymoides splendens (Soapwort). 1 foot. Elegant trailer with showy rose flowers in spring. Used for homemade soap.

Savory, winter *(Satureja montana)*. 1 foot. Evergreen good for flavoring beans.

Sorrel, large-leaved French *(Rumex acetosa)*. 3 feet. Used to add flavor to salads and to make a delicious French soup.

Spearmint *(Mentha x spicata)*. 2 feet. For flavoring beverages, sauces, and meats.

Tansy *(Tanacetum vulgare)*. Leaves used fresh as dye, dried as insect repellent.

Thea sinensis. Tea plant.

Thyme, English *(Thymus vulgaris)*. 6 inches. Excellent for flavoring lamb and other meats. Try other varieties of thyme for more intense flavor.

True watercress *(Nasturtium officinale)*. Tangy leaves for garnishes and salads.

Woodruff, sweet *(Asperula odorata)*. Small star-shaped blossoms. Excellent ground cover, exudes a sweet perfume. Leaves used in May wine. Used in medicinal teas. Attractive to bees.

Annual Herbs

Ambrosia *(Feather geranium)*. Intensely fragrant, used for dry bouquets.

Anise *(Pimpinella anisum)*. 1 foot. White flowers. Flavors drinks and pastries.

Basil *(Ocimum basilicum, sweet basil)*. Very fragrant and handsome, used for flavoring.

Basil *(Ocimum basilicum "minimum")*. The "good basil" of French cuisine. Small, tender, sweet leaves, fragrant friend of the tomato.

Basil, dark opal. Deep purple, attractive in bed or border as well as fine for flavoring.

Basil, Italian *(Ocimum basilicum Neapolitaneum)*. For Neopolitan cuisine.

Basil piccolo. Small-leaved, crisp green. Best variety for growing in pots. Very fragrant.

Borage *(Borago officinalis)*. 2 feet. Blue flowers. Used for flavoring, attracts bees.

Caraway, Russian *(Carum carvi)*. 1 foot. Fragrant seeds flavor breads, meats, and liquors.

Chamomile *(Matricaria recutita)*. Scented foliate. Flowers used in medicinal teas.

Chervil, Curled *(Anthriscus cerefolium)*. 1 foot. For eggs, chicken, and vegetables.

Chia, blue-seeded *(Salvia hispanica)*. Young leaves provide high-protein food.

Chili pepper serrano *(Capsicum frutescens)*. The Tabasco pepper, small, pungent ingredient of Mexican hot sauces.

Cumin *(Cuminum cyminum)*. 6 inches. Seeds used in flavoring curries.

Dill *(Anethum graveolens)*. 2 feet. Seeds used in pickling, leaves to flavor fish or potatoes.

Dill bouquet. The same as above, but with dwarf compact habit. Very tasty.

Marjoram, sweet *(Origanum majorana)*. 2 feet. Sweet flowers in purple spikes. Leaves used to flavor sauces, meats, and vegetables.

Mignonette, sweet-scented *(Reseda odorata)*. For sweet, long-lasting bouquets.

Mustard, black *(Brassica nigra)*. 4 feet. Seeds crushed to make the condiment mustard.

Mustard, yellow *(Brassica alba)*. 1 foot. Seed used for condiment mustard.

Parsley. Excellent for flavoring and garnishing and as an attractive basket plant.

Perilla frutescens. Leaves and seeds used in tempura sauce, seeds salted and eaten like peanuts, oil for perfume.

Rocket or **rucola** *(Eruca vesicaria)*. Young, peppery leaves used in salads.

Savory, summer *(Satureja hortensis)*. 18 inches. Aromatic tops for seasoning, vegetables.

Sesame *(Sesamum indicum)*. Seeds used in baking and for sprouts.

Tarragon, Russian *(Artemesia dracunculus)*. Flavors salads, chicken, and fish.

Fragrant Herbs Are a Turn-On

I said earlier that fragrant herbs hanging near windows and doors were a refreshing change. Planting fragrant herbs in and around your yard gives your garden a whole new personality and makes the little bit of physical effort easier to accept when at every turn another fragrance teases your sense of smell; even mowing the lawn can become a pleasure. Here is a pleasant start:

Angelica	Lavender	Savory
Basil	Lemon balm	Scented geranium
Bayberry	Lemon verbena	Sweet cicely
Burnet	Lily of the valley	Sweet flag
Catnip	Marjoram	Sweet olive
Chamomile	Mint	Tansy
Costmary	Oregano	Tarragon
Good King Henry	Pennyroyal	Thyme
Heliotrope	Roses	Yarrow
Hyssop	Rosemary	
Jasmine	Sage	

GET A WHIFF OF THIS

Plants or Seeds Matter Not, Just Start!

In most cases dozens and dozens of small herb plants are available from your local nurseryman, garden department, or seedhouse. If you would like more information on herb growing than I am able to provide you with in these pages, I suggest that you send a self-addressed, stamped business-sized envelope to:

Herb Society of America
300 Massachusetts Avenue
Boston, MA 02115

The Herb Society has several excellent books and pamphlets as well as an Herb Buyers Guide for 25 cents. You can also write to these mail-order dealers:

SIT RIGHT DOWN AND WRITE A LETTER

Carrol Gardens
Box 310
Westminster, MD 21157

Green Herb Gardens
Green, RI 02827

Growing Is a Snap!

You can really say that herbs are in the easy-to-grow class. Many a science teacher begins the second-graders on herbs in paper cups to be taken home as a gift on Mother's Day. Young folks who go off to live alone or first-marrieds will often begin with chives or parsley on a windowsill. As a matter of fact, they are as easy to grow as weeds. Yes, many an herb is considered a weed.

YOU'RE NEVER TOO YOUNG TO LEARN

Growing Herbs Outdoors!

These instructions will please even the most impatient vegetable gardeners.

Light
Most like 5 to 8 hours of full sun, but most will take light shade.

Soil
Just like the light, they want the best soil when they can get it. They want a good light organic sandy loam that drains well but retains a little moisture. If you have poor soil, clay or wet, grow your herbs in raised gardens or pots and hanging baskets.

Watering
Soak your herbs, letting the water run all the way through if they're in planters. For garden-grown herbs, deep watering is needed, 12 to 18 inches.

Food
I use Super K-Gro Fish Emulsion at 25 percent of the recommended rate once a month. Don't spoil herbs or they will become fat and sassy.

Insect and Disease Control
Since we are going to eat many of the herbs we grow, use an insect control recommended for fruit and vegetables. K Mart has one called Super K-Gro All Purpose Fruit & Vegetable Spray. It includes a fungicide that is harmless to humans when used as directed.

TRY THE SPICES IN LIFE

Dried herbs don't compare with fresh-picked for gourmet seasonings, good cooks agree. Though shelves are filled with a bountiful dried harvest, three or four times as much are required as for fresh, and always lack that elusive just-picked flavor. Some of the most useful herbs can be grown indoors through winter as easily as house plants. Since chives do not dry well, this is the only way to keep a ready supply other than by freezing, which has decided limitations.

To have plants handy, a kitchen window with 4 to 5 hours sun is ideal; higher humidity near the sink is an asset. Most herbs are ornamental and may be included with other plants in bright places. Large trays with gravel and water are useful for holding pots together. Most herbs require light, porous, quickly drained soil: Use 1 part peat, 1 part sand, and 2 parts garden loam (sterilized). For annual herbs in particular, 9- or 10-inch bulb pans (shallow clay pots) work very well. A 50° minimum night temperature is beneficial. Pots should be given a half turn each week to keep plants shapely. Never permit flowers indoors.

Woody perennial herbs are started from 4-to- 5-inch soft-wood cuttings in late spring. These make nice plants for potting singly in late summer or early fall, but are not taken indoors until late freezes are expected in late October. Examples: rosemary, sage, thyme. Tender perennials may also be increased by cuttings in spring. A cold frame is useful for starting as well as holding safely through early-fall frost periods. Heights shown in the lists are maximum outdoors; with frequent snippings most will be less than half this size indoors.

Family preference and usage will determine how many plants are needed for normal winter pickings. Usually five or six different kinds will suffice. Unlike summer-grown, only the leaves are used from winter-grown plants, other than mint. Liquid-feed sparingly during sunless periods. For convenience, a few such as basil and mint can be grown for several months in water only, adding Super K-Gro Water Soluble from time to time.

HOW TO GROW AND COOK YOUR OWN HERBS

Herb	Growing Instructions	Cooking Suggestions
Basil, sweet Annual 18″	Start seeds in July, transplant to 4- or 6-inch pots after second pair of true leaves appear; keep flower spikes cut out as they appear.	Tea, tomato dishes, hot biscuits, vinegars and stew; use to garnish soups and salads, vegetables (beans).
Chervil Annual to 2′	Start from seeds in July. Give slight shade.	Salads, egg and fish dishes, soups (as for parsley)
Chives Perennial, 10″	Use garden clumps; cut back tops, pot in 9- or 10-inch bulb pans in September. Leave outside until late October.	Salads, cottage cheese, spreads
Coriander Annual to 2′	Use whole seed from grocery spice shelf, as seldom found in packets. Sow in early July; as for dill, no transplanting! Keep flowers pinched out.	Leaves season and garnish Chinese, Indonesian, or Mexican foods. Wild and pungent (it may take time to learn to like this one).
Dill Annual 2 to 3′	Start seeds in pot where they are to grow, by July. Thin to a dozen in a 9- or 10-inch pot, no transplanting.	Dressings, fish sauces, salads, dips, mayonnaise, potato salad, sprinkled on boiled potatoes; leaves only, usually chopped
Lemon balm Perennial 2′	Pot up a good garden plant in early fall, cut back to make a tidy shape.	Tea, eggs; add to tarragon vinegar; in cool drinks.
Mint Perennial 2′	Pot in fall but leave out in open until cold weather nears. Trim back to shape up. Rich, moist soil; takes light shade.	Tea, meatballs, cold drinks, lamb
Parsley Annual or biennial, 12″	Cut back and pot garden plants; or start seed by early July. Space seedlings 2″ apart in large pots.	Salads, garnishes, soups, hot breads
Rosemary Perennial 3′	Can grow year-round in large pot, set outside in summer only. One plant in a 6-inch pot. Soil must be fast-draining. Likes lime; moderately dry side.	Tea, biscuits, stews; use to season tomato sauce, garlic bread; sprinkle over pork, lamb, and roast beef before cooking.
Sage Perennial 2′	Garden-grown shrublets, 2 years from cuttings. Pot up in fall in light, gritty soil. Keep moderately dry.	Tea, stuffing; sprinkle on poultry and pork
Summer savory Annual 18″	Start from seeds in July, keep outside until mid-September. Use singly in 4- or 6-inch pots, or three to four in a 9-inch pot. Clip twigs for compactness	Tea, meat loaf, salads, fish; with green snap beans
Sweet marjoram Perennial 8–12″	Pot up garden-grown plant in fall. We start these from seed each year, as they do not overwinter in the garden.	Tea, stews, meats, salads

Herb	Growing Instructions	Cooking Suggestions
Tarragon (French is preferred) Perennial 2'	Cut a section of garden-grown crown or rhizome with six buds and plant in a 6- or 8-inch pot with richer soil. A period of dormancy follows summer.	Vinegar, salad, meat and fish sauces; use sparingly as has a strong flavor (as of licorice).
Thyme, common Perennial 6–10"	Pot up garden-grown clump in fall, cut back to force branching. Keep on the dry side.	Tea, stuffing, soup, stew, meat and fish sauces

HOW TO HARVEST AND STORE FOR TOP FLAVOR

Along with canning and pickling, seasoning herbs deserve careful harvest and preparation for storage. During summer we prefer herbs freshly picked; but for the cold months we must rely on dried supplies, frozen or salted herbs, or infusions in salad vinegars. Flavors are fleeting; plan for only one year's supply at a time, as none should be carried over. When attractively packaged, dried herbs make very acceptable gifts at bazaars and for discerning cooks.

Optimum time to pick herb foliage is on the morning of a warm, dry day. For most kinds that flower, strongest-flavoring oils develop just before blooming, and both leaves and sprigs are cut from then on, with potency diminishing after the flowering season. Pick only the green leaves, and never overpick any one stem or plant. Pinch back longer stems to promote fuller growth; if future seeds are not needed, clip off flower stems well before blooming.

As a final note: To taste the true flavor of an herb you've never tried before, mix ½ teaspoon crushed herb with 1 tablespoon cream cheese or sweet butter. Let stand 10 to 15 minutes, then spread the mixture on a small piece of bread and taste.

Drying

The simplest method requires quick drying after picking. Wash springs and leaves, damp-dry without crushing, spread very thinly to dry in an airy, shady place. Screens are ideal for drying trays and can be set up in an attic. Small bunches of sprigs are hung from rafters. Slow oven heat of 100° F. dries well. Process only until material is crisp, not longer than two weeks.

Savory twigs are kept whole. Leaves only can be crushed and rubbed through a sieve; some cooks prefer to keep leaves whole until time to use—it is considered this preserves more of the valuable oils. Place at once in glass jars and screw covers on tightly. Label with care; in fact, lots should be labeled from time of picking, as many look alike when dried. Keep jars out of strong light or in a darkened cabinet, cool if possible. Check occasionally to make certain no moisture remains to make a musty odor. Never attempt to store in paper bags except for the initial short drying period.

Freezing

Tender sprigs can be frozen, usually in small lots only as they cannot be refrozen. Leaves turn limp and begin to darken soon after thawing; time their use at the very last minute. After picking fresh, wash and damp-dry, roll-wrap in plastic with a single layer, seal with freezer tape. Label each roll.

Herbs frozen in ice cubes are decorative and flavorful in cold tea or fruit drinks. Mint is commonly used for drinks; rosemary, thyme, and basil can be cubed to garnish cold consommé or broth. To make cubes, freeze a layer of water in the cube tray, place the herb in the middle, add more water, and refreeze.

Herbs can also be cube-frozen for flavoring. Use whole, minced, or finely chopped by blender. For each two cups of water use a cup of herb leaves. Pour into ice trays to freeze. Wrap each cube separately in plastic and store the lot in a large freezer bag. At cooking time, melt, and add just the herbs to the dish.

Vinegars

French tarragon is best used in vinegars, though thyme, dill, basil, marjoram, and mint, alone or in combination, can be

VINEGAR and SPICE DO MIX!

used. These are the exquisite salad vinegars, preferably based on white or red wines. Bruise the leaves, put in a glass jar or crock, and cover with warm vinegar (some prefer boiling apple vinegar). Tightly cover and allow to steep for a week or two. Use plenty of foliage in the infusion and stir every two days. Taste; when it seems strong enough, strain and bottle.

Salting

Mints and parsley lose flavor in drying, unless a salt solution is used as a fixative. Add 1 teaspoon of salt to each quart of water and bring to a boil. Wash leaves, place in a strainer, and immerse for 2 or 3 seconds in the boiling salt solution. Then shake out excess moisture and place leaves on a screen to dry out rapidly.

Sweet basil can be preserved for winter by salting down in alternate layers in a crock. Foliage remains fresh and green to be used as needed. Other herbs can also be preserved in this way.

Seeds

Anise, caraway, coriander, dill, sweet fennel, poppy, and mustard all provide flavorful seeds. Watch carefully after blooming, as seeds ripen quickly and fall at the touch. Find a time when heads can be cut without shattering, invert in bags to finish. Later screen or sort out debris, wash and quick-dry if necessary before storing as for leaves. Seeds of sweet cicely (Myrrhis) are used green only.

Roots

Angelica and lovage are dug in the fall when dormant. Wash and scrape the roots, and cut larger ones lengthwise. Dry as for leaves, up to six weeks until brittle. Seal in glass jars.

9

It's a Battleground in the Spring
WEATHER AND WOOLLIES

ONE LAST CHILL

When it comes to protecting your spring garden I just never know where to start. The woollies (furry varmints) are sitting on the sideline, licking their lips anticipating the tasty morsels you are about to put on the garden table. At the same time Jack Frost is peeking around a big gray cloud in the north just waiting to rip your enthusiasm with a frosty little paint job on your newly planted tomatoes and peppers.

Pre-Planting Projects

Before I begin to plan my garden, I usually find an evening or two to begin to collect 1-gallon plastic milk and bleach bottles, small cardboard boxes (12 × 12 × 12 inches). I make a couple dozen newspaper soldier hats like those we use to make when we were kids. I cut chicken wire into 30 × 20-inch rectangles and bend the ends up and stack them. Then I cut pieces of clear plastic sheeting into 30 × 30-inch squares to cover the chicken wire. Now I am ready for Jack Frost.

Post-Planting Projects

This job still calls for a little "pre" as well. I begin to watch the newspaper ads and hunt the K Mart Home Centers on my appearance tours for steel drive-in fence posts and inexpensive fencing, either wire or snow fence. And I look for an old gate at a garage sale. All of this junk is used to keep Ricky Raccoon, Peter Rabbit, Bambi Jo, and Willard Woodchuck out of my cabbage patch.

This Is a Hair Raiser!

My last scavenger trip is to the barber shop with two large brown grocery bags. You've got it! I get them full of hair. No, not mine. If you have seen me on TV or in magazine ads you would know we would all be long gone before I ever covered the bottom of the bag. Any hair will do. What I use the hair for is Joel Mole. More about this in a moment!

PLEASE FENCE ME IN

SO LET THE BOTTOM DROP OUT

GOING TO DO WHAT WITH MY HAIR?

Covers, Caps, and Collars

The plastic jugs are washed out with warm soapy water and rinsed well and then the bottoms are cut off, but not thrown away. Keep the tops. These will now be used for portable greenhouses.

The boxes and paper hats are sprayed with any of the cheap waterproof sprays. Spray twice lightly—you know, like Scotchguard. This will make them moistureproof enough to last a couple of weeks as hot caps and covers.

The chicken wire and plastic are used as domes for row crops. You can make the plastic more than 6 inches wider than the wire so that you can anchor it down with bricks.

Please Fence Me In!

Now for the fence, I get my garden all set to plant. The sides are almost raised as far as I want. Now, I dig an 8 × 6-foot trench all around the outside of my garden and cover the bottom with hair. I fill half the soil in and add more hair. I add a quarter more and add the rest of the hair and cover with the rest of the soil (dirt) and press it down with my foot. If Joel Mole comes bug hunting in my garden he gets hair on his fur and scratches himself near to death and never comes back. Don't get excited—I haven't forgotten the fence. Drive the four corner posts in straight (use a level); next, space the rest of the posts so that the fence will be firm and neat and not sag or bow. Place your gate and secure the fencing.

P. U.!

Spray the fence and grass all around the garden with a deer repellent containing bone tar oil. Even you won't want to stick around after you plant.

This Is a Shady Project

Since you are in a constructive mood, you can get four 10-foot poles and secure them to your corner poles. Stretch wire between all four poles all the way around and place a

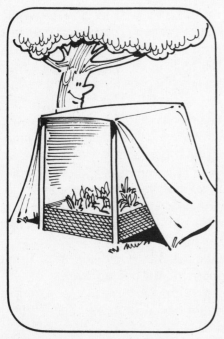

SUMMER CAMP FOR VEGETABLES

shade cloth cover when the hot dry summer arrives. Make sure you attach the cover so that you can slide it back and forth. Friends of mine have some of the most attractive garden canopies you have ever seen. It will make vegetable gardening more comfortable for both you and the vegetables.

Support Your Local Vegetable Garden

This is something most of you never think of. You just plant the peas, beans, cucumbers, melons, and squash, mulch them, and then forget them. Any plant that creeps, crawls, or climbs in your garden needs uplift and support. They need this for varying reasons, such as:

1. If you allow cucumbers, squash, and pole beans up on a trellis, they don't take up as much space.

2. If melons, cucumbers, and squash are allowed to grow up through a rack, air can pass beneath the foliage, and water can get through and help prevent fungus and disease growth—not to mention getting at insects better.

3. Tomatoes should never be allowed to grow along the ground for all of the above reasons; plus, vegetables that grow up on racks are tastier, sweeter, and more wholesome. They also will look more attractive, since they don't sit on the soil where they develop a faded spot or rot.

I always prefer you use metal rather than wood or plastic. Metal attracts static electricity, which charges the atmosphere with nitrogen. Old bedsprings (single, double, queen, or king whichever fits your vegetable bed, pardon the pun) look super as soon as they are covered with foliage. In the fall, clean the bedsprings with a hose and store them. Bedsprings can be laid flat or on edge and stakes driven to support the weight.

For tomatoes, I use the metal (heavy-duty) cages. Don't buy cheap light-duty ones; you will end up sorry.

If you want looks, a storm fence nailed to a simple wooden frame and set up on bricks looks great. Paint it whatever color you prefer.

Always use old nylon stocking strips to tie plants, not

GETTING UP IN THE WORLD

string, wire, plastic, or rope. The nylon is strong, soft, flexible. It also attracts static electricity.

You Can Extend the Growing Season with a Simple Cold Frame

With very little effort you can add 10 to 15 days to the vegetable-growing season. Planting cold-susceptible crops early and protecting them from late cold snaps by using hot caps, jars, plastic jugs, cardboard boxes, or plastic coverings help extend the gardening season. But the best method is to use a cold frame.

Cold frames have been called a poor man's greenhouse. A cold frame can simply be a box which gives plants protection from wind, rain, and cold and is not artificially heated. If artificial heat is supplied, the cold frame becomes a hotbed.

Using a cold frame allows you to get an early start on the gardening season. Although you can start tomatoes, cucumbers, and other seedlings in a sunny area in the house, these seedlings often become leggy and weak from growing too fast. If moved outside these plants may not be able to make the sudden adjustment to fluctuating day and night temperatures and may not grow well. The best solution is to germinate the seeds inside. As soon as the seedlings have formed a set of true leaves, move the plants to a protected area outdoors where they can gradually become acclimated to outside conditions. Although cold frames usually are used to get an early start on the spring gardening season, they can be used during winter to protect crops such as lettuce, radishes, beets, and carrots from severe cold weather.

Locate the cold frame on a well-drained site facing the south to take advantage of the sun. Some type of barrier on the north side, such as a fence or wall, will protect the cold frame from northerly winds and also reflect heat back to the cold frame.

Cold frames can be built in many different shapes and sizes. A convenient size is 3 to 6 feet wide with a 12-inch front and an 18-inch back. Use plywood for the sides and light lumber or old window or glass-door frames for the top.

YOU'RE NOT A HOT BOX? YOU'RE A COLD FRAME? YOU'RE NUTS!

Treat the wood with a preservative which is nontoxic to plants. It is also good to paint the inside either white or silver to reflect more light to the plants. Attach the top to the high side of the cold frame with hinges to open and close it.

Sink cold frames 4 to 6 inches into the soil to provide adequate protection from extremes in weather conditions. Also bank soil up around the cold frame for added insulation. Although not absolutely necessary, it is often advantageous to remove 4 to 6 inches of soil from beneath the cold frame and replace it with a layer of gravel or sand. If seedlings are to be grown directly in the cold frame rather than in some type of planting flat or container, put 2 inches of gravel and 4 inches of a good, fertile topsoil or soil mix in the bottom of the cold frame.

Operation of the cold frame is relatively simple. To help maintain optimum growing temperatures equip the cold frame with a thermometer. Check the thermometer to determine whether or not the top "sash" of the cold frame should be opened for ventilation. When the temperature reads above optimum growing conditions, open the sash and permit air circulation to reduce the temperatures. When the sun goes down or temperatures drop, close the sash to retain the heat absorbed from the sun by the soil.

The secret to successful plant growing in a cold frame is plenty of ventilation, but do not open the cold frame directly into a gusty wind. Optimum growing temperatures for seedlings of most cold-hardy plants range from 50° to 70° F. and for most tender plants from 60° to 75° F. When it is cold outside and the sun is shining, it may be necessary to raise the top to keep plants from overheating. It can get over 90° F. in a cold frame in full sun even when the temperature is 20° to 25° F. outside. On extremely cold nights or during extended cold periods the cold frame may need the extra protection of covering it with a quilt or blanket.

By the same token, if the sun is bright and temperatures are high, you may need some shading to keep the plants from burning.

Consider building a cold frame to extend your garden season. You may find that a sheet of plywood and an old window frame is your best garden investment ever.

These few handy jobs will save you time, money, space, and food.

HELLO DEARY

10

Bugs and Blotches
INSECT CONTROL

Pestilence and plagues are no big thing when it comes to home gardening. Oh, don't get me wrong, I'm not referring to a full-blown MGM production with casts of thousands. I'm talking about an anthill or two who attack the picnic table that is covered with cake crumbs and carry the crumbs into the shade so they can enjoy the feast; or the slugs who march three abreast up your garden patch to a John Philip Sousa march to taste your tomatoes; or, say, a cabbage looper chorus line who rhumba on your nearly ripe cabbage heads. These we can contend with in a fast, safe, efficient, and in most cases inexpensive way.

Garden Sprayers Do the Trick!

At some time gardeners must spray their vegetable plants to protect them. Pest control is a hard fact of life, especially where gardening is concerned.

Some gardeners make costly mistakes. Plants can be damaged if too much spray material is applied. Or if not enough is applied, insects and diseases may not be controlled. Improper care of spray equipment is also costly, since frequent replacement of sprayers is expensive. Let's look at the kinds of sprayers available and the proper maintenance of this equipment.

First of all, decide what kind of sprayer is needed. Factors such as garden size, intended use, location, and layout influence the decision. The main sprayers used are the compressed-air and hose-on types. Compressed-air sprayers are mobile, self-contained units which are pressurized by periodic pumping. These come in various gallon capacities and have either galvanized or longer-lasting plastic tanks. The hose-on sprayer receives its spray pressure from a garden hose.

There are advantages and disadvantages with each type. The compressed-air sprayer is completely portable, but its portability and effectiveness are directly proportional to the strength of the person toting it. A 5-gallon sprayer is heavy, and unless you are fairly strong do not try it. A 2-gallon sprayer is lighter, easier to handle, and adequate for small gardens. With smaller sprayers, the gardener can mix exactly the amount of pesticide needed and not overspray plants with extra mix.

Care of the compressed-air sprayer is most important. Rinse the sprayer, tank, nozzle, and hose after each use to avoid clogging during the next use. Store the compressed-air sprayer bottom-side up with hose drained. This prevents water from settling and pooling in the bottom of the sprayer after rinsing. Improper storage of the sprayer can cause rust in the tank, which will then flake and clog your nozzle. Some industrious people coat the insides of their sprayers with oil for prolonged storage.

The hose-on sprayer is used by many people, and abused by many, too. It is popular because it is light and does not have to be repressurized by periodic pumping. Problems arise in mixing ingredients, in portability, and in calibration. Hose-on sprayers operate on the principle of siphoning a concentrate spray material and mixing it with a stream of water. Problems occur in siphoning and mixing the concentrate spray material. For something to be siphoned, it must be liquid; yet, many insecticides and fungicides are in a wettable powder form. The powder can be suspended in water, but sometimes thorough mixing is a problem. Because the hose-on sprayer siphons suspensions and not large particles, premix wettable powder pesticides in a small bowl. This ensures that all large particles are broken up and will not clog the siphon hose. Use a small strainer to filter out larger particles when pouring the mixture into the sprayer tank.

Also, remember you are mixing a *concentrate* spray for a hose-on sprayer. If the jar says 6 gallons, put enough concentrate material in that small sprayer jar to be siphoned and dilute into 6 gallons. Calibrate the sprayer periodically. Use a gallon container, fill the hose-on sprayer to the gallon mark, and spray into the container. Theoretically, the sprayer should be empty when the container is full. If not, you have a problem and may be putting out too much or too little spray material.

In summary, get the sprayer that is easiest for you to handle and best fits your gardening situation. Regardless of the type you choose, operate and maintain it properly for maximum efficiency.

Squeaky Clean Makes Bugs Nasty and Mean

AND YOU THOUGHT EX-LAX DID THE TRICK

What I mean is that you should lay down a good plastic mulch, remove any broken or sick foliage, and wash your plants at least once a week (twice if you want real insurance) with ordinary liquid dishwashing soap. Don't go looking for your glasses, you read it right! I said liquid dishwashing soap. Use 3 to 5 drops to the quart, 1 tablespoon to the gallon, 1 cup to 10 gallons. Shower everything in sight— vegetable gardens, fruit trees, shrubs, grass, evergreens, the new car, aluminum siding, driveway, and dog. Shower almost anything but the passing postman. This soap is now sold on the shelves of your local garden centers as insecticide soap, and from time to time I use it, but for the most part I use whatever is on sale at the corner store.

The fact that the soap upsets a bug's stomach is a bonus. I use it to remove airborne disease particles, surface tension, and pollution so that photosynthesis and osmosis can take place. To further P.O. the bugs, I take four fingers of Red Man chewing tobacco and place it in the toe of an old nylon stocking. I tie a knot and drop it in a quart of hot water and let it steep. I now add 2 tablespoons per quart of soap to water (or 2 cups to 10 gallons) and spray only the plant world with this solution. What happens is the bugs get diarrhea from the soap and sick to their stomach from the tobacco juice. They are so busy in the bug bathroom that they don't have time to bother your garden.

Don't Be a Thrill Killer of Bugs—It's Dangerous

COME AND GET IT, I DARE YOU

Insecticides and pesticides don't pollute; people pollute through misuse and abuse. If you have one or two houseflies cruising your kitchen or screened porch looking for the "beef," or an occasional mosquito doing night flights over the patio, why not just swat? Instead you grab a can of spray and splot or you grab some other big bug fog spray and proceed to contaminate your own airspace. The bugs, they're smart—they get the dickens out of the way.

I don't mean to tell you how to keep house, but if you will just dust, sweep, wash, and wipe entertainment centers real well after you have eaten, and then spray the bushes, under chairs, eaves, tables, trees, and other cool shady spots once a week (when no one is around) with soap and water followed with methoxychlor, you should have few problems. Especially if you have containers of vegetables and flowers growing in your entertainment area.

Prepare for Insects

Home gardeners should prepare for encounters with insects and diseases. These pests fit into two categories—apparent and unnoticed.

The apparent category includes pests which can be seen easily after the initial invasion. They include pill (sow) bugs, tomato hornworms, potato beetles, stinkbugs, and powdery mildew fungus.

The unnoticed category includes those sneaky pests which go unnoticed until they have practically killed garden plants. They include spider mites, loopers, nematodes, cutworms, and most fungus diseases.

These pests are the trickiest to control, since preventive action must be taken before damage is seen. If a gardener waits until he sees the pest's damage, control measures probably will be ineffective.

The cutworm is a good example. This insect larva eats plant stems in two, so plants lying on the ground are the

WANTED
FOR DESTRUCTION of PROPERTY

first sign of damage. By this time it's too late for control measures.

To complicate matters, cutworms eat only at night, so you may never see them. If you plant another plant, the worm will eat it off, too. If a large number of these pests are detected during soil preparation, a soil application of diazinon will control them. After plants are established in the garden, foil cutworms by placing a can around each plant. Since the cutworm moves on top of the soil, the can protects the plant effectively. Gardeners also can dig around damaged plants and find cutworms.

Getting to Know Your Local Bugs

There are more bugs to bother the home gardener than you would care to count, and I refuse to. In this list I have listed the most likely ones to make a move on your garden; so, be alert for them.

Aphid. Adult: Winged or wingless, soft body. Cornicles or tubes project from rear. Nymph: Resembles adult but wingless. Small insect.

Armyworm. Light green to black; striped; white inverted Y on front of head; up to 1½ inches long.

Cutworm. Adult: Dull grayish or brownish front wings. Wingspread 1 to 1¾ inches. Larva: Dull-colored; curls into a light C shape when disturbed. 1½ inches long.

Bean leaf beetle. Adult: ¼ inch long. Beetle reddish to yellowish with six black spots. Larva: ⅜ inch long, slender, white with black head and tail.

Mexican bean beetle. Adult: ⅓ inch long. Brownish with sixteen black spots arranged in three rows across back. Larva: ⅓ inch when full-grown. Lemon yellow with spines on back.

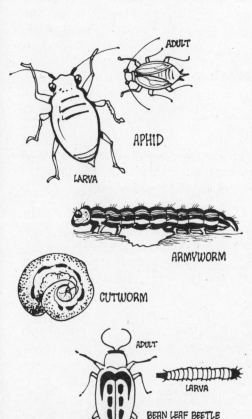

ADULT

APHID

LARVA

ARMYWORM

CUTWORM

ADULT

LARVA

BEAN LEAF BEETLE

ADULT

MEXICAN BEAN BEETLE

LARVA

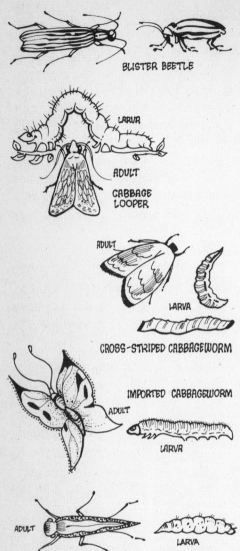

BLISTER BEETLE

LARVA

ADULT

CABBAGE LOOPER

ADULT

LARVA

CROSS-STRIPED CABBAGEWORM

IMPORTED CABBAGEWORM

ADULT

LARVA

ADULT

LARVA

DIAMONDBACK MOTH CATERPILLAR

Blister beetle. Adult: Elongated, dark with necklike region between head and base of wings. Some species are striped. ½ to 1 inch long. Larva: Yellow and about ⅖ inch long.

Cabbage looper. Adult: Brownish; silvery markings on front wings. Wingspread 1½ inch. Larva: Greenish "looper" 1½ inches long; four white lines along the body.

Cross-striped cabbageworm. Adult: Moth has yellow to brown wings with dark brown zigzag lines. Young worms are gray. The mature worms are ⅗ inch in length with tiny black stripes across bluish-gray backs.

Imported cabbageworm. Adult: White butterfly with three or four black markings and wingspread of about 2 inches. Larva: 1½ inches when full-grown, velvety green with three gold stripes.

Diamondback moth caterpillar. Larva: Light green; slender; up to ⅓ inch long. It wriggles rapidly when disturbed, and often drops from the plant and hangs by a silken thread, which it produces.

Colorado potato beetle. Adult: ⅜ inch long, ¼ inch wide. Ten black and ten yellowish longitudinal stripes. Larva: ½ inch when grown. Reddish with two rows of black spots, humpbacked, soft.

Corn earworm. Adult: Grayish-brown; darker areas near wing tips; 1½-inch wingspread. Larva: Brown to green or even pink. About 2 inches long with yellow heads.

Hornworm. Adult: Moth gray with five yellow spots on each side. Front wings have white and dark markings. Hind wings lighter. Larva: Green, eight white L-shaped marks on side. 3 to 3½ inches long when full-grown.

CORN EARWORM

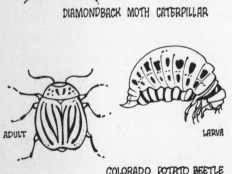

ADULT

LARVA

COLORADO POTATO BEETLE

HORNWORM

Eggplant lace bug. Adult: Grayish to light brown; flat; lacelike wings; 1/6 inch long. Nymph: Yellowish; louselike; spiny; up to 1/10 inch long.

Flea beetle. Adult: Small dark beetle that jumps like a flea. Many species about 1/16 inch long. Larva: White-bodied, brown-headed, cylindrical, about 1/5 inch when full-grown.

Harlequin cabbage bug. Adult: Flat, shield-shaped, 3/8 inch long. Reddish or orange with black markings. Nymph: Resembles adult, but smaller and wingless.

Leafhopper. Several species. Adult: Green; wedge-shaped; up to 1/8 inch long; flies quickly when disturbed. Nymph: Resembles adult but smaller; crawls sidewise like a crab.

Mite. Adult: Reddish, yellowish, or greenish; four pairs of legs. Body oval in outline, 1/16 to 1/20 inch. Young: Resembles adult but smaller.

Melonworm and pickleworm. Adult: Wingspread 1 inch. Wings fragile, yellowish-brown margins, white centers. Larva: 3/4 inch. White to greenish caterpillar with black spots. Head brown.

Root maggot. Adult: 1/4 inch long, gray, two-winged fly. Larva: 1/4 inch long when full-grown. White, wedge-shaped maggot. Feeds on roots of cabbage and related crops.

Seed-corn maggot. Adult: 1/5 inch long, grayish brown fly. Larva: Maggot; wedge-shaped, legless, cream-colored. 1/4 inch long when full-grown. Narrow end is the head.

Striped cucumber beetle. Adult: About 1/5 inch long, yellow with three longitudinal black stripes on top wings. Larva: Whitish, about 1/3 inch when grown. Feeds on the roots of plants.

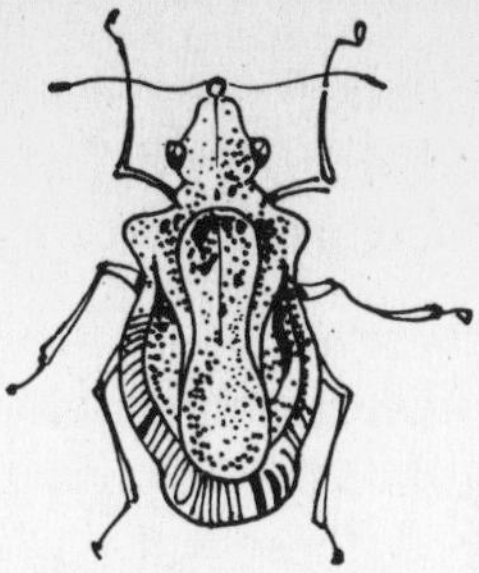
EGGPLANT LACEBUG

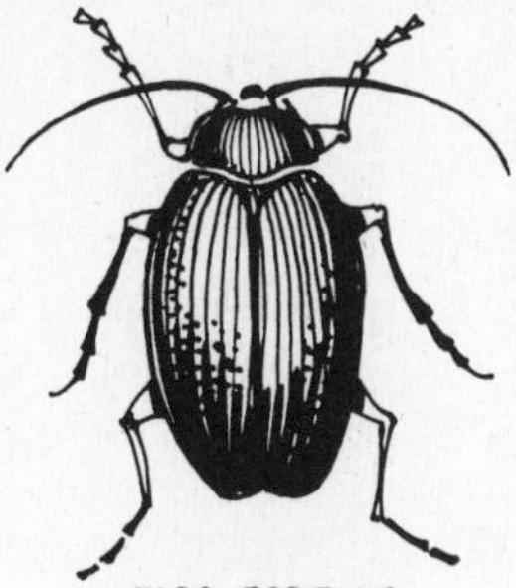
FLEA BEETLES

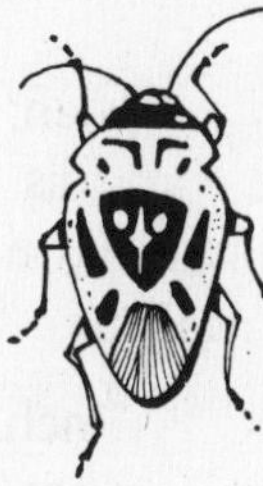
HARLEQUIN BUG

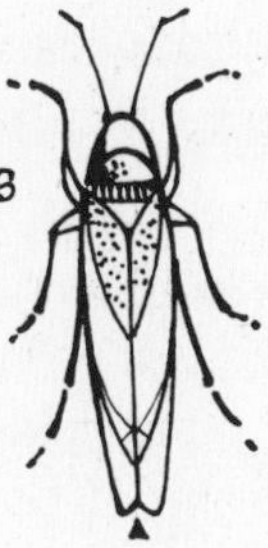
LEAFHOPPERS

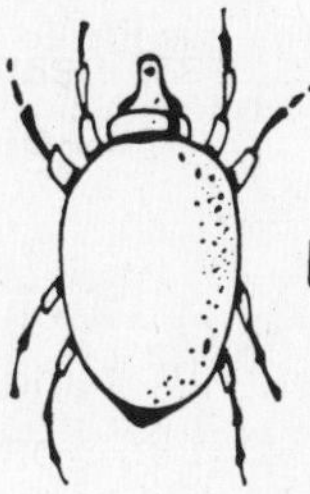
MITE

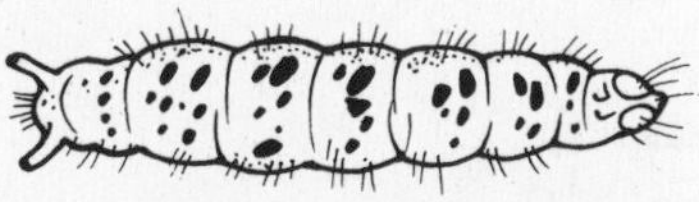
MELONWORM – PICKLEWORM

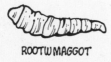

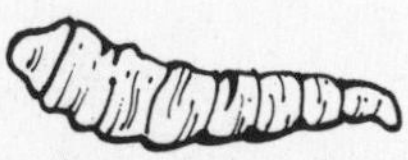
ROOTW MAGGOT

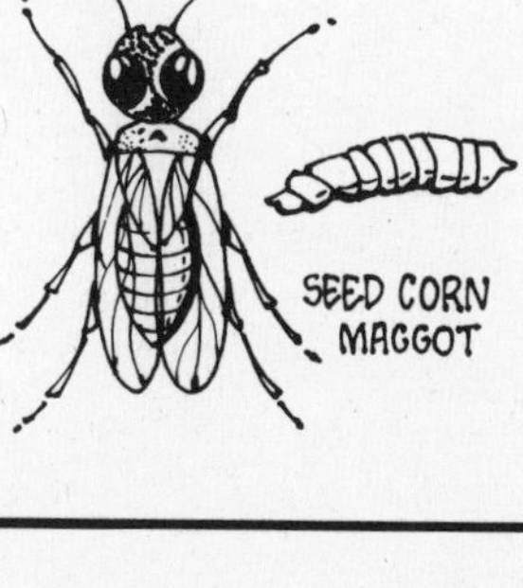
SEED CORN MAGGOT

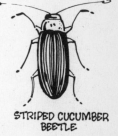

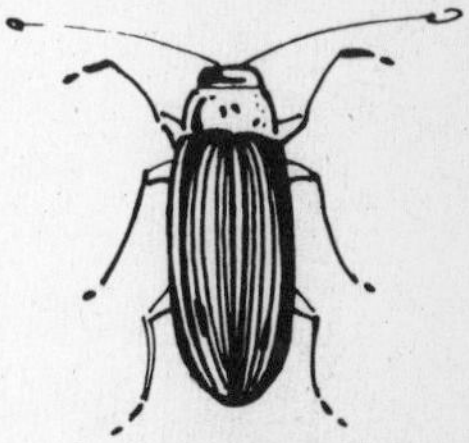
STRIPED CUCUMBER BEETLE

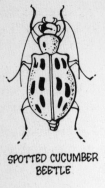

Spotted cucumber beetle. Adult: Yellowish-green with eleven black spots. Head and antennae black. Larva: Yellowish-white, brown-headed, ¾ inch long when grown.

Lygus bug (tarnished plant bug). Several related species including tarnished plant bug. Flat, oval; mottled with white, yellow, and black splotches that give it a tarnished appearance; ¼ inch long. When disturbed, these active insects fly or move to opposite side of stems; are seldom seen.

SPOTTED CUCUMBER
BEETLE

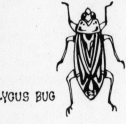

Stinkbug. Several species. Adult: Brown, green, or black, with or without markings; shield-shaped; up to ⅝ inch long and ⅓ inch wide. Nymph: Resembles adult but smaller. Stinkbugs discharge a foul odor.

LYGUS BUG

Squash bug. Adult: About ⅝ inch. Brownish-black to gray; flat across back. Top wings are leathery at base, membranous at the tips. Nymph: Resembles adult, wingless, smaller.

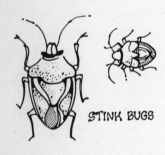

Squash vine borer. Adult: Wingspread 1½ inch. Front wings have greenish-black scales, hind wings transparent. Abdomen has red rings and black scales. Larva: White, smooth. Brown head.

STINK BUGS

Common stalk borer. Slender; up to 1¼ inches long. Young borer: Creamy white; dark purple band around the body; several brown or purple stripes running lengthwise down the body. Full-grown borer: Creamy white to light purple without band and stripes.

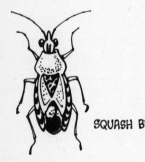

European corn borer. Adult: Pale yellowish with irregular dark bands across wings. Wingspread 1 inch. Larva: Flesh-colored, brown heads, brown spots on body; 1 inch long when grown.

SQUASH BUG

COMMON STALK BORER

SQUASH VINE BORER

EUROPEAN CORN BORER

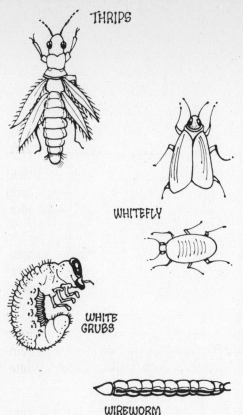

THRIPS

WHITEFLY

WHITE GRUBS

WIREWORM

Thrip. Adult: Slender, louselike, about 1/20 inch long; varies from light to dark brown. Wings narrow with fringe of hair. Nymph: Lighter, smaller, and wingless.

Whitefly. Adult: Minute; looks like a tiny white moth, with two pairs of broadly oval wings covered with snow-white, waxy powder. Nymph: Active; pale yellow; later becomes flat, oval, with a marginal, fringed, white, waxy filament.

White grub. Adult: Dark brown to black, hard-shelled, 1/2 to 1 inch long. Larva: White with brown head. Usually rests in a C shape.

Wireworm. Adult: Elongated, hard-shelled, dull-colored; 1/2 to 1 1/2 inches long. Often called "click" beetle. Larva: Yellowish, tough-bodied, 1/2 to 2 inches long.

Slug and snail. Wormlike, legless, horned, shiny body, 1/2 to 8 inches long. Snails have hard shells. Usually found in damp, protected places.

Garden symphylan (also called symphilid). White; fragile; twelve pairs of legs on adult (fewer legs on young); up to 3/8 inch long. Not classified as insect. Found in moist soils that contain decayed plant material, particularly near greenhouses.

SLUG AND SNAIL

GARDEN SYMPHYLAN

Here Is What He Likes Just for Supper

Since this book is designed to speed up your garden enjoyment, just check the critter and the crop and you'll have full identification:

I have found that the best control for the home gardener is Super K-Gro All Purpose Fruit Tree & Vegetable Spray. It contains Sevin, malathion, methoxychlor, and captan. It is available at K Mart stores.

GIVE HIM WHAT HE WANTS...ONCE!

Bugs \ Vegetables	Asparagus	Beans	Beets	Broccoli	Cabbage	Cantaloupes	Carrots	Corn	Cucumbers	Eggplant	Lettuce	Okra	Onions	Peas	Peppers	Potatoes	Pumpkins	Radishes	Rhubarb	Squash	Sweet potatoes	Tomatoes	Turnips	Watermelons
Aphid	✓	✓	✓	✓	✓	✓	✓	✓	✓	✓	✓	✓	✓	✓	✓	✓		✓	✓		✓	✓	✓	✓
Armyworm		✓			✓	✓		✓	✓				✓	✓	✓	✓		✓				✓	✓	✓
Asparagus beetle	✓																							
Bean leaf beetle		✓						✓																
Blister beetle		✓	✓		✓	✓	✓	✓			✓			✓	✓	✓	✓	✓				✓	✓	✓
Cabbage looper			✓	✓	✓						✓		✓		✓	✓		✓						
Cabbage webworm			✓	✓	✓													✓						
Celery leaf tier		✓			✓				✓		✓		✓											
Colorado potato beetle										✓					✓	✓						✓		
Corn earworm		✓			✓			✓			✓	✓	✓		✓					✓		✓		
Cowpea weevil		✓												✓										
Cutworm	✓	✓	✓		✓			✓	✓	✓			✓		✓						✓	✓		
Diamondback moth					✓														✓					
Eggplant lace bug										✓														
European corn borer		✓	✓					✓							✓	✓			✓					
Flea beetle		✓	✓	✓	✓	✓	✓	✓	✓	✓	✓	✓			✓	✓	✓	✓	✓	✓	✓	✓	✓	✓
Garden symphylan	✓								✓		✓						✓					✓		
Grasshopper						✓												✓						
Green June beetle		✓						✓																
Harlequin cabbage bug		✓	✓		✓			✓	✓	✓					✓			✓			✓			
Hornworm										✓					✓	✓						✓	✓	
Imported cabbageworm			✓		✓						✓							✓					✓	
Japanese beetle	✓							✓													✓			
Leafhopper		✓	✓	✓		✓	✓	✓	✓	✓					✓	✓			✓	✓		✓		
Leaf miner		✓	✓		✓			✓			✓		✓	✓	✓			✓					✓	✓

Bugs \ Vegetables	Asparagus	Beans	Beets	Broccoli	Cabbage	Cantaloupes	Carrots	Corn	Cucumbers	Eggplant	Lettuce	Okra	Onions	Peas	Peppers	Potatoes	Pumpkins	Radishes	Rhubarb	Squash	Sweet potatoes	Tomatoes	Turnips	Watermelons
Lima bean pod borer		√												√										
Melonworm						√			√								√							
Mexican bean beetle		√																						
Mites	√	√				√	√			√		√	√	√	√							√		
Pepper maggot										√					√							√		
Pea weevil														√										
Pickleworm						√			√					·			√			√				√
Potato tuberworm										√						√						√		
Rhubarb curculio																			√					
Root maggot					√	√																		
Seed-corn maggot		√	√	√				√	√				√	√			√							
Spotted cucumber beetle	√	√	√		√	√		√							√	√	√			√		√		√
Squash bug					√	√											√	√		√				√
Squash vine borer						√			√								√	√		√				
Stalk borer							√		√						√	√			√			√		
Stinkbug		√					√	√	√	√	√	√			√							√		
Striped cucumber beetle		√	√		√			√	√	√	√				√	√	√			√		√		√
Tarnished plant bug		√	√	√			√			√	√					√								
Thrip		√	√		√	√	√	√					√	√						√		√	√	
Vegetable weevil		√			√						√		√			√		√				√	√	
Whitefly								√	√	√							√					√	√	√
White fringed beetle		√			√			√								√					√			
White grub								√			√													
Wireworm		√	√			√	√						√			√		√				√		√

How You Spray or Dust Does Make a Difference

In the beginning of this chapter, I made the comment that it is unnecessary to fill the air with material that is designed to kill insects (let alone airplanes, birds, and kites). I have learned most of my garden techniques from experienced longtime gardeners in both this country and abroad, where I gardened for several years when I was at Great Ruffins, a

STINKING — THINKING

TAKE YOUR BEST SHOT

stately mansion in Essex County, England, in the town of Wikham Bishops. I worked with a man named Burgess who was well over ninety. Whenever it was necessary to dust or spray small plants, he would cover them with a bag or two or three sheets of newspaper and spray up underneath. This would control the spray or dust. Fruit trees or shrubs were covered with a light tarp and sprayed the same way. I still do this today.

When You Spray and Dust
Also Makes a Difference

Insects tend to eat when it's cool and comfortable. That's all right. Spray after 6:00 p.m. when the temperature is below 85°, the wind is less than 5 mph, and no rain is expected within 24 hours.

What You Spray with
Is the Critical Step

As a rule you can destroy insects by drowning, fire, squashing, or poison. Fire is out! I mean O-U-T! I have over the years seen some awful, awful results from this method of insect control—loss of human and animal life, timber, buildings, and equipment. So don't ever consider it. Drowning takes too long, and besides, 60 percent of all insects can swim. Swat and squash your insects—it's a good method if you have just a few.

Try Grandma Putt's soap-and-tobacco recipe on page 00. If that doesn't work, let's get a medication that will. It must be recommended for both the plant and the insect. Use it as recommended, in both strength and duration. I do not want you to combine different insecticides into one container unless the instructions are on the bottle or in a reputable publication. Listed here are the current insect controls available in retail garden centers, and they can be found under many brand names. For controlling less common pests that may damage crops or pests of vegetables not listed, contact your County Agricultural Agent.

NOTE: Most pesticides can be used only up to a given number of days before harvest. Read the label and follow directions.

HOW TO CONTROL BUGS AND BLOTCHES

Vegetable	Insect or Disease	Damage	Treatment or Control
Beans (dry, lima, shell, or snap)	Flea beetles (small beetle and larva)	Makes small round shot holes in leaves.	Carbaryl (Sevin)
	Leafhopper (small flying green insect)	Leaves crinkle, turn yellow, then brown.	Carbaryl (Sevin) or malathion
	Mexican bean beetle (brown beetle; yellow larva)	Eats partway through leaves and later makes holes.	Carbaryl (Sevin), two or more applications at 7-to-10-day intervals when present
	Seed-corn maggot (yellowish-white fly maggot)	Destroys seed. Kills or stunts plants by feeding on seeds, roots and lower stem. Plants wilt.	Buy treated seed.
	Spider mite	Causes yellowing leaves	Kelthane
	Sclerotinia (white mold)	Water-soaked spots on stems, leaves, and pods are later covered with a white mold. Plant is stunted and dies.	Plant on land not used for beans, lettuce, potatoes or tomatoes. Zineb.
Beets	Flea beetle (small beetle and larva)	Makes small, round shot holes in leaves	Carbaryl (Sevin)
Swiss chard	Spinach leafminer (whitish fly maggot)	Circular mines (tunnels) in leaf caused by a white maggot	Diazinon (first choice), malathion
Broccoli Brussels sprouts Cabbage Cauliflower	Aphid	Leaves become curled and wrinkled. Look for aphids on undersurface of leaves and on stems.	Malathion, Diazinon, or Meta-Systox R. Complete coverage important. Thorough schedule necessary (5-to-7-day interval).
Chinese cabbage Kohlrabi Radish Rutabaga Turnip	Cabbage root maggot (yellowish-white fly maggot)	Kills or stunts plants by feeding on roots and lower stem. Plants wilt. Root crops (radish, turnip, etc.) are susceptible. Damage period may last till August.	Diazinon in transplant water or broadcast before seeding or transplanting. Most common in spring and early summer.
	Cabbageworm (green or green-and-yellow caterpillar)	Makes notches and holes, particularly in young leaves, or feeds at base of the head.	Weekly application of carbaryl (Sevin), malathion, methoxychlor, or Dipel. Begin when plants are small or just coming into head. Repeat every 7 days.
	Cabbage looper (green with white stripes)	Makes holes in leaves and burrows into the head. Young (smaller) larvae are easier to control.	Dipel is first choice. Same as the cabbageworm. Usually not common before August. Repeat every 7 days. Complete coverage necessary.

Vegetable	Insect or Disease	Damage	Treatment or Control
Turnip (continued)	Cutworms (brownish or black caterpillar)	Snips plants off at ground level or just below ground level. Damage must be anticipated for effective control.	Carbaryl (Sevin) or Dylox baits or Diazinon spray. Direct post-plant treatments at soil surface and away from edible plant parts.
	Flea beetles (small beetle and larva)	Makes shot holes in leaf.	Carbaryl (Sevin)
	Club root (slime mold)	Swollen, deformed roots. Plants yellowish and stunted.	Rotate plantings in disease-free soil or Lime soil to pH 7.2.
	Damping-off (fungi)		Treat soil with fungicide (Captan or Thiram) before planting.
Carrot	Celery worm (green-yellow-black caterpillar)	Eats leaves.	Hand picking
	Carrot rust fly (yellowish fly maggot)	Burrows in carrot roots.	Diazinon to the furrow at planting time
	Leafhopper (small flying green insect)	Leaves crinkle and turn yellow.	Carbaryl (Sevin) or methoxychlor
	Leaf blight (fungus)	Brown spots on leaves.	Maneb or zineb every 7 days during wet periods
	Yellows (virus)	Young leaves yellowed, old leaves twisted and reddened. Roots stunted and useless.	Control leafhoppers, which transmit virus.
Corn (sweet)	Aphid	Feeds on tassels and destroys pollen; poorly formed ears and sticky, unsightly husks can result.	Malathion or diazinon
	Corn earworm (green to brown striped caterpillar)	Feeds on tips of ears. Damage not noticeable till husk removed. Eggs are tiny and laid on fresh silk.	Apply carbaryl (Sevin) to fresh silk at 2-to-4-day intervals from mid-July on, particularly in southern half of New Hampshire.
	European corn borer (larva with dark brown head)	Makes shot holes in knee-high corn, feeds on tassel, then enters stalk and/or ear. White egg masses laid on undersides of lower leaves.	Apply carbaryl (Sevin), 2 or 4 applications to corn in the 6-to-8-leaf stage (10″) at 4-to-6-day intervals, and again when ear is present at 4-to-6-day intervals till harvest.
	Seed-corn maggot (yellowish-white fly maggot)	Destroys seed and young seedlings. Also a pest on cucumbers and melons.	Buy treated seed.

Vegetable	Insect or Disease	Damage	Treatment or Control
Cucumber melons	Aphid	Sucks plant juice, causes leaves to curl. Transmits cucumber mosaic disease.	Malathion or Meta-Systox R
Pumpkin Squash	Spider mite	Sucks plant juices.	Kelthane
	Spotted cucumber beetle (beetle yellow-green with black spots; larva yellowish-white)	Eats flowers, leaves, and stems. Spreads bacterial wilt disease organism.	Methoxychlor once a week as needed or carbaryl (Sevin) except during bloom because of hazard to bees
	Striped cucumber beetle (beetle yellow with black stripes; larva whitish)	Same as spotted cucumber beetle. Attacks plants in very young seedling stage (1"-3").	Same as spotted cucumber beetle. Sevin first choice. Treat very early when seedlings are emerging. Repeat in 4 days.
	Squash bug (brown sucking insect; adult winged)	Plants wilt and may die. The young nymphs are easier to control.	Malathion or carbaryl (Sevin). Repeat in 5 to 7 days.
	Squash vine borer (whitish caterpillar)	Bores in stems and roots. Plants wilt and die.	Malathion or methoxychlor (a dust mixture of methoxychlor and zineb is available in some stores), particularly to the base of plants, about June 30, 3 times at 10-day intervals or when vines begin to run.
	Bacterial wilt	Plants turn yellow, wilt and die. Sap from stem milky or sticky.	Control cucumber beetles which transmit bacteria; plant resistant varieties
	Fruit rots (fungus)	Occurs primarily in stored squash.	Captan or maneb before storage
	Leaf spots (fungus)	Dead areas on leaves	Captan, zineb (a dust mixture of methoxychlor and zineb is available in some stores).
	Scab (fungus)	Light green or water-soaked spots on leaves, stems, and fruit which turn gray to white	Resistant varieties.
Eggplant	Aphid	Leaves become curled and yellow.	Malathion or Meta-Systox R
	Colorado potato beetle (adult yellowish with black stripes; larva brick-red with black-spots)	See potatoes.	Carbaryl (Sevin) or methoxychlor

Vegetable	Insect or Disease	Damage	Treatment or Control
Eggplant (continued)	Flea beetle (small beetle and larva)	Eats leaves and new shoots.	Carbaryl (Sevin)
	Tomato hornworm (large green-and-white caterpillar)	Eats foliage.	*Bacillus thuringensis*
	Damping-off (fungus)	Stem wilts.	Treat soil with Captan before planting.
	Verticillium wilt (fungus)	Plants are stunted and wilt; leaves die and drop off. Stems show dark discoloration when peeled.	Use disease-free seed. Rotate crops. Do not plant after tomatoes or potatoes.
Lettuce (leaf, head endive, or escarole)	Aphid	Sucks juice and curls leaves.	Malathion
	Leafhopper (small flying green insect)	Same as above.	Carbaryl (Sevin) or malathion
	Yellows (virus)	Plants are yellow-green, stunted.	Control leafhoppers, which transmit virus.
Onion (bulb, green)	Onion maggot (yellowish-white fly maggot)	Destroys bulbs; plants wilt.	Diazinon in the furrow at planting
	Thrip (tiny yellowish to brownish insect)	Its feeding causes white stippling or patches on leaves. Leaf tips turn brown first.	Malathion or diazinon
	Purple blotch (fungus)	White spots on leaves which later turn purplish with a yellow margin	Maneb weekly from late June on, particularly for sweet Spanish-type onions
Parsley	Aphid	See cucumber.	Malathion
	Celery worm (green-yellow-black caterpillar)	Eats leaves.	Hand picking
Parsnip	Aphid	Leaves become curled and yellow.	Malathion
	Carrot rust fly (yellowish fly maggot)	Burrows into roots.	Diazinon applied to soil before planting
	Parsnip canker (fungus)	Reddish-brown, later black areas over most of the root	Keep roots covered with soil. Control carrot rust fly.
Peas	Aphid	Leaves become curled and yellow.	Malathion or diazinon
	Mosaic (virus)	Distorted plants, stunting, mottling of leaves	Plant early; control aphids.

Vegetable	Insect or Disease	Damage	Treatment or Control
Peas (continued)	Root rots and fusarium wilt (fungi)	Yellow, stunted plants; wilt	Rotate location; use resistant varieties.
	Damping-off and seed rots (fungi)	Stem wilts.	Treat seed with chloranil (Spergon).
Pepper	Aphid	Leaves become curled and yellow.	Malathion, dimethoate, or Meta-Systox R
	Flea beetles (small beetle and larva)	Eats leaves and new shoots.	Carbaryl (Sevin)
	European corn borer (larva with dark brown head)	Bores into stems and fruit.	Carbaryl (Sevin). Begin when fruit begins to form and repeat every 5 days.
	Mosaic (virus)	Mottled, curled leaves, stunted plants	Control aphids.
Potato	Aphid	Leaves become curled and yellow.	Dimethoate, Meta-Systox R, or malathion. Repeat every 7 days.
	Colorado potato beetle (adult yellowish with black stripes; larva brick-red with black spots)	Eat leaves and new shoots.	Carbaryl (Sevin) or methoxychlor. Repeat application every 7 days till good control is attained.
	Flea beetle (small beetle and larva)	Eats leaves and new shoots.	Same as above
	Leafhopper (small flying green insect)	Leaves crinkle and yellow.	Same as above
	White grub (adult hard-shelled, dark; larva white with brown head)	Eats roots.	No registered insecticide
	Wireworm (adult hard-shelled, called "click beetle"; larva yellowish)	Stems cut at soil.	No registered insecticide
	Early blight (fungus)	Usually begins on lower leaves as small, irregular brown spots, targetlike markings.	Maneb or zineb every 7 to 10 days after plants are up to 8" to 10"
	Late blight (fungus)	Irregular water-soaked areas on leaves which turn gray-brown. Entire plant may be killed, may infest tubers.	Maneb or zineb every 7 to 10 days after plants are up 8" to 10". Most common during cool, wet weather. Use resistant varieties, disease-free seed potatoes.

Vegetable	Insect or Disease	Damage	Treatment or Control
Potato (continued)	Scab (fungus)	Rough cankers or lesions on tubers.	Adjust pH between 5 to 5.3. Rotate crop. Use resistant varieties.
	Seed-piece decay (fungi or bacteria)	Seed pieces rot.	Use disease-free seed potatoes. Treat seed potatoes with captan or Polyram before planting.
	Verticillium wilt (fungus)	Plants turn yellow, wilt, and die early in season.	Use disease-free seed potatoes. Rotate crops. Use resistant varieties.
Spinach	Aphid	Leaves curl and yellow.	Dimethoate or diazinon.
	Flea beetle (small beetle and larva)	Eats leaves and new shoots.	Carbaryl (Sevin); a dust mixture of methoxychlor and zineb is available in some stores.
	Spinach leaf miner (whitish fly maggot)	Feeds between upper and lower leaf surfaces, causing brown blotches.	Diazinon or dimethoate starting when miners first appear or when leaves are 4″ high
Tomato	Aphid	Sucks plant juice and deforms leaves.	Malathion, diazinon, or dimethoate.
	Flea bettle (small beetle and larva)	Makes round shot holes in the leaves.	Carbaryl (Sevin)
	Tomato hornworm (large green-and-white caterpillar)	Feeds on leaves, can strip plant.	Carbaryl (Sevin) or hand pick; *Bacillus thuringensis*
	Early blight (fungus)	Kills seedlings, which damp off, or a collar rot may girdle the stem. Also see under potato.	Maneb or zineb every 7 to 10 days after plants are up 8″ to 10″. Use resistant varieties.
	Late blight (fungus)	Irregular water-soaked areas on leaves, which turn gray-brown	Maneb or zineb every 7 to 10 days after plants are up 8″ to 10″. Most common during cool, wet weather. Use resistant varieties.
	Fusarium wilt (fungus)	Leaves turn yellow and plant may be stunted or wilt and die. Stems near ground level have dark coloration when peeled.	Do not plant in infested soil. Use resistant varieties.

Don't Waste Your Money on Expensive Garden Chemicals

Let economics dictate what you buy. Malathion, methoxychlor, Sevin, and other chemicals are pretty much the same product under all brand names. Another waste is buying more than you need, which then becomes a safety hazard. I have found that most of the above insect problems can be controlled by a combination spray called Super K-Gro All Purpose Fruit Tree & Vegetable Spray. This material contains Sevin, malathion, methoxychlor, and captan and is available at all K Marts.

Plan for Disease Prevention

PREVENTION IS LESS WORK THAN CURE

Home gardeners are constantly pestered with diseases that rob them of their harvest. Many gardeners have found that planning properly and following recommended control practices keep vegetable losses to a minimum.

It's also important to select a well-drained garden site to prevent damping off and other problems associated with wet soils.

Organic matter (straw, leaves, crop residue) is essential to a productive soil, but it can also increase the occurrence of blight. To avoid a buildup of southern blight, bury organic matter below the expected root zone of next year's crop. This should be done in the fall if possible.

Watering plants in the evening causes leaves to remain wet for an extended period and increases the chance of leaf diseases. Plants watered in the morning dry quickly, resulting in fewer leaf disease problems. Drip irrigation also reduces foliage diseases.

Grow vegetables in the same location only once every 3 to 5 years. If this cannot be done, plan your garden to avoid growing vegetables of the same family group in the same area season after season. Family groups are: (1) watermelon, cucumber, squash, cantaloupe, honeydew melon, pumpkin; (2) cabbage, cauliflower, Brussels sprouts, rutabaga, kale, turnip, mustard, radish, collard; (3) Swiss chard, beets, spinach; (4) pepper, tomato, potato, eggplant; (5) carrot, parsley, parsnips; (6) onions, garlic, leek, shallots; (7) sweet corn; and (8) beans, peas, and southern peas.

Certain vegetable diseases are seed-transmitted. To avoid multiplying disease problems, don't save seed from the garden for planting the following year.

A number of diseases attack the foliage and fruit of vegetables. Diseases caused by fungi cannot be cured, so they must be prevented. When you see a fungus problem, irreversible damage has already been done. Cloudy, damp mornings encourage the growth of fungus spores. So when such conditions exist, follow a preventive spray schedule.

The spray schedule should consist of an application of maneb and captan every 7 to 10 days. Mix benomyl fungicide with one of the chemicals on every second spray or every 14 to 20 days. Use 1 teaspoon of liquid detergent with each gallon of spray to ensure uniform coverage. A uniform coverage of fungicide is important so fungus spores will be killed when they land on the plant tissue.

The diseases mentioned probably do more damage than any other problem encountered by most gardeners. The difficulty in controlling these destructive organisms makes them a formidable adversary for home gardeners.

Garden Diseases Look Worse Than They Are

It always seems that vegetable plant diseases appear from nowhere and, as a rule, overnight. Fungus and bacterial diseases cause more damage to most vegetable crops than any bugs do. Most plant diseases are tough to find before they do a ton of damage, so if your soil gets too moist, use an ounce of prevention in the form of liquid dish soap and non-sweet mouthwash in a gallon of warm water with a teaspoonful of dry powdered milk. Make a paste out of the powdered milk before you mix it in the water. Add 1 ounce each of liquid soap and the mouthwash and spray it lightly on the plants.

If a disease rears its ugly head, then don't be afraid to use fungicides, as they are not as toxic to man as insecticides. Be very careful, however, when using them around ponds and streams. Even though most of you don't know the names of these diseases, you are painfully aware of them in your garden. The moldy grays, yellows, and rusts and cankers, shankers, and oozes are all sure signs that fungus is among us. Fungicides that control most vegetable diseases are maneb, zineb, and captan. Read the labels before mixing and spraying. Powdery mildew is controlled by Benomyl.

VEGETABLE DISEASE CHART

Crop	Diseases to Guard Against
Asparagus	Rust, Fus. Rot, Gray Mold
Snap Beans	Rust, Virus Bact. Blight, White Mold
Table beets	Leaf Spot, Virus, Rhizoct. R. Rot
Broccoli	Clubroot, Wilt, Bact. Blight
Cabbage	Fus. Ylws., Wirestem
Carrots	Leaf Spot, Aster Ylws., Storage Rot
Cauliflower	R. Rot, Gray Mold, Mildew
Sweet corn	Smut, R. Rot, Leaf Spot
Swiss chard	Seed Rot, Anthr., Leaf Spot, Downy Mildew
Cucumbers	Bact. Wilt, Mosaic, Leaf Spot
Eggplant	Fus. Vert. Wilt, Leaf Spot
Endive	Seed Rot, Aster Ylws., Gray Mold, Mosaic
Kale	R. Rot, Gray Mold, Mildew
Kohlrabi	Cottony Rot, Fus. Ylws.
Leaf lettuce	Aster Ylws., Leaf Spot, Soft Rot
Head lettuce	Aster Ylws., Leaf Spot, Soft Rot
Onions	Botrytis Neck Rot, Smut, Smudge, Bulb Rot
Bunching onions	Botrytis Neck Rot, Smut, Smudge, Bulb Rot
Parsley	Aster Ylws., Leaf Spot, Soft Rot
Parsnips	Mosaic, Watery Soft Rot, R. Rot
Peas	Bact. Blight, Fus. Wilt, Mold, R. Rot
Peppers	Mosaic, Vert. Wilt, Bact. Spot
Potatoes	Use Clean Seed
Pumpkins	Leaf Blight, Bact. Wilt, Anthr.
Radish	Scab, Downy Mildew
Rhubarb	Root and Crown Rot, Leaf Spot, Anthr., Mosaic, Ring Spot Virus

I'M THE ONE WITH THE INGROWN TOENAIL

Rutabaga	Boron Deficiency, Downy Mildew, Wirestem
Salsify	Mildew, Aster Ylws., Soft Rot
Spinach	Damping-off, Leaf Spot, Virus Ylws.
Squash, summer	Leaf Spot, Scab, Anthr., Angular Leaf Spot, Fus. Wilt
Squash, winter	Leaf Spot, Fus. Wilt
Tomatoes	Fus., Vert. Wilt, Canker, Blossom End Rot
Turnips	Spot, Fus. and Vert. Wilt, Mosaic, Soft Rot, Blackleg

Abbreviations used in Vegetable Disease Charts
Anthr. = Anthractnose

Bact. = Bacteria
Fus. = Fusarium
Rhizoct. = Rhizoctonia

R. Rot = Root Rot
Vert. = Verticillium
Ylws. = Yellows

Check the Pesticide Label

When buying a pesticide and again before using it, read the label carefully.

A pesticide label contains a considerable amount of useful information. It identifies the pest for which the material is effective. Use the pesticide to control only those pests listed. The rate of material to use also is given. Follow this rate, for if you exceed the recommended rate and problems occur, the company is not responsible. Also, you waste material and stand a chance of polluting an area with a chemical.

The pesticide label also lists the interval to use in applying the materials. This varies with materials but generally it is between 3 and 21 days.

How soon can you eat a crop after an application? That information also is found on the label. On many labels special precautions are given such as washing fruit or not spraying past a certain development stage. Follow these warnings closely.

Root knot nematodes are the single most important home garden pest in the South and Southwest. Conservative estimates show at least 50 percent of home gardens are damaged by root knot.

One problem with controlling this pest is that it's hard to detect the problem early enough to take preventive measures. Once nematodes are found on plant roots, little can be done to save the crop.

It's important to inspect plant roots for galls as you remove them from the garden in the fall. Galls or knots on roots indicate the presence of root knot nematodes. Another symptom of nematodes is stunted, yellow plants.

As soon as root knot nematodes are found in the garden, immediately remove all diseased plants. Get as much of the root system as possible, because the nematode carries over in the egg stage to the next crop in these roots. Root tissue around the eggs protects them from chemical treatment and drying.

Once plant roots are removed, till or spade the area as deep as possible. This breaks up remaining roots, making them decay faster, and it dries the soil, reducing the number of young nematodes (larvae) in the soil. If nematodes are detected in the spring garden, continue tilling or spading the garden at 2-to-3 week intervals until fall planting time. This continual tilling reduces the nematode population even further.

In that portion of the garden not being used for winter vegetables, plant rye (cereal) in mid-September. Water the garden regularly for maximum fall growth of the rye.

Cereal rye acts as a control for nematodes. Many of the nematodes entering the roots will not be able to undergo complete development and will be killed. When the rye is spaded or tilled under it decays and produces an organic acid toxic to nematodes.

In addition, rye serves as a source of organic material encouraging the growth of fungi which feed on nematodes. Turn the rye under as soon as possible in early spring. This allows time for plant decay before spring planting.

When soil temperature reaches 50° F. for 7 days at a

AND YOU THOUGHT ATHLETE'S FOOT WAS BAD

depth of 6 inches, treat the garden with Vapam fumigant, using 1 quart per 100 square feet. Water the chemical into the soil using about 1 inch of water at the time of treatment.

Vapam is water-soluble and leaches down into the soil with the water. It is important that the chemical move into the soil as deep as possible for maximum control. Repeat the application of water 24 and 48 hours after treatment.

After treatment, leave the area undisturbed for 7 days. Then till the soil to get the chemical out. Wait an additional 2 weeks before planting.

Additional steps can be taken at planting to further ensure nematode control. In those areas where root knot is most severe, plant onions, garlic, or sweet corn. These crops are not susceptible to root knot, and their presence further reduces nematode population.

Also, plant nematode-resistant varieties when available. Some of the varieties that have done well include:

Tomatoes: Bigset, Better Boy, Terrific, Bonus, Small-Fry (cherry type)

Southern peas: Mississippi Silver (cream)

Sweet potatoes: Jewell, Centennial

You may find that you are able to follow only one or two of the control practices because of planting or economic restrictions. Remember, once nematodes are found in your garden, it is impossible to eliminate them completely. However, a sound control program keeps the population at a manageable level.

IT WAS GOOD ENOUGH FOR THE INDIANS

11

The Natural Way to Grow
ORGANIC GARDENING

In the last dozen years, millions upon millions of folks have become seriously concerned with their personal health and longevity. They are jogging, slogging, bending, dipping, and dancing to improve their health. Organic restaurants and organic foods are popular and in increasing demand. We are in the natural food revolution. Organic gardening has come into its own. Now the organic nut that used to live down the block is a practicing ecologist.

My mail is full of questions on organic gardening each week. I think it's commendable and should be the way to grow. But I also think that occasionally we get carried away with the promises of magic motions, potions, and lotions. We become disillusioned and discouraged when we find that our crops don't grow larger, more colorful, or tastier than they did the old way when we bought chemicals. And we discover that the bugs and blights did not read the organic garden book we did and ate the dickens out of our tomatoes, potatoes, cucumbers, and watermelon before we ever got a taste. So I cannot write a book on vegetable gardening without giving you my experience and knowledge about how to reduce your depending on synthetics

The Word "Organic" Is What Causes the Confusion

I'LL HAVE HORSE MANURE SOUP and COW PIE

Organic Dining for Plants —Natural Plant Food Menu

and properly use the natural materials for soil building, plant feeding, and insect and disease control.

The difference between organic gardeners and most other gardeners is the use of synthetic versus natural gardening products. The organic gardener is really a natural gardener who refuses to use materials that have been chemically manufactured or changed from their original form. For example, organic gardeners use dried blood meal, phosphate rock, and wood ashes as a fertilizer instead of a manufactured or blended chemical fertilizer like 5-10-5 or 4-12-4.

To control insects in the organic garden, rotenone or pyrethrum are used instead of a chemically manufactured pest control like Sevin, malathion, or methoxychlor.

Any gardener soon discovers the importance of and need for organic materials for plant growth and soil building. The term "organic gardener" implies that only a select group of gardeners use organic materials. To some degree that's true, but my experience leads me to believe that nearly all of the some 35 million home vegetable gardeners use the organic concept to some degree, while some who claim to be completely organic accept the use of plastic, a synthetic product, as a mulch.

What all of us should do is make every effort to use any and all natural methods available to us in producing and protecting our gardens. We should not choose sides or ridicule one method or another but rather work in harmony to improve the environment for our own benefit and generations to come. So, let's begin with the natural way to grow.

For good healthy growth, plants need several essential elements. They need these elements in addition to air, light, water, and carbon dioxide. They need:

1. *Primary elements*—nitrogen (N), phosphorus (P), and potash-Potassium (K)
2. *Secondary elements*—magnesium (Mg.), manganese, and copper

3. *Minor elements*—zinc, iron, sulfur, calcium (Ca), molybdenum, and boron
4. *Elements from water and air*—carbon, oxygen, and hydrogen

These elements can be added to the soil in different ways and forms, but in the soil they have to be converted into a chemical form that the plant can take in through its roots. Nitrogen can be added to the soil as manure, blood meal, urea, or ammonium nitrate, and then changed to ammonia 00 nitrate ions before the plant can eat it. By the way, plants don't give a darn what kind it is, just "how much."

Here is a table of some common natural plant food sources and what they contain.

Material	Kind	N	P	K	Ca.	Mg.
Manure	Cattle	0.53	0.29	0.48	0.29	0.11
	Fresh chicken	0.89	0.48	0.83	0.38	0.13
	Fresh horse	0.55	0.27	0.57	0.27	0.11
	Fresh sheep	0.89	0.48	0.83	0.21	0.13
	Fresh swine	0.63	0.46	0.41	0.19	0.03
	Dried cattle	2.0	1.8	2.2	—	—
	Dried sheep and goat	1.4	1.0	3.0	—	—
Animal tankage	Dried blood	9-14	—	—	—	—
	Steamed bone meal	1.6-2.5	23-25	—	—	—
	Dried fish scrap	6.5-10	4-8	—	—	—
	Dried hoof and horn meal	10.75-15.6	—	—	—	—
	Tankage	5-10	10	—	—	—
Crushed rock powders	Rock phosphate	—	38-41	—	—	
	Basic slag	—	8-17	—	33	—
	Limestone	—	—	—	40	—
	Dolomite	—	—	—	22	—
	Greensand	—	1.35	4.15-9.54	—	1.63
Vegetable waste	Castor pomace	4.1-6.1	1-2	1.0-1.5	—	—
	Cottonseed meal	6.7-7.4	2-3	1.5-2.0	—	—
	Kelp	1.6-3.3	1-1	4-13	—	—
	Soy meal	6	1	2	—	—
	Unbleached wood ash	—	—	5	23	—

Material	Kind	N	P	K	Ca.	Mg.
Sewage sludge	Dried digested sludge	1.5-2.2	1.1-2.0	0.2-1.0	—	—
	Dried activated sludge	4.1-6.4	2.5-2.0	2	—	—

Some common organic fertilizers are listed below.

Name of Fertilizer	Analysis in Percent			Remarks
	N	P	K	
Blood	10	1.5	0	A very rapidly available organic fertilizer.
Fish scrap	9	7	0	Do no confuse with fish emulsives, which generally are quite low in fertilizer content.
Guano, bat	6	9	3	Partially decomposed bat manure from caves.
MEAL				
Bone, raw	4	22	0	Main value is nitrogen, since most of the phosphorus is not soluble.
Bone, steamed	2	27	0	As a result of steaming under pressure some nitrogen is lost but more phosphorus is soluble for use by plants.
Cocoa shell	2.5	1	3	Primarily a conditioner for complete fertilizers.
Cottonseed	6	2.5	2	Generally very acid. Useful in alkaline soils.
Hoof and horn	14	0	0	The steam-treated and gound material is a rather quickly available source of nitrogen.
MANURE				
Cattle	0.5	0.3	0.5	Although manures in general are low in fertilizer, when they are used in relatively large amounts to improve soil structure, damage may occur because of too much fertilizer.
Chicken	0.9	0.5	0.8	
Horse	0.6	0.3	0.6	
Sheep	0.9	0.5	0.8	
Swine	0.6	0.5	0.4	
Mushroom manure (spent)	1	1	1	
Oyster shells	0.2	0.3	0	Because of their alkalinity these are better used for raising pH than as a fertilizer.
Peat (reed or sedge)	2	0.3	0.3	Better used as a soil conditioner than as a fertilizer. Breaks down too rapidly.
Rice hulls (ground)	0.5	0.2	0.5	
SLUDGE				
Sewage	2	1	1	Examples of activated sludge are Milorganite (Milwaukee, Wis.), Hu-Acinite (Houston, Tex.)

Name of Fertilizer	Analysis in Percent			Remarks
	N	P	K	
Sewage, activated (special micro organisms added)	6	5	0	Chicagrow (Chicago, Ill.) and Nitroganic (Pasadena, Calif.)
TANKAGE				
Cocoa	4	1.5	2	
Garbage	3	3	1	
Process (leather, hair, wool, felt, feathers, etc.)	8	2	0	
Wood ashes	0	2	6	Quite alkaline. Do not use on high-pH soils.

The Real Thing— Organic Material

IT'S LIKE A BREATH OF FRESH AIR

Your organic collection is the real life in soil. In heavy soil (like clay and silt) it binds the fine soil together in aggregates so the excess water drains free. Heavy soil like clay will warm up faster with organics tilled in; on light sandy soil the organic material fills the extra pore space and slows down and holds the moisture. To make it simple, it breaks down clay and retains food and water in sandy soil.

Adding large amounts of organics isn't always the magic answer, and contrary to what some organic gardeners believe, organic material won't prevent insect or disease damage. Large amounts of organic material in the soil just before you plant can lead to real damage by the corn maggot. On the other hand, it can also control the wireworm on corn roots. Large amounts of corncobs, straw, and leaves draw the nitrogen out of the soil as well as reduce the phosphorus, which means another source is necessary.

Hide and Seek for a Source Is Not Necessary

No sir-re-Bob! You can smell it in the barnyard. Along with a good assortment of manure there are grass, leaves, thatch collection, ground tablescraps, coffee, and tea leaves. Apply evenly and plow in nice and deep.

You're Talking Big Numbers When It Comes to Animal Manure

All manure is not the same. You would have to consider the age of the animal, its diet, the type of bedding, and the time of year. Fresh manure is low in phosphorus, so you will have to add 2 pints of rock phosphate per bushel. Use 20 bushels of cow, hog, or horse manure, 700 pounds per 100 square feet, and 350 pounds of rabbit, goat, or sheep —it's stronger. Are you thinking what I was when I first saw these figures, that you'd have to live next to a stockyard or zoo?

A Perking Pile Is Barnyard Gold on Simmer

GET YOUR FINGER OUT OF THE PIE

The compost pile is the single most important source of organic material any gardener can possibly have, build, or find. But you know something? Most of you folks turn your noses up at the thought of a pile of crap (as it is referred to by those who don't know), grass clippings, woodchips, sawdust, weeds (not gone to seed), old garden-flower and vegetable plant (not with disease), manure, table scraps, shredded newspaper (black-and-white only), and any other organic material you can find piled up in a corner of your yard, simmering in the hot summer sun, giving off an odor that makes the birds change course. A well-planned and well-cared-for compost pile smells good, looks good, and tastes good to your garden charges. A compost pile is worth $30 to $70 in fertilizer value if you were to buy it. Compost piles can be attractive if you let your imagination work a little while. I grow tomatoes on the outside of the working pile, growing up the wire cage that contains my compost cookery.

To make a compost pile, take a piece of wire fencing 4 or 5 feet high and bend it into a round or square figure 4 to 5 feet wide and long. Spread on an 8-to-10-inch layer of any or all of the compost materials mentioned above, throw on a light layer of garden soil, and add 1 pound of limestone, dried blood, or bone meal. Next, sprinkle half a can of beer over the top and dampen the pile. Stir it up once a month. My garden friends, you've got gold in that there pile.

Green Manure Is Just Grass with a Fancy Name

When you hear farmers or natural gardeners talk about green manure or a cover crop, they are referring to the same thing. For the home gardener practicing natural-method gardening, a fall-sown crop of annual-rye grass (as soon as you have removed the old vegetation to the compost pile) will fill the bill. In the early spring you simple spade or plow it under. Alfalfa, clover, and winter rye will do as well.

Vegetative Residue Sounds a Little Highbrow

FLOPPED IN DAILY

This refers to peat moss, kelp, sawdust, leaves, chopped hay, and dry grass clippings. Whenever these are added to the soil you must sprinkle 10 to 15 pounds of dried blood per 700 square feet of garden surface and spray with a can of beer to help speed up the breakdown process and not rob the soil of its nitrogen.

Tankage Is Not from the Honey Bucket

Animal tankage is processed by-products of the meat industry: fish scraps, hooves, horns, blood, meat, and bone. The best of these products are dried blood meal and fish; 6 pounds per 1,000 square feet of garden once a month will make your vegetable garden the happiest on the block

Prepared Vegetable Residue Is Just Roasted Peanuts

As a rule, wood ashes, beer and whiskey renderings, cottonseed meal, soybean meal, and peanut shells compose this group. They are a good source of nitrogen—5 to 7 percent, to be sort of exact.

THE TASTE TEST

Sludge Is the Sewage That Made Milwaukee Famous

Milorganite, the most famous and popular organic fertilizer for both garden and golf course, is just processed Milwaukee, Wisconsin, purebred sewage. I don't know just how to write this analogy, but sludge is the organic vegetable soup (sorry, veggies!). It's got everything in it. There are two kinds: *Dried digested* sludge is naturally dried and can from time to time have some bad organisms; *dried activated* sludge is heat-treated and is much safer to use.

Crushed Rock Powders Aren't What They Are Cracked Up to Be

Up to this point the organic materials have been high in nitrogen and low in phosphorus and potash. The rock powders go the other way, low to no N and high in P and K. But there is a hangup: Even though these rock materials are pulverized into fine powders the nutrients in them are not easy for plants to eat, and so a lot is necessary to get the job done. Following is a description of the rocky road to a good natural garden.

Limestone is used to neutralize acid soil.

Rock phosphate is tough for your garden to chew and is needed at a rate of 50 pounds per 1,000 square feet. To make your garden comfortable, apply rock phosphate along with lime.

Potassium is purchased as greensand or granite dust, and since they are low, low on solubility, you will need 500 pounds per 1,000 square feet.

Make a V-8 Cocktail for Your Garden

You can mix and mush any of the organics and rocks together, since time is the key word for action that makes these available to your plants, and they move slow. You will need large quantities of each.

Make sure that you take a fall, spring, and midseason soil

MIX, MIX, MIX THEM JUICES UP

sample. Either test it yourself or send it to the state soil test laboratory. With simple kits and low-cost meters, you and your neighbors can do your own if you prefer.

Here is the rate in pounds per 1,000 square feet:

NITROGEN

Dried blood meal	15–20 lbs.
Cottonseed meal	35–50 lbs.

PHOSPHORUS

Rock phosphate	25–75 lbs.
Steamed bone meal	10–40 lbs.

POTASSIUM

Greensand	250–750 lbs.
Dry wood ashes	30–100 lbs.

Bug and Blotch Battle Organically— Insect and Disease Damage Is Not Funny Any Way You Garden!

The natural or organic gardener is no more immune from bugs and blights than any other gardener, since most natural insect controls are more gentle and subtle. The natural gardener must be more observing and use more cultural preventions. Cultural prevention is simply keeping your garden and plants clean. Pick up plant material that may have broken off or vegetables that fall off or rot and remove them.

Wash the foliage with ½ cup of liquid soap per 20 gallons of water once a month. Pick off and destroy a stray bug, worm, or other pest. Encourage birds to visit your yard. Protect fruit and ripe vegetables from these visitors with nets designed just for this purpose:

Naturals are insecticides that are derived from plant and other natural sources. They are not a panacea and as a rule are much more expensive than synthetics.

Pyrethrum is a floral extraction from Kenya and Ecuador. Pyrethrum is a contact poison, knocking down and paralyzing insects instantly. Science now has a synthetic pyrethrum.

Rotenone comes from Timbo, Derris, or Cube and is used for control of many sucking insects. It is both a contact and a stomach poison. You must not use rotenone near ponds, lakes, and streams, as it kills fish.

Ryania is a contact and stomach poison. It is, however, slow-acting. It is used on fruit trees for codling moth, and for the corn borer. Ryania is made from the roots of *Ryania seciosa,* from the Amazon Basin and Trinidad.

Sabadilla is a natural insecticide made from the seeds of *schoenocaulon officinale,* which grows in South America. Sabadilla is both a contact and stomach poison. This control works on a large variety of insects but is no control over aphids.

Bacillus thuringensis is a bacterium that gives caterpillars ulcers, so to speak.

I want you to keep one thing in mind: Even though these chemicals are considered safe, you must read directions and use only as recommended.

INSECTS AND DISEASES—NATURAL CONTROLS

Insects / Diseases	Pyrethrum	Rotenone	Ryania	Sabadilla	Bacillus Thuringensis	Sulphur	Birds	Good Insects
Ants	✓						✓	✓
Aphids	✓	✓	✓				✓	✓
Mealybugs			✓				✓	✓
Scale							✓	✓
Mites		✓	✓					✓
Caterpillars	✓	✓	✓	✓	✓	✓	✓	✓
Moths			✓		✓		✓	
Leafhoppers	✓	✓	✓	✓		✓	✓	✓
Borers			✓					✓
Snails and Slugs							✓	
Thrips	✓	✓	✓					
Beetles and True Bugs	✓	✓	✓	✓			✓	✓
Powder Mildew						✓		
Rust						✓		
Leaf Spot						✓		

NOT ALL BUGS ARE BAD, ARE THEY?

Good Bugs—Bugs, Bugs, Bugs!

Believe it or not, there are insects that are our friends. They cause you and me no discomfort, don't eat plants, don't lay eggs that develop into larvae that attack our gardens. These insects only destroy other insects. They are:

Ant lion (doodlebug)	Minute pirate bug	Predaceous wasp
Ladybug	Praying mantis	Spider
Damsel bug	Syrphid fly	Predaceous mite
Assassin bug	Ground beetle	

Bees Are Necessary If You Really Want a Bumper Crop

When you think of insects you may envision all kinds of serious problems in the garden. It's true that insects can be a real problem; some insects are harmful, but not all of them. It's been estimated that less than 5 percent of known insects are harmful to man or his food crops. The rest either pose no known threat or are considered beneficial.

As a matter of fact, it can be a real problem not having some insects in your garden; bees are a good example. As bees collect nectar and pollen, they visit flowers and carry out one of the most important acts in nature—pollination. Pollination is the transfer of pollen from the anther of the flower to the stigma. This process must be carried out before fruit set will occur. Just how important is pollination to your vegetable garden? For the common vine crops such as cucumbers, squash, cantaloupes, watermelons, and pumpkins, pollinating insects are essential, because these crops have separate male and female flowers. Without bees or other pollinating insects of some type, pollen transfer does not normally occur; the result is nothing to eat from your vine crops.

If you've grown vine crops in the past and had them bloom but not set any fruit, chances are the problem was no pollination. Putting a hive of bees in the middle of your garden may not be practical. One thing you can do is avoid spraying your garden for damaging insects during the morning when honeybees are most active. Remember, there are

YOU GOT TWO AT 12 O'CLOCK HIGH

fewer pollinating insects in urban areas than in suburban or rural areas.

Look out for damaging insects; however, also be aware that some insects are there to do a very important job.

While Birds of a Feather Flock Together, So Do the Ones That Like Bugs!

I must admit that there are times when I get so mad at the birds around my garden I could scream and shout. I know, however, that they do more than their share of good. It is an excellent idea to do things to attract birds. Feeders in the winter help—but cover your ripe fruit. Here is a list of some of the birds that help:

Kinglet	Sparrow	Bluebird
Brown creeper	Scarlet tanager	Catbird
Nuthatch	Red-eyed vireo	Meadowlark
Titmouse	Flycatcher	Downy
Ruby-crowned	Gnatcatcher	woodpecker
kinglet	Barn swallow	Towhee
Junco	Warbler	

Smashing, Sticking, and Blinding 'Em Is as Natural as You Can Get

The secret and most effective method of killing bugs is still a fly swatter or hand picking and squashing underfoot; these methods are called *physical control*. Bug lights, aluminum foil, sticky traps, and stem barriers are called *medicinal methods*. Both of these methods are used to a degree professionally, but in the home garden they can be a plant lifesaver and are practical.

Light the Way to Bug Disaster

There are more bug lights added each weekend than new cars every spring, and some of them cost just about as much. When you are placing a bug light trap for garden

GET 'EM COMING and GOING

STICK AROUND FOR AN ELECTRIFYING EXPERIENCE

SHOW ME THE WAY TO GO HOME

protection or patio comfort, place it in a position to draw the insects away—not show them where you and the tomatoes are resting.

They Really Stick to This Method

Barriers and traps covered with a sticky substance, like Tree Tanglefoot, spread into a band of tree wrap and tacked with the sticky side out 4 feet up, are a sure catcher for creeps and crawlers on the way to dinner in your tree each night or on the way home to sleep in the daytime.

Tangletrap, an adhesive in a spray can from Tanglefoot Company, can be sprayed on yellow plastic disks or coffee-can covers (the yellow plastic ones) and hung in trees or over your garden plants to attract and catch most flying insects. Paper collars on stems for cutworms and tar-paper disks spread with stickum around young cabbage stems get loopers.

Slugs Are Suckers for a Beer

So, fill a pie tin with beer and place the edge at ground level. They will belly up to the bar and drown. But to make sure that they are done in, lightly sprinkle diatomaceous earth (used in swimming-pool filters) on the soil. When they crawl over this it cuts and dehydrates their skin. Boy, do they scream when they fall into the beer.

Diseases Are the Toughest for the Natural Gardener

If disease control is difficult for science to find a solution for, it stands to reason that you and I with bare hands and determination are fighting an uphill battle. But let's fight!

Sulfur is one of the oldest and best for fighting plant disease and will be your most useful disease-fighting material. Powdered milk or skimmed milk has long been used to help control diseases on tomatoes. Use 2 tablespoons per gallon of water and spray lightly on fruit and plants if they show signs of disease.

Vaccinated Plants Are Still the Best Bet!

If you look at the list of varieties in Chapter 2, you will find dozens of virus-free varieties of vegetables—so try them! Your worry load will be less.

Room to Grow Is Just Common Sense

It's common sense, that is, if you don't crowd or overplant your garden. Leave plenty of room between plants and rows for fresh air to get into, and you will stand less of a chance of having to battle disease.

IT'S NOT WHAT YOU THINK

THIS IS MY SIDE OF THE BED

Rotating the Lineup Wins Games

In the garden game you should move each crop's position around from year to year. It replenishes the soil as well as hides the crop plant from last year's blight.

JONES, IN FOR SMITH

Trap Them with a Plant

It would be nice if we could hang carnivorous plants (like the Venus flytrap, pitcher plant, and cobra plant) around our garden, but that's dreaming. Trapping crops are merely plants that bugs like better than the one you do. They're planted side by side to detour the bugs. It's "iffy" at this point.

Body Odor Keeps Bugs Away

These are known as repellent plants, and they do a darn good job of guarding your garden plants:

Guard Plant	Enemy	Victim
Asparagus	Soil insects	Tomato
Beans	Colorado potato beetle	Potato
Chives	Scab	Apple
Celery	Cabbage white butterfly	Cabbage crops
Herbs	Cabbage maggot	Cabbage crops
	Carrot fly	Carrots
	Flea beetle	Radish
Leek	Carrot fly	Carrot
Lettuce (head)	Flea beetle	Radish

UM UM GOOD

Guard Plant	Enemy	Victim
Marigold (African and French)	Nematode	Potatoes, roses, and tomatoes
Sugar cane and beets	Nematode	Potatoes, roses, and tomatoes

(NOTE: Marigold flowers should be saved and spaded into the fall and spring garden. Sugar cane and beets can also be shredded or chopped fine and tilled into soil where nematodes are a problem.)

Mint	Ant	Cabbage crops
	Cabbage maggot	
	White cabbage butterfly	
Mole plant	Mole and mouse	Garden soil

(NOTE: This plant is a spurge and it does its job; but if you get it on your skin it can make open sores.)

Nasturtium	Aphid	Apples, cabbage crops, and radish
	Squash bug	Vine crops
	White fly	Greenhouse
Onion	Carrot fly	Carrots
Radish	Cucumber beetle	Vine crops
Tomato	Asparagus beetle	Asparagus
	Cabbage maggot	Cabbage crops
	White cabbage butterfly	Cabbage crops

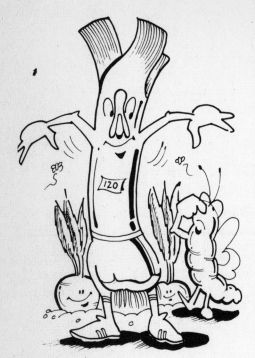

MUSK YOUR GRASS

I have found that if you make a special compost pile—a small wire basket will do fine—and fill it with layers of chives, onion tops, leek tops, marigold flowers, mint leaves and stems and nasturtium flowers, and then in the spring of the year till it into your garden, you will seldom, if ever, have bug problems, or at least they will be acceptable and controllable.

Mulch Is the Natural Way to Battle Weeds

Mulch can be defined as "any material spread on the garden to protect plant roots from heat, cold or drought; to reduce problems with weeds; and to keep fruit clean."

Clear plastic warms the soil more than most other mulches. It stimulates weed-seed germination and growth. It also can be laid over seeded rows to stimulate early vegetable-seed germination. Remove the plastic as soon as seedlings emerge from the soil. If weeds are not a problem, clear plastic is an excellent mulching material.

Black plastic makes the soil warmer early in the season and greatly reduces the weed population (it will not control nutgrass). Adequate soil moisture should be available when the black plastic is applied. Cut holes through the plastic after it is applied over the bed to allow for seeding or transplanting. Water by using drip systems or water soakers beneath the plastic, by furrow watering, or by sprinkling. If sprinklers are used, it may be necessary to cut T-slits in the plastic for water penetration.

Paper of various types is used as mulch, with newspaper by far the most common. Several sheets of newspaper laid flat over the surface of the garden row work well as a mulch. However, paper reduces the soil temperature. Paper mulch used early in the spring when the soil is cold causes delayed maturity of many garden vegetables, such as tomatoes, peppers, squash, etc. For these crops paper can be used to greater advantage if applied after the crops are growing and the soil has warmed up. Paper mulch will not delay cool-season, spring-planted crops such as lettuce, broccoli, and cabbage as much as warm-season plants. As with the black plastic, apply the paper when the soil contains good moisture. Unlike plastic, paper deteriorates and does not have to be removed at the end of the garden season.

Organic mulches are by far the most common. The benefits of organic mulches occur primarily in the summer, because they reduce soil temperature and save soil moisture. Do not use organic mulches too early in the spring. If applied to cold garden soils, the soils warm up more slowly and maturity is reduced. Organic mulches prevent soil crust-

THE PAPER WEIGHT CHAMPION

ing, control weeds, prevent erosion, lessen fruit rot, conserve moisture, and reduce summer temperatures. After the soil warms, apply organic mulches at a depth of 0 to 2 inches around growing plants. With organic materials such as sawdust, leaves, rice hulls, etc., it usually is necessary to increase the amount of garden fertilizer by about one-fourth to compensate for the nutrients used by microorganisms during the breakdown process. At the end of the season, turn under organic mulches to improve the soil's physical condition.

Grow Naturally

The quality and quantity of your harvest is in direct balance with the degree of your involvement. The same goes for career, marriage, and friendships. Just be yourself—be natural.

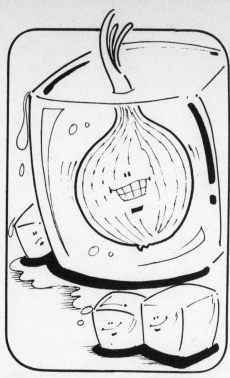

THERE HAS GOT TO BE A BETTER WAY

12

Freeze It, Squeeze It, or Dry It
STORING FOOD

It bothers me no end when I see gardeners produce a bumper crop only to let it go to waste, because they can't eat it all and because they have never stored and preserved food.

As a rule, whenever I mention preserving food, I get a distressed look and a reply like "Oh, canning is dangerous, and besides, it's too much work." Neither of these two assumptions is true. Yes, there are rare occasions when improper sanitation steps aren't taken and an *ism* appears. But it is seldom a real problem. Too much work? Well, I must admit, it takes time and it does get hot in the kitchen; but don't despair, there are other ways to "lay food away," as they say. The large variety of garden vegetables that can be frozen comes as a surprise to most home gardeners.

Harvest Hints for Better Taste

Make it a point to harvest all vegetables as they mature. To get the most from your garden, harvest vegetables at their best stage for eating. Many vegetables such as beans, okra, and squash quit producing if not harvested on a regular basis, so regular harvesting is very important.

Harvesting at the right stage is also a must if you plan to do any canning or freezing. The final quality of your preserved vegetables is no better than the quality you begin with. Many gardeners consume most of their vegetables fresh; they can or freeze what is left over. Avoid this practice if at all possible. Vegetables that you can or freeze should be identical in quality to those that are consumed fresh.

To maintain the quality after harvest, handle vegetables very carefully. Avoid bruising or damaging them, as this encourages decay and a shorter storage life. Some vegetables, such as sweet corn, peas, asparagus, and leafy vegetables, should be cooled to between 35° and 40° F. as soon as possible unless they are to be eaten immediately.

Another important point is to keep the time between harvesting and eating or preserving vegetables as short as possible. This helps you enjoy their full flavor and nutrient value. Many vegetables lose flavor and vitamin content if kept too long.

To get the most out of your garden this year, harvest vegetables at the right time and stage of maturity. This may mean delivering some produce to your neighbors rather than swamping your kitchen with the third bushel of squash in a week.

VEGETABLES FOR FREEZING OR DRYING		
Vegetable	*Freezing*	*Drying*
Artichokes	√	
Asparagus	√	√
Beans	√	√
Beets	√	√
Broccoli	√	√
Brussels sprouts	√	
Cabbage	√	√
Carrots	√	√
Cauliflower	√	
Corn	√	√

Vegetable	Freezing	Drying
Endive		
Greens (all)	√	√
Herbs	√	√
Kale	√	√
Okra	√	
Onions		√
Parsnips	√	√
Peas	√	√
Peppers	√	√
Potatoes	√	
Pumpkins	√	√
Rutabagas	√	√
Squash	√	√
Tomatoes	√	
Turnips	√	√

INSURING THE FLAVOR

Gray Peppers and Brown Tomatoes Don't Look Too Appetizing

It is important to maintain good color in frozen food, and this can be done if you select only firm, attractive vegetables to begin with. Color can also be protected if you use an antidarkening agent. Lemon juice and citric acid are two of the most common and are added to the hot blanching water.

Ascorbic acid is a crystalline powder form of Vitamin C.

Blanching Is Boiling Plain and Simple

In most cases, it will be necessary to blanch vegetables before freezing them to stop the enzyme action of ripening and the bacteria that cause spoilage.

Basic Rules for Freezing Are a Chilling Subject

CHRRRRRRISP, IT'S COLD IN HERE

Before you decide to freeze your bumper crop, make sure that you have the freezer capacity to hold your needs. I'm sorry to say that a small freezer on top of your refrigerator won't work too well. The real secret to proper, tasty freezing is to freeze it fast and keep it that way—10° to below zero. Most small freezers won't do this.

Frozen Dirt Tastes Terrible

It may sound funny but it happens all too often. Folks get in a hurry and don't properly wash or peel the vegetables before they slice, dice, or chop them and a particle or two of your garden compost goes into the bag or box only to be discovered when you cook them—in muddy water! A small scrub brush will avoid this.

Bite Sizes Save Space and Lockjaw

BIG MOUTH

I have been asked to judge more than my share of county fair entries of frozen and dried fruit and vegetables. What always surprises me is the large number of folks with extremely big mouths! Not loud—big in size. Why do I say this? Well, from the looks of the sizes vegetables are cut into for freezing. You would need a mouth the size of a wolf to eat a great deal of them. When you chop, dice, or slice for freezing, take into consideration the eating habits of your family and make the pieces a comfortable size. Smaller sizes and thinner slices cook, boil, fry, or microwave faster.

Don't Be Boiling Mad the Second Time—Boil It the First Time!

This is what we call blanching, and it is used to slow down the ripening process and lock in the flavor and natural sweetness. When the chart calls for blanching, darn it, do it! A short cut here tastes like heck later. Make sure that the water is at a rumbling boil before placing the vegetables into it. Change water for each different vegetable or you will end up with some strange flavors.

OH SOAP-O-ME-O

BLANCHING TIME FOR VEGETABLES

Vegetable	Minutes	Vegetable	Minutes
Artichokes	10*	Okra	2
Asparagus	4	Onions	0
Beans	2	Parsnips	2
Beets	5	Peas	1
Broccoli	3	Peppers	0
Brussels sprouts	4	Potatoes	0
Cabbage	0	Pumpkins	0
Carrots	3	Rutabagas	1
Cauliflower	3	Squash	3
Corn	6	Tomatoes	4 as a sauce
Endive	0	Turnips	1
Greens	2	Celery	3
Herbs	0	Eggplant	4
Kale	0	Kohlrabi	2

* Citric Acid
0—Do Not Blanch

THE TOUGH TASTE TEST

Contain Your Vegetable Harvest

Here is where trouble can really begin. Don't use cheap, ill-fitting bags, boxes, or bottles. Packaging materials must be top-quality, vapor- and moisture-resistant, pliable and durable at very cold temperature, odorless and flavorless. Don't use old or used bags. Use nonabsorbent bags, easy to seal and the right size for the job. I have found that placing my sliced, diced, and chopped vegetables into

TIGHT FIT MEANS FRESH TASTE

freezer bags first and then into a box or container gives me added insurance of both flavor and no freezer burn.

Drying Food Can Be Child's Play

As a matter of fact, that is how I first ran into food drying. My Grandma Putnam, the lady I write about in all of my books, the one that taught me gardening at six years old, sliced up apples one rainy day to occupy my time and proceeded to show me how to oven-dry and light-dry fruit. Next, she showed me how to sun-dry fruit. The methods may have seemed crude, but the end result was delicious.

You can dry and store a great number of vegetables and herbs, to be reconstituted and used in soups, meat dishes, snacks, and many other cooking uses. The same steps are necessary for preparing vegetables for drying as for freezing. They must be clean, fresh, firm, and of good color, and must be blanched, with an antidarkening agent used. Quicker drying occurs when pieces are smaller and thinner.

VEGETABLES FOR DRYING

Vegetable	End Result	Vegetable	End Result
Artichokes	Crisp	Eggplant	Brittle
Asparagus	Leathery	Horseradish	Powdery
Beans	Brittle	Mushrooms	Leathery
Beets	Leathery	Okra	Brittle
Broccoli	Brittle	Onions	Brittle
Brussels sprouts	Brittle	Parsley	Flaky
Cabbage	Brittle	Peas	Wrinkled—crisp
Carrots	Leathery	Peppers	Brittle
Cauliflower	Brittle	Potatoes	Brittle
Celery, leaves and stalks	Brittle	Spinach, all greens	Brittle
Corn, cob and cut	Brittle	Squash	Brittle
		Tomatoes	Leathery

How You Dry Depends on Your Time

I WOULD RATHER LIE IN THE SUN

I just mentioned that there are a few ways to dry vegetables. The oldest and slowest is *sun drying*. You must have several consecutive days of 85° to 90°, with low humidity.

Oven drying is faster and can be done while you sleep. Place vegetables to be dried on cookie sheets and place in oven at 140° until dry. *Turbo oven* is the fastest way to dry, since you have dry, hot circulating air. Check the manufacturer's recommendation. The *food dehydrator* is really a great investment for a serious gardener. They are not expensive and are available at most retail department and mass merchandiser stores. The professionally designed dehydrator constantly circulates low even heat for uniform drying. Trays are specially designed to allow the constant flow.

Keep Dried Foods Dry or Don't Even Try

As soon as your vegetables are dry, place them in plastic Ziploc bags; pack them rather tight. Store them in a cool, dry, dark location. The basement or spare bedroom closet does nicely. Dried food should keep up to a year. If you put it in the freezer, you can count on two years.

Reconstituting Is a Snap

Just add 1½ cups of boiling water or broth for each cup of vegetables and let set for 30 minutes. That's about all there is to avoid wasting your rewards from your pride, patience, and persistence.

Storing Produce Is Not for Most of You

Storing fresh produce is really a lot bigger job than some books make it sound, and building a food cellar is a job most of you wouldn't tackle, so I won't go into it. Here are the temperature and humidity you would need if you try and the length of time you might expect to eat from your vegetable stash:

Vegetable	Recommended Temperature (°F.)	Recommended Relative Humidity (%)	Approximate Length of Storage (Months)
Artichoke	34	90–95	1
Artichoke, Jerusalem	34	90–95	2–5
Asparagus	34	90–95	1/3–3/4
Bean	45–50	85–90	1/4–1/3
Bean, lima, unshelled	34	90–95	1/2
Beet, topped	34	90–95	5–6
Broccoli	34	90–95	1/4–1/3
Brussels sprouts	34	90–95	1
Cabbage	34	90–95	3–4
Carrot, topped	34	90–95	4–5
Cauliflower	34	90–95	1/2–3/4
Celery	34	90–95	2–3
Chinese cabbage	34	90–95	2–3
Corn	34	90–95	1/6–1/4
Cucumber	50–55	90–95	1/2–3/4
Eggplant	50–55	85–90	1/3–1/2
Endive or escarole	34	90–95	1/2–3/4
Garlic	34	70–75	6–7
Greens and salads	34	90–95	1/2–3/4
Horseradish	34	90–95	5–6
Kohlrabi	34	90–95	1–2
Leek	34	90–95	2–3
Lettuce, head	34	90–95	1/2–3/4
Muskmelon	45–50	85–90	1/4–1/2
Okra	45–50	85–90	1/2–1/3
Onions, dry	34	70–75	6–7

Vegetable	Recommended Temperature (°F.)	Recommended Relative Humidity (%)	Approximate Length of Storage (Months)
Parsnips, topped	34	90–95	5–6
Peas	34	85–90	¼–½
Pepper, sweet	45–50	85–90	¼–⅓
Potato	38–40	85–90	5–6
Pumpkin	50–55	70–75	3–6
Radish	34	90–95	¼–⅓
Rutabaga	34	90–95	2–4
Salsify, topped	34	90–95	2–4
Spinach	34	90–95	⅓–½
Squash, summer	50–55	85–95	⅙–¼
Squash, winter	55–60	70–75	5–6
Sweet potato	55–60	80–85	4–6
Tomato, mature green	55–60	85–90	⅓–½
Tomato, ripe	45–55	85–90	¼–⅓
Turnip	34	90–95	4–5
Watermelon	50–55	85–90	¼–½

NO, NO, BOZO! I KNOW I SAID PLANTS ARE LIKE PEOPLE!

Calories, Vitamins, Good Health

These numbers in the following chart are the amounts of vitamins and calories in about ½ cup, cooked unless you ordinarily eat it raw. Vitamin A is in International Units, Vitamin C in milligrams. Active adults require 5,000 I.U. of Vitamin A each day for men and 4,000 for women, 45 mg of Vitamin C are recommended for both.

Since we are all conscious of our weight and the calories are the culprit that gets us in dutch, I thought I would show you just how much good your garden can do for your weight—2,700 calories are a plateful for you guys and 2,000 a day will keep your girlish figure intact.

In recent tests involving ordinary green vegetables, it was concluded that higher quantities influenced a reduction in colon and intestinal diseases.

EAT YOURSELF HEALTHY
Nutritional Value of Some Popular Vegetables

	Vegetable	Vitamin Content		Calories
		A (I.U.)	C (mg)	
GROUP 1 High in A and C	Parsley (raw)	8,500	172	44
	Spinach	8,100	28	23
	Collards	7,800	76	33
	Kale	7,400	62	28
	Turnip greens	6,300	69	20
	Mustard greens	5,800	48	23
	Cantaloupe	3,400	33	30
	Broccoli	2,500	90	26
GROUP 2 High in A	Carrots (raw)	11,000	8	42
	Carrots (cooked)	10,500	6	31
	Sweet potato	8,100	22	141
	Swiss chard	5,400	16	18
	Winter squash	4,200	13	63
	Green onions	2,000	32	36
GROUP 3 High in C	Peppers	420	128	22
	Brussels sprouts	520	87	36
	Cauliflower	60	55	22
	Kohlrabi	20	43	24
	Cabbage	130	33	20
	Chinese cabbage	150	25	14
	Asparagus	900	26	20
	Rutabagas	550	26	35
	Radishes (raw)	322	26	17
	Tomatoes (raw)	900	23	22
	Tomatoes (cooked)	1,000	24	26

| | | Vitamin Content | | |
	Vegetable	A (I.U.)	C (mg)	Calories
GROUP 4 Green vegetables	Green beans	540	12	25
	Celery	240	9	17
	Lettuce, leaf	1,900	18	18
	Lettuce, head	330	6	13
	Okra	490	20	29
	Peas (garden-fresh)	540	20	71
GROUP 5 Starchy vegetables	Lima beans	280	17	111
	Sweet corn (yellow)	400	9	91
	Onions (dry)	40	10	38
	Peas (southern field)	350	17	108
	Potatoes (baked in skin)	Trace	20	93
GROUP 6 Flavor, color, and texture	Beets	20	6	32
	Cucumber	250	11	15
	Eggplant	10	3	19
	Pumpkin	1,600	9	26
	Rhubarb	80	6	141
	Summer squash	440	11	15
	Turnips (roots)	Trace	22	23

Freezing and Drying Are Fun but the Squeezing Is Pure Joy!

Over the years I have tasted about every kind of wine you could possibly dream of that could be fermented. Some were excellent, others passable, and others pure poison. So I know exactly what one can do with excess root crops, like beets, parsnips, turnips, carrots, and potatoes. Make vegetable wine from the beets, carrots, parsnips, and turnips and make champagne out of potatoes. While we are at it, let's try a little mint wine as well.

NO WONDER HE'S IN A.A.

VEGETABLE WINE

10 pounds of vegetable
of your choice:
beets, parsnips,
carrots, or turnips
1 pound of raisins

3 lemons (cut-up)
8 pounds of sugar
1 package of
powdered yeast

Boil vegetable until it is tender. Add enough additional water to juice to make 2 gallons. Now add the above ingredients. To fix yeast: Mix yeast and 1 teaspoon of sugar in ½ cup of lukewarm water and pour over the vegetable mix. Pour into a crock and cover with cheesecloth and let sit for 3 weeks. Strain and bottle.

POTATO CHAMPAGNE

7 potatoes
7 oranges
7 lemons
7 pounds of sugar

1 pound of raisins
(ground)
1 package of dry yeast
1 slice of dry hard toast

Peel and slice potatoes, oranges, and lemons. Place in crock with 7 gallons of water and add the rest of the ingredients. Place yeast on top of toast and float on top of mix. Do not stir in. Cover with cheesecloth. Carefully remove the toast-yeast in a week. Let set for another week and then strain. Let set another week and strain again. Let set two days and bottle.

MINT WINE

1 quart of mint leaves
4 pounds of sugar
1 gallon of water

1 package of
dry yeast
1 slice of dry hard toast

Pour a gallon of cold water over clean mint leaves, add 4 pounds of sugar, and stir well. Place dry yeast on toast and float. Cover for a week, remove yeast-toast at end of one week. Let stand for another 10 days. Strain and balloon-seal. After gases no longer fill balloon bottle, seal and wait 3 months. Bottoms up!

13

The Most Asked Vegetable Questions and Their Answers

THERE ARE NO DUMB VEGETABLE GARDEN QUESTIONS!

Of the thousands and thousands of questions I receive in letters each year, the following, compiled by R. R. Rothenberger and A. E. Gaus, Department of Horticulture, College of Agriculture, University of Missouri–Columbia, are the most common on vegetable gardening.

Asparagus

Q. *How soon after planting may asparagus be cut?*

A. Wait until the bed is well established. If it has started well, a few spears may be cut the second year, and it may be cut for several weeks the third year. A full crop should not normally be harvested until the fourth year.

Q. *How long may asparagus be harvested?*

A. After it is well established, harvest for 6 to 10 weeks.

Q. *Should asparagus be mulched in winter?*

A. Asparagus is winter-hardy, so mulching is not essential. Mulching is nevertheless beneficial for weed control and moisture retention.

Q. *Is it safe to use salt on asparagus plantings?*

A. Salt is not beneficial to the healthy growth of asparagus. Salt was once used as a weed killer in asparagus beds; 2 pounds of salt per gallon of water was sprayed on the bed early in the season. We now have very effective herbicides, and they are better for weed control. Salt will gradually deteriorate the physical nature of the soil.

Beans

Q. *Do pole beans or bush beans provide the most efficient use of garden space?*

A. Bush beans can be spaced closer and will produce a greater quantity at any one time than a planting of pole beans. Pole beans will continue to produce, so that a more constant supply is available. In limited space, pole beans provide too much shade for neighboring crops, and the bush types would then be preferable.

Q. *Why do lima beans flower, but not set pods?*

A. Blossom drop in lima beans may be caused by hot, dry weather or cool, wet weather. Large-seeded limas react more to unfavorable weather conditions.

Beets

Q. *Why do beets produce lush top growth and little root development?*

A. Excess top growth with no bottoms generally results from too much nitrogen fertilizer, seeding too thickly without thinning, or planting so late in the season that weather becomes too hot before good growth has developed.

Q. *Do beets prefer acid or alkaline soil?*

A. Beets prefer a pH between 6.5 and 7. Therefore, the addition of lime is necessary in many soils for best beet growth.

Broccoli

Q. *Why does broccoli flower without forming heads?*

A. This may occur if plants have been stunted by poor growing conditions, or have been set out too late in the spring. Broccoli needs cool weather for best head formation.

Q. *Should broccoli be left in the garden after the center head has been cut?*

A. Green sprouting broccoli varieties will produce smaller side heads for a time after the center head has been cut. The plants may be allowed to remain until hot weather makes heads tough and poor-tasting.

Brussels Sprouts

Q. *Should a beginning gardener plant Brussels sprouts?*

A. Generally, no. Although their needs are similar to those of cabbage, they will take space throughout the summer, and begin production only in the fall after weather cools.

Cabbage

Q. *Why have the cabbage seedlings I started indoors become leggy even though in good light?*

A. Cabbage likes cool temperatures. Normal house temperature is too hot. Move the seedlings outdoors to a hotbed or cold frame as soon as germination is completed.

Q. *How can cabbage heads be kept from splitting?*

A. Heavy rains after heads are well developed often cause splitting. Prompt harvest is essential. If not possible, twist or pull the plant slightly to tear some of the roots, and cut down on water absorption and consequent splitting. Some varieties are more prone to splitting.

Cauliflower

Q. *Why are cauliflower heads greenish and bitter?*

A. Most likely the head has received too much light and growth has been slow. When the new head is about the size of a half-dollar, tie the large leaves together over the head to shade it. This keeps it white. Bitter flavor may also be associated with slow growth caused by low fertility or hot weather.

Q. *The cauliflower I planted was self-blanching, but leaves did not cover the head totally. Why?*

A. These varieties work best in cool climates. Late planting or low fertility would reduce vigor, and prevent leaves curling over the center from being large enough to give good cover. These same conditions result in poor head formation.

Carrot

Q. What makes carrot roots short, knobby, and sometimes split?

A. Heavy soils, rocky soils, low fertility, and crowding can lead to stubby short roots. Hot weather may stunt growth, but when followed by a period of wet favorable weather, roots may rapidly expand and develop cracks. Knobby roots indicate nematode problems.

Corn

Q. Is it necessary to pull suckers from the base of the plant?

A. No. There is no benefit, and crop may even be reduced.

Q. Why do ears of corn not fill properly?

A. Hot, dry weather results in poor pollination. Periods of heavy rain at pollen shedding or planting a very small patch or single row may lead to poor filling of the ears. Other reasons may be nutrient imbalances, particularly high nitrogen and low potassium.

Q. What makes corn tassel while plants are still very short?

A. Assuming that this is not an early, naturally short variety, lack of nitrogen, poor soil condition, or drought might cause this.

Q. Do sweet corn, field corn, popcorn, and ornamental corn mix? If so, how far apart should they be planted to prevent this?

A. Popcorn, ornamental corn, and field corn are all able to pollinate sweet corn. The reverse is also true, except in the case of sweet corn, which does not pollinate popcorn. White and yellow corn can also cross-pollinate, producing ears of mixed colors. The effect of these pollinations is not greatly apparent at the roasting-ear stage of sweet corn. Therefore, wide separation is not necessary unless there is some reason to save seeds for another crop. However, since most corn varieties are hybrids, seeds should not be saved.

Cucumber

Q. *Do cucumbers cross with watermelon, muskmelon, pumpkin, or squash?*

A. Although it is a common belief that cucumbers taint the flavor of muskmelons (cantaloupe) by crossing with them, they are not able to cross with each other. Neither can cucumber pollinate any of the other vine crops mentioned.

Q. *What causes bitter cucumbers?*

A. Weather conditions, drought, and low fertility contribute to the malfunction of one of the enzyme systems that prevent bitterness in cucumbers. Wide temperature fluctuations, such as a sharp drop, add to the problem. Cucumber mosaic may also cause bitter fruit. Plant breeders are attempting to overcome the genetic factors involved.

Q. *Why do cucumber flowers drop without producing fruit?*

A. Cucumbers have male and female flowers. Normal types of cucumbers first produce ten to twenty male blooms before female blooms are formed. As a result these first blooms drop without any fruit production. As female fruits are developed, set and fruit development usually begins.

Q. *What are gynecious cucumbers?*

A. These are a more recent development, and are plants that produce only female flowers, thereby resulting in earlier and more abundant set. A few "normal" plants must be included for pollination, and a few such seeds are normally mixed with seeds of gynecious varieties.

Q. *What causes deformed cucumbers?*

A. Poor pollination is the main cause of poor fruit shape. Since cucumbers require cross-pollination, good bee activity is essential. Drought conditions, hot weather, bacterial wilt, and cucumber mosaic may also lead to deformed fruit.

Eggplant

Q. *Why do eggplants sometimes fail to set fruit?*

A. Eggplants are sensitive to temperature. Cool night temperatures early in the season prevent fruit set. Hot dry winds in midsummer may also prevent pollination. Low fertility can also reduce fruit set and development.

Q. *Why do eggplant fruits not ripen properly?*

A. Stunted plants from cool weather, flea beetle damage, or poor soils.

Lettuce

Q. *Why is lettuce tough or bitter?*

A. Slow growth results in these characteristics. Crowding, low fertility, late planting, and hot weather all stunt growth and reduce quality.

Q. *Why does lettuce go to seed instead of producing a lush leafy plant?*

A. Hot weather causes lettuce to "bolt" and flower. Plant early and select varieties listed as heat-tolerant.

Q. *Can I grow head lettuce in Missouri?*

A. This is a difficult crop in Missouri's climate. Summers become too hot too soon. Start plants in a hotbed and shift outdoors as soon as possible. If cool weather lasts long enough, a fair crop may result.

Muskmelon

Q. *Do muskmelons cross with cucumbers to produce a "cucumber taste"?*

A. No. For more details, see the section above on cucumbers.

Q. *Can honeydew melons be grown anywhere?*

A. They need a long growing season, and if fall weather cools before fruits are well developed, the result is limited crop and poor flavor. Early-maturing varieties are being developed, and should be preferred if this melon is to be grown.

Q. *Can muskmelons be transplanted?*

A. Yes. However, care should be taken not to disturb the roots. They are best started indoors, in peat pots which can then easily be moved into the garden with a minimum of root injury.

Q. *What's the secret for growing good-tasting melons?*

A. There is no secret, just the best growing conditions possible. Fertilize early in the season, but not as fruit development begins, as too much fertilizer produces vines and no fruit.

Keep moisture levels even, with either irrigation or a deep mulch. Use disease-resistant varieties, and maintain good insect control.

Okra

Q. *Why doesn't my okra bear? All the flowers drop off until the end of summer.*

A. Temperature extremes; either too hot or too cool will prevent okra from setting. Poor soil fertility or drainage can aggravate the problem.

Q. *Why are my okra pods tough and stringy?*

A. Pods have become too old. Pick when pods are about 2 inches long.

Onion

Q. *Is it best to plant onion seeds, onion plants, or onion sets in the garden?*

A. Onion sets are easiest to handle, and they develop quickly for green onions as well as onions for winter storage. Onion plants are slower to develop but also produce good crops. Plants are usually used for growing Bermuda and Spanish onions. Seeds for onions may be started early in cold frames, or in the garden and thinned. They are suitable for green onions in early summer, but usually hot weather arrives and long daylengths stop growth before large onions can develop.

Q. *Is there any way to prevent onions from going to seed?*

A. Plant onion sets of bulbs no larger than ⅝ inch in diameter. Larger bulbs have a greater tendency to seed in the garden.

Q. *When am I supposed to break the tops of my onions over?*

A. Tops of onions should fall over naturally. After about two-thirds to three-fourths of them have fallen over the others may be broken down to help close the necks. However, onions which do not fall over naturally tend to be poor keepers and should be kept separate and used first.

Q. *What is a "multiplier" onion?*

A. This is a hardy type of onion that is allowed to remain in the garden over winter. In summer the tops produce new bulblets that drop to the ground and start a new group. They are suitable for green onions for home use.

Parsley

Q. *Why does my parsley often die out after flowering?*
A. Parsley is a biennial plant. Therefore, in the second year it flowers, produces seeds, and dies. Yearly seeding ensures continuous production. Poor drainage may also lead to root rot and death of younger plants.

Pea

Q. *What makes pea plants die, often as they are just coming into production?*
A. The cause may be wilt, root rot diseases, or hot weather. Use wilt-resistant varieties, and rotate pea plantings to prevent buildup of soil diseases. Mulch between rows to keep soil cool longer. Plant early to get maximum growth and production before hot weather arrives.

Pepper

Q. *Why do peppers flower, but not set fruit?*
A. Peppers are sensitive to high temperatures, low humidity, and drying winds. Under these conditions, plants of many varieties do not set fruit well and flowers drop off. Well-developed plants set in the garden often flower and set ample fruit before these extreme weather conditions arrive.

Q. *Are red peppers different from green peppers?*
A. No. All green peppers will color to red or yellow as they become more mature.

Potato

Q. *Why is there sometimes a poor stand in the potato planting?*
A. Very wet weather, poorly drained soils, or planting too deep may lead to the development of rhizoctonia or other diseases that rot the seedling pieces or young shoots before they become established.

Q. *Are "certified seed" potatoes really necessary for the home planting?*

A. Yes. This means that the potatoes used for planting were inspected in the growing fields, and are free of the many diseases that may be carried on the seed piece. Potatoes grown for table use do not have this guarantee of freedom from disease.

Q. *Are you supposed to cut potato seed pieces a certain number of days before planting?*

A. This is not necessary. Potatoes can be cut and planted directly. If they are cut a day or more ahead of planting, place them in a covered container in a warm location to help the cut ends to heal over without excessive drying.

Q. *There are little tomatoes on my potato plants. What should I do about them?*

A. These are the seed fruits of the potato, which form more abundantly some years under favorable weather conditions. Since the potato and tomato are closely related, the structures are somewhat similar. Potato seeds do not normally produce good-quality potatoes, and therefore should not be saved and planted.

Q. *How can I keep potatoes from sprouting?*

A. There are no longer chemicals available to the home gardener to place on potatoes to keep down sprouting in storage. Cool, moist storage temperatures of less that 40° are necessary for best storage.

Q. *Are green-skinned potatoes really dangerous?*

A. Green skins are caused by exposing potatoes to light. The green portion contains an alkaloid, solanine, that can cause illness. All green portions should be thoroughly cut off before cooking.

Q. *What causes hollow potatoes?*

A. This is due to extremely rapid growth, usually in periods of abundant moisture after drier growing conditions.

Q. *What causes deformed potatoes?*

A. This occurs when certain varieties have stopped growing because of unfavorable weather conditions, and then a period of favorable growing weather develops, and new growth develops on the potato rather than a continued enlargement of the potato.

Q. *What causes potatoes to have black spots or streaks inside them?*

A. Many factors may cause blackening. Most common are fusarium wilt, virus, and high temperature prior to harvest.

Pumpkin

Q. *Do pumpkins, squash, and ornamental gourds cross?*

A. Pumpkins, squash, and ornamental gourds, all in the genus *Cucurbita,* are divided into three species: *pepo, moschata,* and *maxima.* The *pepo* and *moschata* may be identified by their woody, ridged, five-angled fruit stem, and are generally called the true pumpkins. The *maxima* types have soft, cylindrical fruit stems, swollen at the base, and are called the true squashes. Crosses take place very readily within any one of these species, but less commonly between them. The *pepo* types cannot cross with the *maxima* types. The *moschata* is apparently more intermediate, and crosses have been made between this and other types, although these crosses are relatively rare in the garden.

The *pepo* group includes Connecticut field pumpkin, jack-o'-lantern pumpkin, sugar pumpkin, acorn squash, summer crookneck squash, zucchini squash, cocozelle squash, white bush scallop, vegetable marrow, small ornamental gourds, vegetable spaghetti, and vegetable gourd.

The *moschata* group includes butternut squash, cushaw pumpkin, and Kentucky field pumpkin.

The *maxima* group includes mainly winter squashes such as banana, buttercup, hubbard, mammoth marblehead, and Turk's turban, and large-fruited pumpkins such as Big Max.

Q. *Do pumpkins need to be "frosted" before harvest?*
A. No. Actually, freezing will reduce the storage life of the pumpkin.

Q. *How can I grow the biggest pumpkin?*
A. Remove all blossoms and fruit except one, so that all strength goes into the one fruit. Provide best possible moisture and fertility conditions.

Radish

Q. *Why do radishes become pithy and hot?*
A. Slow growth because of hot weather, drought, or poor fertility can lead to pithy, hot roots. Early planting and adequate moisture are best precautions against this.

Q. *Why do radishes form abundant tops and few edible roots?*
A. Too much nitrogen in the soil or planting too late will usually be the cause of this problem.

Rhubarb

Q. *How can rhubarb be kept from seeding? Should these flower stalks be removed?*
A. All rhubarb will eventually flower. However, poor growing conditions, drought, and hot weather stimulate flowering. Cut out the flower stalks as soon as they are noticed to help prevent weakening the plant.

Q. *Why are the "stems" of my rhubarb green rather than red?*
A. There is some varietal variation in stem color. However, lack of color development in plants that once had red color may mean too much shade.

Q. *What causes rhubarb to die out?*
A. In poorly drained areas rhubarb is subject to damage from one of the crown rot fungi. Damage may also result from stalk borers or rhubarb curculio.

Q. *Does rhubarb need to be mulched?*
A. Mulching is not essential; however, 3 to 4 inches of a strawy mulch may be put around the plants in fall after freezing weather. The mulch should not be put directly on the crowns.

Spinach

Q. *Is there a spinach that can be grown in hot weather?*
A. There is no true spinach that will grow well in hot weather. New Zealand spinach is not a true spinach, but is a good summer substitute for it.

Q. *Is it true that spinach likes lime?*

A. Spinach does not grow well in an acid soil. Therefore in most areas the addition of some lime is beneficial.

Squash

Q. *Do pumpkins and squash cross?*
A. See section above on pumpkins for details.

Q. *What causes squash blossoms to drop without setting fruit?*
A. Dropped blossoms are normally male (see section on cucumber for details). Poor pollination or certain fungus diseases may cause drop of female blossoms.

Q. *Is it true that you can eat the blossoms of squash?*
A. Yes. They may be washed, dipped in batter, and deep-fried.

Sweet Potato

Q. *Why do sweet potato plants fail to produce large roots?*
A. Late planting, cool, poorly drained soils, low fertility, or excess nitrogen.

Q. *What causes sweet potatoes to turn black on the surface?*
A. This is caused by a disease called scurf. Don't replant sweet potatoes in the same area, and don't use infected potatoes for planting stock.

Q. *Is it necessary to plant sweet potatoes on a ridge?*
A. It is not essential, but root growth in heavy soils may be better in ridge planting. As plants develop, additional soil may be thrown on the row to build up a ridge.

Tomatoes

Q. *Can tomatoes be seeded directly into the garden, or must plants be started indoors?*
A. Tomato seeds may be planted directly in the garden, but several weeks can usually be gained in earlier harvest if vigorous plants are moved into the garden after weather and soil have warmed up. Direct seeding in the garden results in much poorer germination. Therefore, expensive hybrid tomato seed is usually started indoors.

Q. *What are some low-acid tomatoes?*

A. Although acidity in tomatoes is influenced by variety, it is also greatly influenced by time of harvest and growing conditions. Taste is also not an indication of acidity, since taste is more highly influenced by sugars and other materials than by the acids present. Generally, there is not a great variation in the acidity of popular tomato varieties grown under the same conditions and harvested at the same stage of ripening. Yellow and white varieties are not less acid than many red varieties.

Q. *Will blossom-set hormone sprays increase tomato production?*

A. These materials may not increase production, but aid in setting fruit under unfavorable temperatures. They are effective when temperatures drop slightly below 60° at night and fruit is not set naturally. They are less effective at temperatures of 80°, which also prevent fruit from setting naturally. They are not a substitute for good cultural practices.

Q. *There is much publicity given to hybrid tomatoes. Are they really worth the extra money?*

A. Yes. Most hybrids have some disease resistance bred into them, as well as more vigor and improved fruit quality.

Q. *Why do tomatoes produce a lot of leaves and few or no fruit?*

A. This condition usually occurs when too much nitrogen, either in manure or in commercial fertilizer, has been applied to the plants early in the season before fruit production begins. Fertilize lightly at planting, and side-dress as nitrogen is needed after fruit set has begun.

Q. *Is it really necessary to stake tomatoes?*

A. No. However, staking can save space in the small garden, prevent ground rot on fruit, and make tomatoes easier to pick and spray.

Q. *When is the best time to start pruning tomatoes?*

A. Pruning is generally begun in June as flowering begins.

Q. *My tomatoes flower well, but the flowers drop without setting fruit. What is causing this?*

A. Temperatures too high or too low will prevent fruit from developing. Night temperatures below 60° and day temperatures above 90° will keep flowers from setting fruit.

Q. *Can I get a bigger crop from "tree tomatoes"?*

A. The plant sometimes sold as a tree tomato is not a tomato; it's a tropical plant of the same family. Plants must be at least two years old to fruit, and sometimes fruit under greenhouse conditions, but seldom under normal home conditions. A tomato variety Giant Tree has a large, stout plant and large fruit, but does not outyield popular hybrid varieties.

Q. *What causes tomatoes to crack?*
A. There is a varietal difference in the tendency to crack and type of cracking. However, cracking in susceptible varieties is more severe after periods of heavy rain and humidity.

Q. *What causes the end of the tomato to have a blackened spot?*
A. This problem, blossom-end rot, is caused by moisture fluctuation, especially low soil moisture following abundant soil moisture. Keep plants well watered and mulched to reduce this problem. Maintain optimum calcium levels in the soil, and avoid deep cultivation that may damage roots.

Q. *What causes my tomatoes to be deformed?*
A. Cold weather at time of fruit set may cause deformation. Some varieties of the "beefsteak" type are more likely to have the problem.

Q. *What are the little white bumps that develop on the stems of my tomato plants?*
A. The little bumps are root primordia. If the tomato falls down or the stem is covered, they can develop into roots. They are a natural characteristic of the plant. They become most evident in wet weather, if the normal plant roots have been damaged or partially killed, or if the plant has been exposed to certain types of herbicides.

Q. *Should Epsom salts be used around tomato plants?*
A. In good soils it is doubtful that there is any real advantage to this practice. However, Epsom salts are a source of magnesium, which is essential to good plant growth. In soils where magnesium is low, it would be better to use dolomite limestone for a source of magnesium.

Q. *Do walnut trees really cause tomato plants to wilt and die?*
A. Yes. Roots of walnut produce a toxic substance (juglone) that causes tomato plants to wilt and die.

Turnip

Q. *Why do turnips sometimes fail to produce large roots?*

A. Poor general cultural conditions or excess nitrogen at planting time may lead to poor root development. Another cause might be broadcasting seeds too thickly.

Q. *What makes turnips tough and hot?*

A. Slow growth of the roots because of low fertility or hot weather can result in poor-quality roots.

Watermelon

Q. *Can good watermelons really be grown in the home garden?*

A. Yes, provided there is adequate space. Small icebox types are easiest to grow and often most satisfactory. Watermelons need a loose, well-drained soil and ample moisture for best growth.

Q. *How do you get seed to plant from a seedless watermelon?*

A. The seedless watermelon is produced from two special parent lines which when crossed form a seed which is "trisomic." This seed, although able to grow into a plant, is not capable of producing fruits that contain seeds. Seeds are harder to germinate than those of most watermelons, and therefore they are often started indoors in peat pots at warm temperatures.

General Questions

Q. *Why did the seeds I planted in the garden (snap beans, lima beans, corn, melons, etc.) germinate poorly?*

A. Much poor germination is a result of unfavorable weather conditions at planting time. These crops like warm weather, and soil should be well warmed before planting them. Planting in cold soil reduces germination, and is especially harmful to lima beans and melons. Too much drainage also reduces germination. Seedling diseases are especially destructive under excessively moist conditions.

Seeds sown in summer for a fall crop (such as turnip and lettuce) may suffer from excessive heat and drying. When planting seeds of cool-season crops at that time, keep the soil surface moist at all times for best germination. Some shading during the germination period is also beneficial.

Other causes of poor germination include planting too deeply, and crusting of the soil surface after heavy rains or careless watering. Mechanical injury to the seeds from insects, rodents, or soil diseases may also cause poor germination.

Seed which is old or improperly stored will also germinate poorly or not at all.

Whenever seeds germinate poorly, it is best to dig up and replant promptly, rather than to try to fill spaces with another seeding.

Q. *Should I plant the vegetable seeds I had left over from planting last season's garden?*

A. Generally, if the seeds have been stored well, many of them will germinate fairly well the second year. Expect reduced germination, however, so plant slightly thicker than suggested. If good germination results, then thin seedlings appropriately. Many garden seeds may be kept for two years or even longer in a cool, dry location. Place in a tight jar or can to keep them dry. Seeds that lose germination ability most rapidly include sweet corn, okra, onion, parsley, parsnip, and salsify.

Q. *Can I grow my own vegetable seeds?*

A. Most vegetable seeds purchased for the garden are grown under ideal conditions from selected parentage, or from special crosses known as hybrids. Seeds grown, or saved from the home garden, are not true to type in many cases, and the resulting plants vary in type of growth and quality of crop produced.

Generally, the cost of seeds is a relatively small part of the total cost of gardening, compared to fertilizers, labor, insect control, etc. Therefore, clean, disease-free seeds of selected varieties are one of the best investments for a successful garden.

Q. *Do some vegetables produce more if planted side by side?*

A. Interplanting to conserve space and following an early crop with a later crop (called "succession" planting) can be useful practices.

Q. *How can I tell if my garden needs fertilizer before planting?*

A. A soil test is the best tool available, especially for evaluating a new garden, or if there has been no test for several years. In an established garden, poor growth the previous season is a good indication that a soil test might be needed to evaluate soil fertility and pH.

Q. *How can I tell if my garden needs fertilizer during the growing season?*

A. Plant growth is the best indication of fertility needs. If plants tend to be pale green or stunted or to lose lower leaves, additional fertilization, particularly nitrogen, may be necessary. Evaluate these poor growing conditions carefully, because diseases may also cause similar problems.

Q. *What is the best kind of manure for the garden?*

A. Generally, cattle, horse, or swine manures containing straw are best. Poultry and sheep manure have higher levels of nitrogen and may supply more nitrogen than needed early in the season. Whatever manure is used, don't apply fresh manure to the garden before planting. It is preferable to compost the manure for about a year before using. It may also be plowed under in late summer for planting a garden the following spring.

Q. *Can I apply too much lime to the garden?*

A. Yes. Most vegetables grow best in soils slightly acid. Excess liming can make the soil too alkaline, which reduces the availability of some nutrients and reduces plant growth.

Q. *Are wood ashes harmful to the garden?*

A. No. Wood ashes supply potassium as well as some other nutrients to the soil. They also make the soil more alkaline. Have soil tested every five years to determine pH. Don't use wood ashes when pH reading is above 7.0.

Q. *Are vegetables grown with organic plant foods more nutritious than those grown with commercial plant foods?*

A. Tests have shown that vegetables grown under the same environmental conditions had the same nutrient qualities regardless of the type of fertilization used.

Q. *Can sewage sludge be applied directly to the vegetable garden?*

A. Sometimes. There are two types of sewage sludge: digested sludge and dried activated sludge. The dried activated sludge has been heat-treated and is safe for use on gardens. This is available in bagged form under several different trade names.

Digested sludge is often available from local treatment plants. It has not been heat-treated, and should not be used directly on the garden. It is of relatively low quality as a fertilizer. It should be composted for a year or more for thorough heating before using. There is much variability in sewage sludge, and some contains an abundance of metal ions. The effect of these on soil or crops over a long term has not been established.

Q. *How much cattle or barnyard manure can be used on the garden?*

A. It is generally safe to use composted animal manures at a rate of 50 to 100 pounds per 100 square feet of garden area.

Q. *Is there too much acid in oak leaves for them to be used on or disposed of in the garden?*

A. No. However, oak leaves do have an acid reaction while they are being composted (which should be done before adding them to the garden). Any acidity is easily controlled by adding lime. The real benefit to the soil from the oak leaves is the addition of organic matter.

Q. *Is it safe to add sawdust (shavings and other wood products) to the garden?*

A. Yes. However it is better to have these products composted for a year before addition. Wood products, especially when fresh, tie up nitrogen, so plants may become starved. When wood products are added, additional nitrogen is necessary. A nitrogen fertilizer such as ammonium nitrate may be added at about ¾ cup per bushel of sawdust, or 27 pounds per 1,000 square feet of area with a layer of sawdust 1 inch deep added. Sawdust is excellent for improving the structure of the soil.

Q. *Is it okay to water my garden at night? I hear that watering during the heat of the day will scald the leaves.*

A. Watering during the day does not scald the leaves, but watering in the late evening or at night promotes the development of some diseases. For most efficient use of water, it is best to water the garden in the early morning or in late afternoon, but early enough that the leaves will be dried thoroughly before dark.

Q. *Can I water my tomatoes, trees, melons, etc. by burying a tile (46-ounce juice can, syrup jug, plastic jug, etc.) with a hole in the bottom, and watering in it?*

A. There is nothing wrong with this method of watering. It makes efficient use of water and keeps the foliage dry. For large plantings, however, a large quantity of containers is needed, and installation of them can be a large project.

14

Gardener's Jargon
COMMONLY USED GARDENING WORDS AND PHRASES

Every area of activity has its special words and meanings, and home gardening is no exception. Elizabeth Naegele and J. Lee Taylor of Michigan State University, Department of Horticulture, have captured a collection of the most commonly used words and phrases you are likely to come across in your daily garden practices.

A

ammonium nitrate a high-nitrogen fertilizer (33-0-0).
analysis (of a fertilizer) tells the amount of nitrogen, phosphorus, and potassium in a fertilizer. A fertilizer such as 5-20-20 has 5 percent nitrogen, 20 percent phosphorus (in the form of phosphoric acid), and 20 percent potassium (in the form of potash).

B

biennial a plant that takes two years to complete its life cycle, such as beets, Brussels sprouts, cabbage, and carrots. Biennials sprout from seed and produce leaves the first year. The roots live over the winter and the next year send up shoots, flower, and seed stalks and then die at the end of the second year.

black plastic a dark plastic material, used for mulching, which does not allow light to penetrate it. It usually comes in rolls 2 to 4 feet wide, 1½ mils (.0015 inch) thick.

blanch to take the color out or make white by excluding the light. For example, tying leaves over cauliflower heads blanches them (prevents them from turning green).

blossom-end rot a condition in which the blossom end of fruits or vegetables, such as tomatoes, peppers, and squash, turns black and rots. It is caused by not enough calcium being taken up by plant roots (because of a lack of moisture in the soil). It occurs most often on the first fruits produced by a plant.

booster fertilizer a high-nitrogen fertilizer recommended for most vegetables. It is applied about midseason, usually by side-dressing. Examples are urea (46-0-0) and ammonium nitrate (33-0-0).

burn to damage a plant by applying too much fertilizer or getting it on the leaves. It injures roots, causes browning and wilting of leaves, and may kill the plant.

bush variety a short, compact plant variety, like bush beans or bush squash, that has bushlike growth rather than vining growth.

C

cages used for supporting vining plants, such as tomatoes or cucumbers. They are usually made of concrete reinforcement wire or similar fencing.

catalogs, seed booklets put out by seed companies in which seeds, plants, and garden accessories are sold through the mail. Catalogs have more plant varieties and information than are normally available at seed racks. They are free and available upon request from seed companies beginning in December. Addresses of companies can be found in farm and garden magazines.

clay a type of soil made up of very fine particles. It is very hard, has little air space, and drains poorly. Clay soils are "heavy" soils.

cloves the bulblike sections that make up a bulb, as in garlic.

compost a mixture of many different materials, such as rotten leaves, manure, lime, etc., mixed together and decomposed. It is mixed with garden soil, especially heavy soil, to loosen it up.

cool-season crop a plant that grows best in cool weather (either in spring or fall), such as cabbage and peas. Most cool-season plants can withstand frost. For a spring crop, they are planted when there is still danger of frost. For a fall crop, they are planted in July or late June.

crowns the roots and dormant buds of one-year-old and other perennial plants, such as rhubarb and asparagus.

cultivate to loosen or break up the soil around growing plants in order to kill weeds and let air and water enter the soil more easily.

cultivator a small powered or push-type tiller used to loosen the soil.

cutworm a caterpillar that cuts off the stem of transplants, such as cabbage and tomatoes, at ground level during the night. Placing paper collars around the base of plant stems will prevent cutworm damage. Insecticides may also be used.

D

damping-off a disease of seedlings started indoors, caused by certain fungi that enter a plant near ground level, producing rot. The fungi are always present in the soil. To prevent the disease, sterilize soil and containers before planting seeds in them.

disease-resistant refers to plant varieties that have been bred to withstand attack from certain diseases. Initials of diseases varieties are resistant to are sometimes printed next to the variety name. For example, the tomato variety Supersonic has "(V.F.)" printed next to it, which means it is resistant to verticillium and fusarium wilts.

drainage the ability of a soil to allow water to pass through. Soils such as sand or sandy loams have good drainage.

dwarf variety a plant variety that is shorter than standard varieties of the same species.

E

ear the fruiting spike of sweet corn that includes the kernels, cob, and husks.

elements the basic particles that compose matter. Of the more than a hundred chemical elements, sixteen are known to be essential for plant growth. These include the thirteen mineral elements as well as carbon, oxygen, and hydrogen.
eye the bud of a potato tuber.

F

fall crop vegetables planted from seed during the summer to be harvested in the fall; they usually grow best in cool weather, such as spinach, cauliflower, broccoli, cabbage, Brussels sprouts, etc.
fertilizer a substance that provides nutrients for plant growth. Fertilizers can be organic (rotted animal wastes, plant materials, etc.) or inorganic (processed substances, such as 5-20-20 fertilizer).
flower stalks long stems on which flowers and seeds form; the same as seed stalks. Certain vegetables, such as lettuce and spinach, will form seed stalks if grown in very hot weather. Biennials, such as carrots and parsley, form seed stalks the second year of their growth if they survive over winter.
foliage the mass of plant leaves.
food the nutrients needed for growth, provided to plants by fertilizer. Primary ones are nitrogen, phosphorus, and potassium.
fruit the seed-bearing product of a plant. Many vegetables are actually fruits (for example, tomatoes, peppers, cucumbers and squash).
fungicide a chemical such as captan or maneb used to prevent or control fungus diseases on plants, such as powdery mildew, tomato blight, and fusarium wilt.
furrow a trench in the earth made by a plow or hoe.

G

germinate to begin to grow or sprout.
growing point an area on a plant where new growth is starting. The growing point can be the top bud or buds on the stems on some plants; it can also be at ground level, as in grasses.

growth light a light used to supplement or substitute for sunlight when growing houseplants or transplants indoors. They are generally regular fluorescent bulbs or special bulbs. All fit in regular fluorescent fixtures.

grubs thick, wormlike insects in the immature stage; they later become adult beetles, flies, etc. They eat the roots of many garden plants and are especially numerous in soil that has been in grass.

H

harden off to get plants grown indoors gradually accustomed to the more severe conditions outside (sun, wind, and cooler temperature). This is done by watering less and placing them outdoors on warm spring days and bringing them in at night. Transplants grown indoors should be hardened off before planting in the garden.

harvest to pick or gather a crop.

head the top part of a plant, especially when the leaves are tightly folded together in a clump, as in a head of lettuce or cabbage.

herbicide a chemical that kills or controls weeds.

hill a group of seeds sown together (not a mound of soil). Some vegetables, such as squash, are usually planted in hills.

hot caps or hot tents small covers, placed over plants, that let in light but protect the plants from frost and wind after transplanting.

husk the outer leaflike cover enclosing an ear of corn.

hybrid a crossbred plant or animal. A hybrid is the offspring of a male of one species, variety, etc. and a female of another. Hybrid plants are usually more vigorous than either of the parents. Seeds of hybrid plants, however, should not be saved, because they will not produce the same hybrid plant (will not be true to type).

I

insecticide a chemical such as malathion that kills or controls insects.

irrigation watering with overhead sprinklers, plastic hoses, flooding, etc. to supply growing crops with moisture.

K

kernels seeds (really one-seeded fruits) of sweet corn that form on the cob.

K symbol for potassium.

L

loam a good garden soil consisting of a loose mixture of clay, sand, and organic matter.

M

mature the stage at which a vegetable is full-grown. Note: maturity and ripeness do not mean the same thing. Some vegetables are ready to eat (ripe) before they are fully mature, such as summer squash, sweet corn, and cucumbers.

minerals any chemical element or combination of elements occuring naturally in soil, rocks, etc., such as lime. Of the sixteen elements needed by plants, thirteen are derived from minerals and are called mineral elements. The other three, carbon, oxygen, and hydrogen, are obtained from water and carbon dioxide.

mulch any substance such as straw, leaves, etc., spread on the ground to protect the roots of plants from heat, cold, or drought, to keep fruit clean, to prevent weeds from growing, and to conserve moisture.

N

N symbol for nitrogen.

nitrogen one of the major nutrients needed by plants for growth. Nitrogen promotes leafy growth and dark green color. In a 50-20-20 fertilizer, the first number stands for the percentage of nitrogen. Thus in a 100-pound bag of 5-20-20 fertilizer, there would be 5 pounds of nitrogen. Signs of nitrogen deficiency are pale yellow leaves, especially in the lower portions, and slow, stunted growth.

nutrients the mineral elements necessary for plant growth: nitrogen, phosphorus, potassium, calcium, magnesium, iron, copper, zinc, molybdenum, sulfur, manganese, cobalt, and boron. Plants take these nutrients from the soil. Fertilizers replace them.

O

organic gardening gardening without man-made materials such as chemical fertilizers, pesticides, etc. and using only natural materials for fertilizers or pesticides.

organic matter or material material derived from living organisms. Examples are leaves, grass clippings, rotted plants, and animal wastes. Adding organic matter to soil loosens it and improves drainage as well as adds nutrients.

P

P symbol for phosphorus

peat moss decomposed plant material (especially some bog mosses) added to a soil mix to loosen it up and/or to help it retain moisture.

perennial a plant that continues to live from year to year, such as asparagus and rhubarb. A perennial's roots live over winter and send up shoots, flowers, and fruit during each growing season.

perlite a mineral added to soil mixes to improve drainage by loosening up the soil.

pesticide a substance used to kill or control bacteria, fungi, insects, rodents, weeds, etc. Pesticides include fungicides, insecticides, and herbicides.

phosphorus one of the three major nutrients required by plants for growth. It promotes development of flowers and fruit, as well as root growth. It is the middle number on fertilizer labels; for example, 5-20-20. Signs of phosphorus deficiency are reddish-purple color on stems and veins of leaves, especially on underside, very thin stems, and delayed maturity of fruits.

pinch to remove the growing point of plants. Pinching out the growing point will make most plants send out side shoots and become bushier.

plow to loosen and turn the soil for planting. A plow cuts, lifts, and turns over the soil.

pole a tall, thin stick used to support tall climbing plants.

The word is used to describe vegetable varieties that are tall and climbing, such as pole beans.

pollinate to transfer pollen from the male to the female parts of a flower. Pollen can be carried by wind, insects, or birds to another plant (cross-pollination), or a plant can pollinate itself (self-pollination).

potash potassium carbonate, especially from wood ashes. This form of potassium is often applied as fertilizer to plants.

potassium one of the three major nutrients required by plants. It is the third number on fertilizer labels; for example, 5-20-20. Potassium promotes root growth. Signs of potassium deficiency are curling, browning, and drying of leaf edges, brown spots throughout the leaf, especially on lower parts of the plant, slow growth, and uneven ripening of fruit.

prune to cut off or trim unwanted branches on plants.

R

recommended varieties plant varieties (especially vegetables) considered to be best adapted for growth in a particular climate. These are commonly determined by the agricultural college or university in each state.

ripe ready for picking or eating.

root ball a plant's roots and the soil around them.

rotation the practice of changing the location of vegetable crops in a garden each year. Plants attacked by the same pests should be rotated to avoid diseases or insects that live in the soil. Also, certain vegetables are heavy feeders of certain soil nutrients and would deplete the soil's nutrient supply if they were planted in the same place every year. A garden plan is helpful in remembering where vegetables were planted from one year to another.

rototilling using a motor-driven rotary tiller (Rototiller is one brand name) to churn and loosen the soil to prepare it for planting. It is often used in small gardens instead of a plow.

S

go to seed to form seed stalks. Lettuce does this in hot weather. This reduces yield, since lettuce will not form leaves after going to seed. Biennials such as carrots and onions that survive a winter go to seed the second year.

seed potatoes or seed pieces small potatoes ready to plant or large ones that may be cut up into smaller portions to plant. Seed potatoes are used for growing new potatoes. Therefore, each piece must contain one or more eyes. Certified seed potatoes are free of disease and will sprout easily.

seed stalks stalks on which flowers and then seeds form. When vegetables send up a seed stalk they are going to seed.

seedling a small plant after it has sprouted from seed.

sets small onions grown from seed the previous year. When planted, they will mature faster than onions grown from seeds.

shoot new growth of a plant in the form of a stem and its leaves.

side-dress to apply a fertilizer along rows or around plants (especially nitrogen around July 4, called a booster fertilizer). Side-dressing is placed no closer than 4 inches from plants and should be worked into the soil.

silks those portions of the female flowers on an ear of sweet corn that run from the end of the ear to the kernels; the hairy or silky strands difficult to remove from between the kernels.

sod top layer of soil filled with the roots of grass, weeds, etc. Sod also contains many organisms, such as grubs, cutworms, and earthworms. It should be plowed a full year before planting a garden to reduce the number of grubs and cutworms.

sow to plant seeds.

spear a young shoot of asparagus.

spindly tall and slender, or weak. Spindly growth is usually caused by growing plants in weak light and/or at warm temperatures. Spindly plants are poor transplants.

stake to place stakes (usually wooden) near vining plants, particularly tomatoes, and tie the stems to the stakes at various places for support.

starter solution a fertilizer solution high in phosphorus applied to the soil around transplants when they are placed in the garden. It encourages root growth. A typical starter solution might be 10-55-10.

sterilize to kill most disease organisms in soil or containers before planting seeds or plants in them. This is done by baking soil, treating it with a chemical, or soaking containers in a cleaning solution.

successive planting planting seeds at intervals of a few weeks so that the harvest period is extended, rather than planting all at once and having to harvest all at once.

sucker a shoot from the roots or lower part of the stem of a plant such as corn. These are usually not removed.

T

tassels the male flowers of a corn plant. They produce pollen grains. The time tassels appear on the plant is called tasseling.

thin to reduce the number of plants in a row by removing the extras. Thinnings may be transplanted or eaten if large enough.

till to plow or work the soil; to cultivate.

transplants young plants started from seed and grown indoors. They are then planted in the garden. Tomatoes and peppers are usually started from transplants.

treated seed seed that has been coated with a fungicide to prevent disease from killing it when planted. Seeds planted early in cool, wet soils especially need treating with a fungicide. Sometimes seeds may also be treated with an insecticide.

tuber a short, fleshy, usually underground stem or shoot with buds (or eyes), such as a potato. Pieces of potatoes having one or more eyes can be planted to grow new potato plants.

tuberous root a thick, fleshy root like a tuber but having buds present only at the crown (the stem end), such as a sweet potato. The whole sweet potato must be planted to grow a new plant.

U

urea a high-nitrogen fertilizer (46–0–0).

V

variety a plant that has slightly different characteristics from other members of its species. Tomato varieties have different color, taste, shape, texture, days to maturity, disease resistance, etc.

vegetable plants or plant parts used for food. Tomatoes, cucumbers, peppers, etc., are called vegetables, though they are really fruits.

vermiculite a mineral used in soil mixes to loosen soil. It is also used as a medium in which seedlings are started.

vining a term describing vegetable varieties that are climbing plants, such as pole beans or peas. They are usually supported by a trellis, stake, or cage.

W

warm-season crop a vegetable that grows best in warm weather and is injured by frost, such as bush beans, melons, and tomatoes. Most warm-season crops cannot be planted until May 20 to June 1 in southern lower Michigan, for example.

15

Gardening State by State
HELPFUL PUBLICATIONS

Performance and Results
Depend on Quality Information

At the beginning of this book I suggest that if you have a question about vegetable gardening or a growing problem you contact your Cooperative Extension Service; you can either write or phone your local agent.

The Cooperative Extension Service, in conjunction with the United States Agriculture Department and state universities, designs, writes, consults, and demonstrates. It publishes hundreds of booklets and brochures on how to sew, cook, build, repair, preserve, garden, farm, improve your health, and do just about anything you want to do. Many of them are free; others may cost a fraction of their cost to print.

Under each of the states I have listed any helpful booklets on home vegetable gardening available to you. I have not put in any costs, because costs may change.

If you would like a list of all the helpful information from your Cooperative Extension Service, write and request a full directory of publications and prices. You will be amazed and pleased.

I am a gardener, not a meteorologist, but I could not write a garden book without some advice about weather; after all, the elements are our partners in growing. There are certainly times when I am convinced that it is a one-sided effort and Jupiter Pluvius, the mythical weather (rain) god, doesn't do his fair share. On the following pages I have given you a guide to what you might expect in the way of help from the weather. The figures are from the United States Weather Service and are approximates for the average good growing season in each state. The key cities indicate the different longitudes, latitudes, and altitudes that affect climate. Look to see where your garden patch sets and garden accordingly.

When in doubt, always work on the Murphy's law assumption: If the weather is going to be lousy, it will be directly over your garden. So be safe, not sorry. Use the dates with the shortest growing season.

In order to do what I set out to do in the beginning of this book, which is to appease your impatience and make only the information you really need available to you in a brief and easy-to-understand form, I've tried to capsulize state weather figures.

CODE	MEANING
A	**Number of growing days**
B	**Last frost of spring**
C	**First frost of fall**
D	**Average inches of rain during growing period**
E	**Best growing months**
F	**Number of rainy growing days**

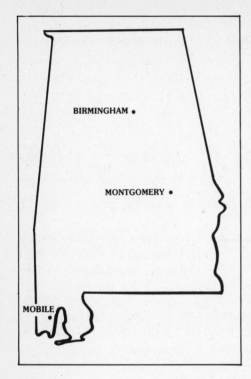

Key Cities

CODE	BIRMINGHAM	MONTGOMERY	MOBILE
A	241	279	298
B	3/19	2/27	2/17
C	11/14	12/3	12/12
D	33"	38"	58"
E	3/15–11/15	3/1–12/1	2/15–12/15
F	75	77	90

The following publications are available to the home vegetable gardener from:

U.S. Cooperative Extension Service
Auburn University
Auburn, AL 36849

ANR-61	Vegetable Garden Handbook
ANR-63	Plant Guide Home Garden, Alabama
ANR-322	Weed Control
HE-35	Gardening Is Fun
HE-209	Grow Your Own Tomatoes
HE-249	Grow Your Own Greens
HE-250	Grow Your Own Collards
HE-251	Grow Your Own Southern Peas
HE-252	Grow Your Own Okra
HE-256	Grow Your Own Beans
HE-257	Grow Your Own Squash
HE-267	Grow Your Own Corn
HE-268	Grow Your Own Lima Beans

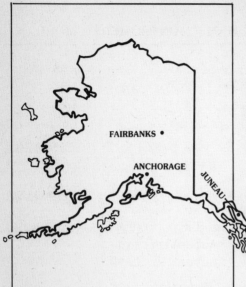

Key Cities

CODE	ANCHORAGE	FAIRBANKS	JUNEAU
A	124	100	181
B	5/15	5/21	4/22
C	9/16	8/30	10/21
D	8″	4″	15″
E	5/17–9/14	5/23–8/28	4/24–10/19
F	49	51	92

The following publications are available for the vegetable gardener from:

Cooperative Extension Service
U.S. Department of Agriculture
University of Alaska
Fairbanks, AK 99701

P-30	Vegetables and Fruits for the Interior
P-31	Vegetables and Fruits for the South Central
P-32	Seed Starting and Transplanting
P-33	Soil for Garden and Greenhouse
P-134	16 Steps to Garden in Alaska
P-136	Mini-Garden with Vegetables
P-137	Insect Control
P-231	Vegetables and Fruits for Southeastern Alaska
P-233	Weed Control, Vegetable Garden
P-237	Gardening in Southeastern Alaska
P-1-022	Compost Heap in Alaska

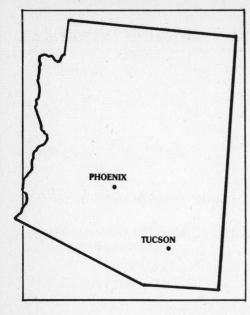

Key Cities

CODE	TUCSON	PHOENIX
A	245	304
B	3/19	2/5
C	11/19	12/6
D	11"	7"
E	3/15–11/15	2/7–12/7
F	38	24

The following publications are available for the home vegetable gardener from:

U.S. Cooperative Extension Service
University of Arizona
College of Agriculture
Tucson, AZ 85721

095	Ten Steps to Successful Vegetable Gardening
0337	Vegetable Varieties for Arizona
130	Arizona Home Gardening
MC-15	Soil Digest for Arizona
MC-2	Soil for Vegetable Gardens
MC-10	Vegetable Gardening in Salty Soil
MC-4	Vegetables, Fruits and Nuts for South Arizona
MC-47	Vegetable Varieties for Arizona

Key Cities

CODE	TEXARKANA	FORT SMITH	LITTLE ROCK
A	233	234	241
B	3/21	3/21	3/17
C	11/19	11/10	11/13
D	28"	29"	31"
E	3/20–11/7	3/20–11/7	3/15–11/10
F	64	60	66

The following publications are available to the home vegetable gardener from:

Cooperative Extension Service
U.S. Department of Agriculture
P.O. Box 391
Little Rock, AR 72203

311 Vegetable Gardens in Arkansas
291 Vegetable Gardens—Insect Controls
148 Growing Tomatoes in Arkansas
217 Spraying and Dusting Tomatoes
495 Vegetables for Arkansas

Key Cities

CODE	SANTA ROSA	FRESNO	EUREKA
A	207	250	253
B	4/10	3/14	3/10
C	11/3	11/19	11/18
D	30"	10"	40"
E	4/12–11/1	3/16–11/17	3/12–11/16
F	—	22	71

CODE	RIVERSIDE	MARYSVILLE	RED BLUFF
A	265	273	274
B	3/6	2/21	3/6
C	11/26	11/21	12/5
D	10"	21"	22"
E	3/8–11/24	2/24–11/20	3/7–12/3
F	—	—	—

CODE	BAKERSFIELD	SAN JOSE	SACRAMENTO
A	277	299	307
B	2/21	2/10	2/6
C	11/25	1/6	12/10
D	6"	14"	17"
E	2/21–11/21	2/12–1/8	2/7–12/8
F	—	—	—

CODE	PASADENA	SANTA BARBARA	PALM SPRINGS
A	313	331	334
B	2/3	1/22	1/8
C	12/13	12/19	12/18
D	19"	17"	31"
E	2/5–12/15	1/21–12/17	1/18–12/16
F	—	—	—

(Continued on page 224)

CODE	SAN FRANCISCO	LOS ANGELES	SAN DIEGO
A	356	359	365
B	1/7	1/3	—
C	12/29	12/28	—
D	21″	14″	9″
E	1/7–	1/3–	1/2–
F	66	33	42

For publications available to the home vegetable gardener write:

——————————— U.S. Cooperative Extension Service
University of California
2200 University Avenue
Berkeley, CA 94720

Colorado

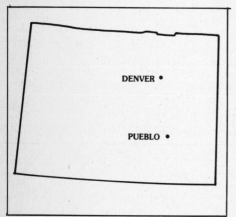

Key Cities

CODE	DENVER	PUEBLO
A	171	174
B	4/26	4/23
C	10/14	10/14
D	15	12
E	4/28–10/12	4/25–10/12
F	42	—

For publications available to the home vegetable gardener write:

——————————— U.S. Cooperative Extension Service
Colorado State University
Fort Collins, CO 80521

Connecticut

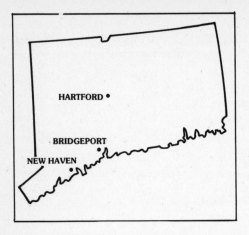

Key Cities

CODE	BRIDGEPORT	HARTFORD	NEW HAVEN
A	174	180	195
B	4/26	4/22	4/15
C	10/16	10/19	10/27
D	18"	21"	21"
E	4/28–10/14	4/24–10/17	4/17–10/25
F	49	59	54

For publications available to the home vegetable gardener write:

U.S. Cooperative Extension Service
University of Connecticut
Storrs, CT 06268

Delaware

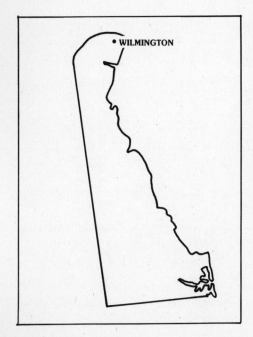

Key Cities

CODE	WILMINGTON
A	191
B	4/18
C	10/26
D	23"
E	4/20–10/24
F	56

For publications available to the home vegetable gardener write:

U.S. Cooperative Extension Service
University of Delaware
Newark, DE 19711

Florida

Key Cities

CODE	JACKSONVILLE	TAMPA	MIAMI
A	313	349	365
B	2/16	1/10	—
C	12/16	12/26	—
D	48″	51″	60″
E	2/18–12/14	1/12–12/24	—
F	103	105	127

For publications available to the home vegetable gardener write:

U.S. Cooperative Extension Service
University of Florida
Gainesville, FL 32611

Georgia

Key Cities

CODE	ATLANTA	AUGUSTA	SAVANNAH
A	242	249	275
B	3/21	3/14	2/27
C	11/18	11/1	11/29
D	29″	34″	41″
E	3/23–11/16	3/16–10/30	2/29–11/27
F	72	74	89

The following publications are available to the home vegetable gardener from:

U.S. Cooperative Extension Service
University of Georgia
Athens, GA 30601

171 Home Vegetable Gardening
173 Vegetables for Georgia Gardens
178 Small Gardens for Georgia

Hawaii

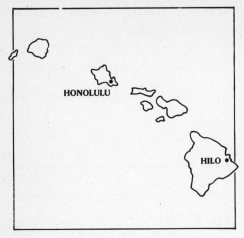

Key Cities

CODE	HILO	HONOLULU
A	365	365
B	—	—
C	—	—
D	119″	25″
E	—	—
F	282	101

The following publications are available to the home vegetable gardener from:

U.S. Cooperative Extension Service
University of Hawaii
Honolulu, HI 96822

489   Vegetable Growing in Containers
WHITE SHEETS
29   Home Garden Series, Sight Selection
30   Home Garden Series, Plan Your Garden
2   Home Garden Series, Chicken Manure
3   Home Garden Series, Soils
4   Home Garden Series, Fertilizers
5   Home Garden Series, Use of Fertilizers
6   Home Garden Series, Compost
7   Home Garden Series, Mulch
GREEN SHEETS
1   Home Garden Series, Carrots
2   Home Garden Series, Lettuce
3   Home Garden Series, Bell Pepper
4   Home Garden Series, Sweet Corn
5   Home Garden Series, Tomatoes
6   Home Garden Series, Cauliflower
8   Home Garden Series, Beans
9   Home Garden Series, Irish Potatoes
10   Home Garden Series, Mustard Cabbage
11   Home Garden Series, Edible Pod Pea
12   Home Garden Series, Sweet Potato

(Continued on page 228)

13	Home Garden Series, Egg Plant
14	Home Garden Series, Vegetable Soy Bean
15	Home Garden Series, Summer Squash
16	Home Garden Series, Onions
17	Home Garden Series, Cucumbers

Idaho

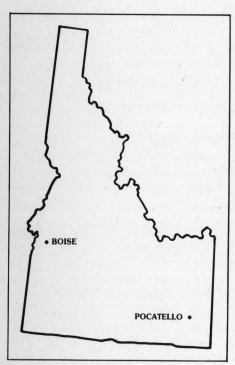

Key Cities

CODE	POCATELLO	BOISE
A	161	177
B	4/28	4/23
C	10/6	10/17
D	23"	11"
E	4/30–10/4	4/25–10/15
F	—	23

For publications available to the home vegetable gardener write:

U.S. Cooperative Extension Service
University of Idaho
Morrill Hall
Moscow, ID 83843

Illinois

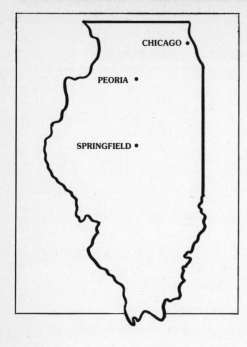

Key Cities

CODE	PEORIA	SPRINGFIELD	CHICAGO
A	181	186	192
B	4/22	4/20	4/19
C	10/20	10/23	10/28
D	21"	21"	21"
E	4/24–10/18	4/22–10/21	4/21–10/26
F	55	59	61

The following publications are available to the home vegetable gardener from:

Cooperative Extension Service
U.S. Department of Agriculture
University of Illinois
Urbana, IL 61801

C-900	Insect Control in Vegetable Gardens
C-1051	Weed Control in Vegetable Gardens
C-1150	Vegetable Gardening in Illinois
C-1155	Mini Vegetable Gardens
SP-56	Vegetable Garden Schedule

Indiana

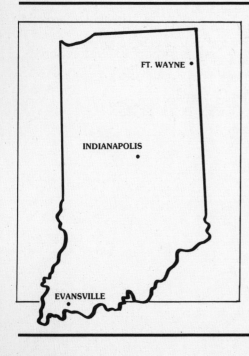

Key Cities

CODE	FT. WAYNE	INDIANAPOLIS	EVANSVILLE
A	179	193	216
B	4/24	4/17	4/2
C	10/20	10/27	11/4
D	20"	22"	24"
E	4/26–10/18	4/19–10/25	4/4–11/2
F	59	60	73

For publications available to the home vegetable gardener write:

U.S. Cooperative Extension Service
Purdue University
Lafayette, IN 47907

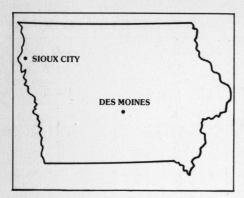

Key Cities

CODE	SIOUX CITY	DES MOINES
A	169	175
B	4/27	4/24
C	10/13	10/16
D	18"	20"
E	4/29–10/10	4/26–10/14
F	52	55

The following publications are available to the home vegetable gardener from:

U.S. Cooperative Extension Service
Iowa State University
Ames, IA 50011

PM-463-9	Common Vegetable Insects
PM-870	Container and Patio Vegetable Gardens
PM-820	Garden Soil
PM-608	How to Plant Tomatoes
PM-203	Insects and Disease Control
PM-819	Home Vegetable Garden
PM-238	Six Steps to a Good Garden
PM-666	Weed Control in Vegetable Gardens
PM-814	Where to Put Your Garden
PM-534	Planting and Harvesting Vegetables
PM-720	Small Plot Gardening
PM-874	Starting Garden Plants Indoors

Kansas

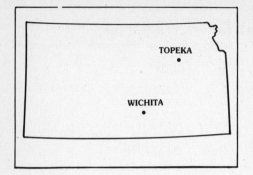

Key Cities

CODE	TOPEKA	WICHITA
A	200	210
B	4/9	4/5
C	10/26	11/1
D	26"	24"
E	4/11–10/24	4/7–10/30
F	57	56

The following publications are available to the home vegetable gardener from:

U.S. Cooperative Extension Service
Kansas State University
Manhattan, KS 66506

XC-436	Kansas Garden Guide
XC-595	Pest Controls in Vegetable Gardening
XL-41	Vegetables for Kansas
XMF-312	Tomatoes
XMF-315	Vegetable Planting Guide
XMF-345	Compost
XMF-661	Harvest and Storage of Vegetables and Fruits
XAF-83	Weed Control in Vegetable Gardening

Kentucky

Key Cities

CODE	LEXINGTON	LOUISVILLE
A	198	220
B	4/13	4/1
C	10/28	11/7
D	24"	25"
E	4/16–10/26	4/3–11/5
F	66	68

For publications available to the home vegetable gardener write:

U.S. Cooperative Extension Service
University of Kentucky
Lexington, KY 40506

Louisiana

Key Cities

CODE	SHREVEPORT	NEW ORLEANS
A	262	292
B	3/8	2/20
C	11/15	12/9
D	29"	47"
E	3/10–11/13	2/22–12/7
F	67	93

For publications available to the home vegetable gardener write:

U.S. Cooperative Extension Service
Louisiana State University
Baton Rouge, LA 70803

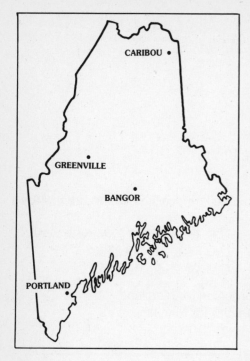

Key Cities

CODE	GREENVILLE	CARIBOU
A	116	125
B	5/27	5/19
C	9/20	9/21
D	14"	15"
E	5/29–9/18	5/21–9/18
F	43	54

Key Cities

CODE	BANGOR	PORTLAND
A	156	169
B	5/1	4/29
C	10/4	10/15
D	17"	16"
E	5/3–10/2	4/31–10/13
F	47	54

The following publications are available to the home vegetable gardener from:

U.S. Cooperative Extension Service
University of Maine
Orono, ME 04473

101 Insect and Disease Control in Your Vegetable Garden
87 Vegetables for Maine
567 Natural Gardening
544 Home Vegetable Gardening

Maryland

Key Cities

CODE	BALTIMORE
A	238
B	3/28
C	11/19
D	26″
E	3/30–11/17
F	68

The following publications are available to the home vegetable gardener from:

U.S. Cooperative Extension Service
University of Maryland
College Park, MD 20742

200	Vegetable Gardening for Maryland
15	Vegetable Varieties for Maryland

Massachusetts

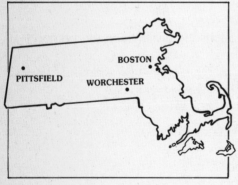

Key Cities

CODE	PITTSFIELD	WORCHESTER	BOSTON
A	138	148	217
B	5/12	5/7	4/5
C	9/27	10/2	11/8
D	19″	18″	23″
E	5/14–9/25	5/9–9/30	4/7–11/6
F	49	50	73

The following publications are available to the home vegetable gardener from:

U.S. Cooperative Extension Service
University of Massachusetts
Amherst, MA 01002

(Continued on page 235)

C-138R Natural Fertilizer for Home Gardens
C-142   Fewer Pesticides for Home Gardens
AB-380 Insects and Diseases—Home Gardens
AB-409 Growing Your Own Vegetables
NE-208 Growing Herbs in the Home Garden

Michigan

Key Cities

CODE	MARQUETTE	DETROIT	GRAND RAPIDS
A	159	182	190
B	5/13	4/21	4/23
C	10/19	10/20	10/30
D	16"	18"	16"
E	5/15–10/17	4/23–10/18	4/25–10/28
F	60	58	52

The following publications are available to the home vegetable gardener from:

Cooperative Extension Service
Michigan State University
East Lansing, MI 48823

EO-760A   Vegetable Variety for Michigan
EO-824-1   Vegetable Gardening, Plan Ahead
EO-824-2   Vegetable Gardening, Start with Soil
EO-824-3   Vegetable Gardening, Planting
EO-824-4   Vegetable Gardening, Keep 'em Growing
EO-824-5   Vegetable Gardening, Herbs
EO-824-6   Vegetable Gardening, Green Beans
EO-824-7   Vegetable Gardening, Root Crops
EO-824-8   Vegetable Gardening, Greens
EO-824-9   Vegetable Gardening, Melons, Cukes, Squash and Pumpkins
EO-824-10   Vegetable Gardening, Salad Stuff
EO-824-11   Vegetable Gardening, Drying and Storing
EO-824-12   Vegetable Gardening, Space Saving
EO-824-13   Vegetable Gardening, Controlling Pests, Weeds, Diseases and Bugs
EO-824-14   Vegetable Gardening, Asparagus and Rhubarb   (Continued on page 236)

EO-824-15	Vegetable Gardening, Start Plants at Home
EO-824-16	Vegetable Gardening, Peas
EO-824-17	Vegetable Gardening, Onion Family
EO-824-18	Vegetable Gardening, Tomatoes
EO-824-19	Vegetable Gardening, When to Harvest
EO-824-20	Vegetable Gardening, Peppers and Eggplants
EO-824-21	Vegetable Gardening, Sweet Corn
EO-824-22	Vegetable Gardening, Lima Beans and Okra
EO-824-23	Vegetable Gardening, Potatoes and Sweet Potatoes
EO-824-24	Vegetable Gardening, Cabbage Family
EO-824-25	Vegetable Gardening, Organic Gardening
EO-824-26	Vegetable Gardening, Dictionary of Terms
E-1650	Using Water in Home Gardens
E-1651	Propagating Garden Plants

This is one of the most humorous, understandable, educational, best-illustrated home garden series I have ever seen. Nancy E. Smith and J. Lee Taylor are to be commended and given a standing ovation.

Minnesota

Key Cities

CODE	DULUTH	MINNEAPOLIS	ST. PAUL
A	125	166	166
B	5/22	4/30	4/30
C	9/24	10/13	10/13
D	15"	17"	17"
E	5/24–9/22	5/4–10/11	5/1–10/11
F	47	55	55

The following publication is available to the home vegetable gardener from:

Cooperative Extension Service
University of Minnesota
St. Paul, MN 55101

4H-BU-0378   Vegetable Gardening in Minnesota

Mississippi

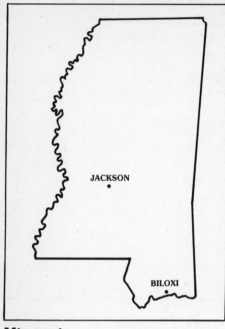

Key Cities

CODE	JACKSON	BILOXI
A	235	298
B	3/18	2/17
C	10/8	12/12
D	27"	58"
E	3/20–10/6	2/15–12/15
F	80	90

For publications available to the home vegetable gardener write:

U.S. Cooperative Extension Service
Mississippi State University
Mississippi State, MS 39762

Missouri

Key Cities

CODE	SPRINGFIELD	ST. LOUIS	KANSAS CITY
A	201	206	207
B	4/12	4/9	4/6
C	10/30	11/1	10/30
D	26"	23"	28"
E	4/14–10/28	4/11–10/30	4/8–10/28
F	59	60	61

The following publications are available to the home vegetable gardener from:

Cooperative Extension Service
University of Missouri
309 University Hall
Columbia, MO 65201

(Continued on page 238)

6201   Vegetable Planting Calendar for Missouri
6202   Disease Prevention for Home Vegetable Gardening
6206   Insect Control for Home Vegetable Gardening
6220   Organic Gardening Techniques
6400   Vegetable Garden Questions and Answers
6950   Fertilizing Your Vegetable Garden
6226   Vegetable Harvest and Storage
6460   Pruning and Training Tomatoes
6461   Growing Tomatoes in Home Gardens
6951   Weed Control
6570   Starting Plants from Seeds

Montana

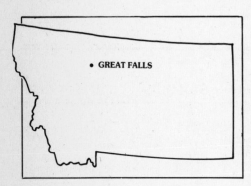

Key Cities

CODE	GREAT FALLS
A	139
B	5/9
C	9/25
D	15"
E	5/11–9/23
F	38

The following publications are available to the home vegetable gardener from:

U.S. Cooperative Extension Service
U.S. Department of Agriculture
Montana State University
Bozeman, MT 59715

1060   Vegetable Variety for Montana
 187   Planting Dates for Vegetables
 297   Tomatoes Growing in Montana

Nebraska

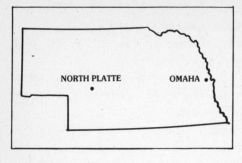

Key Cities

CODE	NORTH PLATTE	OMAHA
A	160	189
B	4/30	4/14
C	10/7	10/20
D	14"	23"
E	5/1–10/5	4/16–10/18
F	45	58

For publications available to the home vegetable gardener write:

U.S. Cooperative Extension Service
University of Nebraska
Lincoln, NE 68508

Nevada

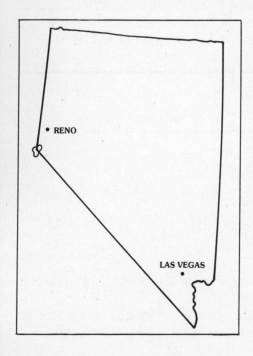

Key Cities

CODE	RENO	LAS VEGAS
A	155	239
B	5/8	3/16
C	10/10	11/10
D	7"	4"
E	5/10–10/8	3/18–11/8
F	—	19

The following publications are available to the home vegetable gardener from:

U.S. Cooperative Extension Service
U.S. Department of Agriculture
University of Nevada
Reno, NV 89507

SNH 83-08-23 Beginning Desert Gardening
(by Linn Mills—a good friend)

73-16 Nevada Gardener: Garden Without
Poison

(Continued on page 240)

73-30	Nevada Gardener: Compost
73-33	Nevada Gardener: Organic Matter
74-9	Nevada Gardener: Where to Plant
74-10	Nevada Gardener: Plan for Cold Frame
74-12	Nevada Gardener: Water Wisely
74-13	Nevada Gardener: Hand Pollination of Vegetables
75-14	Nevada Gardener: Vegetable Spacings
74-17	Nevada Gardener: Planting Guide for South Nevada
75-13	Nevada Gardener: Planting Vegetable Gardens
75-17	Nevada Gardener: Starting Vegetable Transplant
75-18	Nevada Gardener: Protect Vegetables
75-19	Nevada Gardener: Small Area Vegetable Gardens
75-20	Nevada Gardener: Vegetable Garden Fertilization
75-21	Nevada Gardener: Trellising Viney Vegetables
75-23, 24	Nevada Gardener: Tomato Diseases
75-25	Nevada Gardener: When to Harvest

New Hampshire

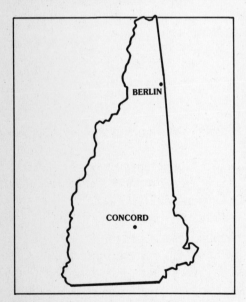

Key Cities

CODE	BERLIN	CONCORD
A	109	142
B	5/29	5/11
C	9/15	9/30
D	12"	14"
E	5/31–9/13	5/13–9/28
F	41	48

For publications available to the home vegetable gardener write:

U.S. Cooperative Extension Service
University of New Hampshire
Taylor Hall
Durham, NH 03824

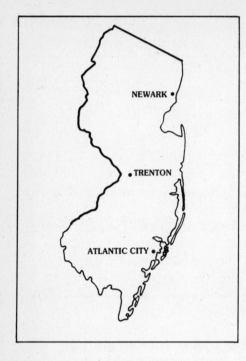

Key Cities

CODE	TRENTON	NEWARK	ATLANTIC CITY
A	218	219	225
B	4/4	4/3	3/31
C	11/8	11/8	11/11
D	25"	24"	27"
E	4/6–11/6	4/5–11/6	4/2–11/9
F	67	69	65

The following publications are available to the home vegetable gardener from:

Cooperative Extension Service
Rutgers State University
P.O. Box 231
New Brunswick, NJ 08903

EB-404   Growing Organically
HG-180   Growing Tomatoes in New Jersey
HG-202   Growing Vegetables at Home
HG-380   Insect and Disease Control
L-518-C Insect Prevention
L-573   Growing Vegetables in Containers
L-615   Your Vegetable Garden

New Mexico

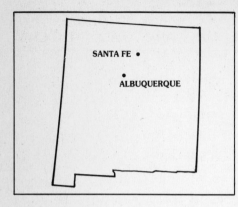

Key Cities

CODE	SANTA FE	ALBUQUERQUE
A	178	198
B	4/24	4/13
C	10/19	10/28
D	13″	8″
E	4/26–10/17	4/11–10/26
F	—	—

Circular #457, entitled *Home Vegetable Gardening for New Mexico,* is available from:

———————————— U.S. Cooperative Extension Service
U.S. Department of Agriculture
New Mexico State University
Las Cruces, NM 88001

New York

Key Cities

CODE	WATERTOWN	BINGHAMTON	SYRACUSE
A	151	154	168
B	5/7	5/4	4/30
C	10/4	10/6	10/15
D	16″	18″	17″
E	5/9–10/2	5/6–10/4	5/2–10/13
F	50	56	60

CODE	ALBANY	BUFFALO	NEW YORK CITY
A	169	179	219
B	4/27	4/30	4/7
C	10/13	10/25	10/12
D	17″	17″	24″
E	4/29–10/11	5/1–10/23	4/9–11/10
F	58	60	69

(Continued on page 243)

The following publications are available to the home vegetable gardener from:

—————————— U.S. Cooperative Extension Service
U.S. Department of Agriculture
New York State College of Agriculture
Ithaca, NY 14853

1B-101	Home Vegetable Gardening for New York
1B-123	Herb Gardening
1B-141	Insect and Disease Control
1B-96	Compost Pile
1B-39	Organic Gardening
1B-36	Facts About Organic Gardening
1B-28	Tomato Diseases

North Carolina

Key Cities

CODE	ASHEVILLE	RALEIGH	WILMINGTON
A	195	237	262
B	4/12	3/24	3/8
C	10/24	11/16	11/24
D	26"	30"	40"
E	4/14–10/22	3/26–11/14	3/10–11/22
F	69	71	79

The following publications are available to the home vegetable gardener from:

—————————— Cooperative Extension Service
North Carolina State University
Raleigh, NC 27607

AG-12	Quick Reference, Home Vegetable Garden Guide
Circular 122	Garden Manual for North Carolina

North Dakota

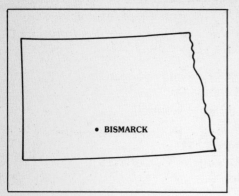

Key Cities

CODE	BISMARCK
A	136
B	5/11
C	9/24
D	10″
E	5/13–9/22
F	42

The following publications are available to the home vegetable gardener from:

U.S. Cooperative Extension Service
U.S. Department of Agriculture
North Dakota State University
Fargo, ND 58102

H-1   Vegetables for North Dakota
H-61   Asparagus and Rhubarb

Ohio

Key Cities

CODE	CINCINNATI	CLEVELAND	COLUMBUS
A	192	195	192
B	4/15	4/21	4/17
C	10/25	11/2	10/30
D	21″	20″	21″
E	4/17–10/23	4/23–10/31	4/19–10/28
F	65	68	64

The following publications are available to the home vegetable gardener from:

U.S. Cooperative Extension Service
Ohio State University
2120 Fyffe Road
Columbus, OH 43210

(Continued on page 245)

555　Organic Gardening
L100　Vegetable Variety for Ohio
287　Home Vegetable Gardening

Oklahoma

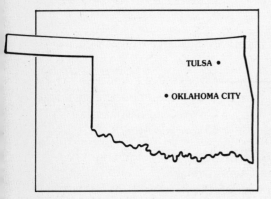

Key Cities

CODE	TULSA	OKLAHOMA CITY
A	221	224
B	3/25	3/28
C	11/1	11/7
D	27″	25″
E	3/27–10/30	3/30–11/5
F	56	56

The following publications are available to the home vegetable gardener from:

U.S. Cooperative Extension Service
Oklahoma State University
Stillwater, OK 74074

6004　Garden Planning Guide
6222　Home Fruit Planting Guide
6007　Improving Your Garden Soil
AF-6001　Vegetable Variety for Oklahoma

Oregon

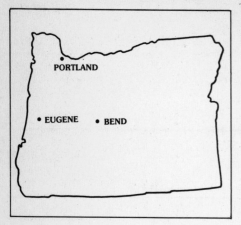

Key Cities

CODE	BEND	EUGENE	PORTLAND
A	91	205	263
B	6/8	4/13	3/6
C	9/7	11/4	11/24
D	12"	43"	34"
E	6/10–9/5	4/15–11/2	3/8–11/22
F	—	—	—

The following publications are available to the home vegetable gardener from:

Cooperative Extension Service
U.S. Department of Agriculture
Oregon State University
Corvallis, OR 97331

EC-871 Home and Farm Vegetable Gardening
EC-874 Grow Your Own Vegetables
EC-884 Vegetable Garden Plan
FS-53   Growing Tomatoes
FS-220 Collecting and Storing Seeds
FS-242 Discourage Plant Disease
FS-246 Cold Frames
FS-270 Raised Beds
FS-276 Mulch and Compost

Pennsylvania

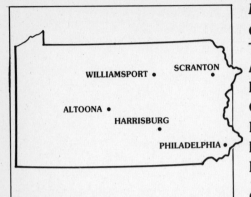

Key Cities

CODE	ALTOONA	WILLIAMSPORT	SCRANTON
A	151	164	174
B	5/6	5/3	4/24
C	10/4	10/13	10/14
D	22"	19"	19"
E	5/8–10/2	5/5–10/11	4/28–10/12
F	62	61	63

CODE	HARRISBURG	PHILADELPHIA
A	204	232
B	4/9	3/30
C	10/30	11/17
D	21"	26"
E	4/11–10/28	4/1–11/15
F	68	70

For publications available to the home vegetable gardener write:

U.S. Cooperative Extension Service
Pennsylvania State University
University Park, PA 16802

Rhode Island

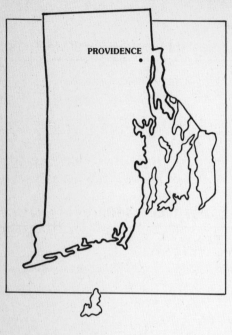

Key Cities

CODE	PROVIDENCE
A	197
B	4/13
C	10/27
D	21″
E	4/15–10/25
F	62

For publications available to the home vegetable gardener write:

U.S. Cooperative Extension Service
University of Rhode Island
Kingston, RI 02881

South Carolina

Key Cities

CODE	COLUMBIA	CHARLESTON
A	262	294
B	3/14	2/19
C	11/21	12/10
D	34″	44″
E	—	—
F	74	94

Circular #570, entitled *Home Vegetable Gardening for South Carolina,* is really good. It's available from:

Cooperative Extension Service
U.S. Department of Agriculture
Clemson University
Clemson, SC 29631

South Dakota

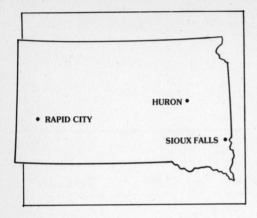

Key Cities

CODE	HURON	RAPID CITY	SIOUX FALLS
A	149	150	152
B	5/4	5/7	5/5
C	9/30	10/4	10/3
D	12"	11"	16"
E	5/6–9/28	5/9–10/1	5/7–10/1
F	44	44	45

The following publications are available to the home vegetable gardener from:

Cooperative Extension Service
South Dakota State University
Brookings, SD 57006

G-202   Home Vegetable Gardening in South Dakota
EC-668   Insect Control

Tennessee

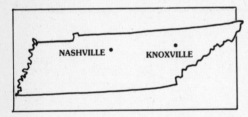

Key Cities

CODE	KNOXVILLE	NASHVILLE
A	220	224
B	3/31	3/28
C	11/6	11/7
D	25"	24"
E	4/2–11/4	4/31–11/9
F	73	68

The following publications are available to the home vegetable gardener from:

Cooperative Extension Service
U.S. Department of Agriculture
University of Tennessee
P.O. Box 1071
Knoxville, TN 37901

(Continued on page 250)

901 Growing Vegetables in Home Gardens in Tennessee
     [very good!]
595 You Can Control Insects

Texas

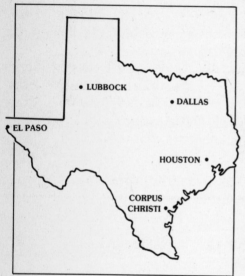

Key Cities

CODE	LUBBOCK	EL PASO	DALLAS
A	205	238	244
B	4/1	3/26	3/18
C	11/9	11/14	11/17
D	15"	6"	23"
E	4/3–11/7	3/28–11/12	3/20–11/15
F	40	33	51

CODE	HOUSTON	CORPUS CHRISTI
A	262	335
B	3/14	1/26
C	11/21	12/27
D	38"	27"
E	3/16–11/23	1/28–12/25
F	80	73

Publication No. B-1397, entitled *Texas Garden Guidelines,*
is a sixteen-page newspaper that is just super. Sam Cotner,
Jerry Parsons, and Jerral Johnson prepared it and Ann Cole
is its editor. They deserve an award—it's great! It is available to home gardeners by writing:

Cooperative Extension Service
U.S. Department of Agriculture
Texas A & M University
College Station, TX 77843

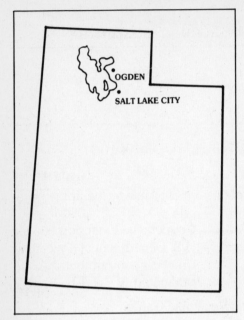

Key Cities

CODE	OGDEN	SALT LAKE CITY
A	155	192
B	5/6	4/13
C	10/8	10/22
D	16″	15″
E	5/8–10/6	4/15–10/20
F	—	—

The following publications are available to the home vegetable gardener from:

Cooperative Extension Service
U.S. Department of Agriculture
Utah State University
Logan, UT 84321

EC-313   Growing Vegetables
EC-332   Home Drying of Fruit and Vegetables
CS-27   Vegetable Garden Insects

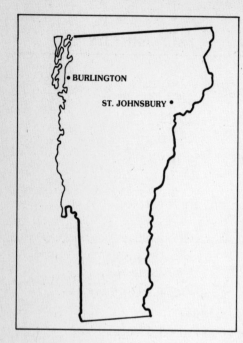

Key Cities

CODE	ST. JOHNSBURY	BURLINGTON
A	127	148
B	5/22	5/8
C	9/23	10/3
D	14″	16″
E	5/24–9/21	5/10–10/1
F	46	58

The following publications are available to the home vegetable gardener from:

Cooperative Extension Service
U.S. Department of Agriculture
University of Vermont
Burlington, VT 05401

C-138	The Home Vegetable Garden
BR-1158	Insect and Disease Control
BR-1172	Herbs
WD-13	Mulch for Weeds
GL-1	Source of Seed
GL-2	Fall Garden Clean Up
GL-3	Storing Vegetables
GL-4	Drying Vegetables
GL-5	Planting Calendar

Virginia

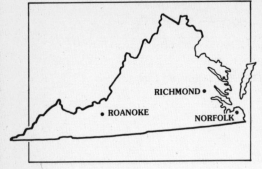

Key Cities

CODE	ROANOKE	RICHMOND	NORFOLK
A	165	218	242
B	4/14	3/29	3/19
C	10/26	11/2	11/16
D	25"	29"	34"
E	4/16–10/24	3/31–10/31	3/21–11/14
F	66	68	79

The following publications are available to the home vegetable gardener from:

Cooperative Extension Service
U.S. Department of Agriculture
Virginia Polytechnic
Institute & State University
Blacksburg, VA 24061

426-313 Soil Preparation
426-316 Seeds and Plants
426-324 Organic vs. Conventional
426-325 Compost Pile
426-331 Planting Guide
426-332 Planting Chart
426-336 Container Gardening

Washington

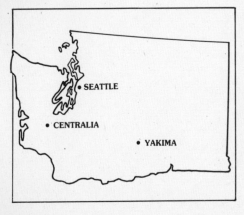

Key Cities

CODE	CENTRALIA	YAKIMA	SEATTLE
A	173	190	255
B	4/27	4/15	3/14
C	10/17	10/22	11/24
D	46"	8"	36"
E	4/29–10/15	4/17–10/20	3/16–11/22
F	—	—	—

(Continued on page 254)

The following publications are available to the home vegetable gardener from:

——————————————— U.S. Cooperative Extension Service
Washington State University
Pullman, WA 99163

EB-0422   Home Gardening for Washington
EB-0648   Organic Gardening
EB-0687   Save Water in Vegetable Gardening

Washington, D.C.

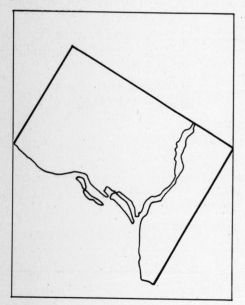

NOTE: See Maryland or Virginia for weather data.

For publications available to the home vegetable gardener write:

——————————————— U.S. Cooperative Extension Service
Federal City College
1424 K Street N.W.
Washington, D.C. 20005

West Virginia

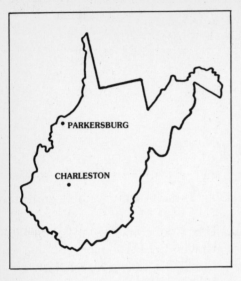

Key Cities

CODE	PARKERSBURG	CHARLESTON
A	159	193
B	4/16	4/18
C	10/21	10/28
D	21"	22"
E	4/18–9/31	4/20–10/26
F	66	71

A publication entitled, "Yearly Garden Calendar Newspaper," is available from:

U.S. Cooperative Extension Service
West Virginia University
294 Coliseur
Morgantown, WV 26505

This newspaper is terrific!

Wisconsin

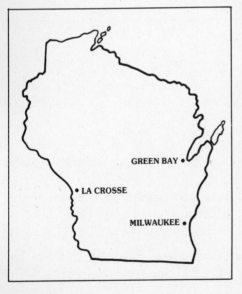

Key Cities

CODE	LA CROSSE	GREEN BAY	MILWAUKEE
A	161	161	188
B	5/1	5/6	4/20
C	10/8	10/13	10/25
D	19"	16"	18"
E	5/3–10/6	5/6–10/10	4/22–10/23
F	54	55	61

For publications available to the home vegetable gardener write:

Dane County Extension Service
57 Fairgrounds Drive
Madison, Wisconsin 53713

Wyoming

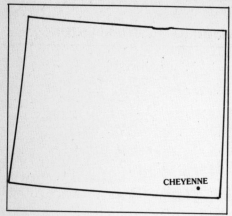

Key Cities

CODE	CHEYENNE
A	141
B	5/14
C	10/2
D	15"
E	5/16–9/30
F	50

For publications available to the home vegetable gardener write:

U.S. Cooperative Extension Service
University of Wyoming
Box 3354, University Station
Laramie, WY 82070

Puerto Rico

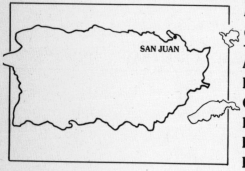

Key Cities

CODE	SAN JUAN
A	365
B	—
C	—
D	70"
E	—
F	219

The following publication is available to the home vegetable gardener from:

U.S. Cooperative Extension Service
University of Puerto Rico
Rio Piedras, PR 00928

H-79   Vegetable Gardening in Puerto Rico [Note: This bulletin is printed in Spanish only.]

Virgin Islands

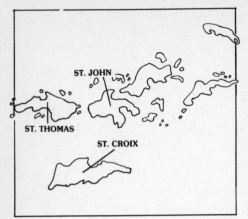

Key Cities

CODE	ST. CROIX	ST. JOHN	ST. THOMAS
A	365	365	365
B	—	—	—
C	—	—	—
D	50"	50"	50"
E	—	—	—
F	180	180	180

NOTE: Cucumbers, peppers, and tomatoes do very well, as do fruit and nuts.

For publications available to the home vegetable gardener write:

U.S. Cooperative Extension Service
P.O. Box 166 Kingshill
St. Croix, VI 00850

Index

Wrap-On Company, 23
Wyatt-Quaries Seed Company, 2
Wyoming, 9, 256

Yarrow, 120

Zineb, 145, 149, 150, 153
Zucchini, 10, 11, 183, 185
  diseases that affect, 154
  varieties, 44
  see also Squash